ENTERTAINING
On the Run

ENTERTAINING
On the Run

Easy Menus for Faster Lives

MARLENE SOROSKY

Photographs by

TERI SANDISON

WILLIAM MORROW AND COMPANY, INC.

NEW YORK

It is the policy of William Morrow and Company, Inc., and its imprints and affiliates,
recognizing the importance of preserving what has been written, to print the books
we publish on acid-free paper, and we exert our best efforts to that end.

Library of Congress Cataloging-in-Publication Data

Sorosky, Marlene.
    Entertaining on the run: easy menus for faster lives / by Marlene Sorosky.
    Includes index.
    ISBN 0-688-12077-6
    1. Entertaining. 2. Cookery. 3. Low-fat diet—Recipes. 4. Menus. I. Title.
TX731.S656   1994
642'.4—dc20   93-43098
                                                                                CIP

Printed in the United States of America

First Edition

2 3 4 5 6 7 8 9 10

Food styling by Rita Calvert and Marlene Sorosky
Book design and illustrations by Beverly Wilson

**To the dear hearts in my life, my children,
who keep me forever active and on the run**

Cheryl, Jim, Samantha, and Max Branman
Caryn Sorosky
Margi, Michael, and Jacob Morrison
Kenny Sorosky

CONTENTS

CONTENTS

ACKNOWLEDGMENTS

The people who helped with this book are so exceptional and cared so much that a mere "thank you" seems barely adequate. I've always believed that two heads are better than one. Throughout the book's concept and development, my assistant, Rita Calvert, was a continual source of inspiration and creativity. Her flair with food is evident in the outstanding food styling she did for the photographs.

A big thank you to photographer Teri Sandison for her commitment to excellence and hard work. And for the extra hours she put in to help with the book's design.

To Beverly Wilson, for bringing my words to life in the layout and design of the book and through her imaginative illustrations.

To my agents, Maureen and Eric Lasher, who were there for me every step of the way and have become dear friends.

To my editor, Harriet Bell, for believing in me and being willing to take risks. To my copy editor, Susan Derecskey, for being such a stickler for detail. And to Barb Durbin for her nutritional analyses.

To my testers, Bonnie Rapoport Marshall, Susan Vohrer, Margaret Biller, and Mary Jane Snyder for being such good sports. And my daughter, Caryn, for her clever centerpiece and invitation ideas and for helping me with my parties.

To Gail and Lenny Kaplan, owners of *The Classic Catering People* in Owings Mills, Maryland; Joann Roth, of *Someone's in the Kitchen* in Los Angeles, California; Ellen Frank and Lynn Kotz of *Celebrations* in Baltimore, Maryland; and *Ridgewell Catering* of Washington, D.C., for generously sharing their party planning expertise.

To the Crate & Barrel Stores, Northbrook, Illinois; Dansk International; Charles Gautreaux, John Nyquist, and Kathy Vanderbilt, of Vanderbilt & Co., Napa Valley, California; and Zyzyx in Owings Mills and Rockville, Maryland, for the beautiful tabletop wares for the photography, and to Claudia "K" Florist, Napa Valley, California. Thank you also to Mr. and Mrs. Allen Horton, and Steve and Cindy Deutch for sharing their lovely homes in Napa Valley for the party photographs.

And a great big hug to my husband and sous-chef, Hal, for his devoted and loyal support, and for sampling the same dishes many more nights than he cares to count.

INTRODUCTION

For many, the thought of hosting a party is nothing short of terrifying. Stage one begins with enthusiastic intent. Then you sit down to plan your guest list and menu and realize that half your friends aren't speaking to one another, or they are on special diets, and your favorite recipes—those you and your family have loved for years—aren't good enough for a party. With lots of trepidation and waning enthusiasm, you send out the invitations. You then move on to stage two: anger. Why did you ever agree to this stupid idea in the first place? Enter stage three: hysteria. You are so high strung, nervous, and snappy, that your family has avoided you for weeks. But that is nothing compared to the emotional outbursts the hour before the doorbell rings. You overseason the sauce, underseason the fish, spill the wine, and can't find the cord to the coffeepot. Your family, unwilling to confront the irrational monster in the kitchen, hides behind closed doors. Stage four: composure. Your guests arrive, they compliment you on the hors d'oeuvres, and you're all smiles. "It was nothing," you assure them, hoping they don't notice the kids, who are supposed to be in bed, groaning and rolling their eyes. Stage five: collapse. They're gone. With relief and dismay, you survey the mountains of dirty dishes. The party was a success. But was it worth it?

There is no question about it, in today's frenetic world, with little time and money to spare, we need to find more casual and relaxed ways to entertain without running ourselves ragged. Today, anything goes. Stuffy rules of etiquette are outdated, and exhausting yourself to impress your friends is passé. There is no right or wrong as long as you're comfortable with what you do. Entertaining should be as individual and unique as your personality and a reflection of your own taste and style.

Entertaining on the Run is entertaining redefined. It's a total concept that expands and broadens the definition to better fit our fast-paced and hectic lives. It is my belief, and the basis for this book, that any time you feed people who don't live in your home, or go to extra efforts to prepare a special meal for those who do, you *are* entertaining—regardless of the place, style, type, or amount of food. It might be chips, dips, and beers for pals who come over to watch a game, or a picnic on a grassy knoll, or breakfast on Christmas morn—each event plays an important part in our lives and shouldn't be valued by the hours spent preparing for it. No longer do we need to bring out a starched tablecloth, polished silver, or sparkling crystal to say we're entertaining. I hope as we accept the fact that it needn't be fancy, or time-consuming, or expensive, we will do it more often.

This book offers innovative ideas for carefree, inexpensive get-togethers, such as combining a workout or sporting activity with a power-packed breakfast buffet, or offering friends mugs for a help-yourself soups-and-suds party. The menus are designed to fulfill every mood, style, and occasion, from a hastily assembled ''don't panic'' dinner for unexpected guests to a detailed and deluxe birthday or anniversary buffet. They span the clock and the calendar with roll-out-of-bed breakfasts, laid-back to luxurious brunches and lunches, Saturday-night dress-up dinners and sportier dress-down ones, and feasts for holidays and life's special milestones. To increase the fun, many menus offer Extra Points, theme ideas that can be carried out through decorations, centerpieces, favors, and entertainment. These are the party enhancers that lift the gathering above and beyond the food.

Entertaining on the Run means saving time by taking shortcuts and reducing steps. I love to cook, so I don't mind spending time to make a dish great, but I do mind wasting it by taking unnecessary steps and using old-fashioned techniques when newer, faster ones are available. My goal in this book is not to make every recipe against a stopwatch but to make each taste delicious, taking advantage of every shortcut available. I continually challenge myself to find yet another way to eliminate steps. When the microwave saves time and dirty dishes, I use it. When the food processor chops food faster than my hand, I choose it. When cut-up salad-bar vegetables and fruits reduce prep time, I try them. When prepared foods offer an alternative, I consider them. I usually prefer fresh ingredients to frozen or canned, but for those who want to run quicker, many recipes include substitute options for even faster preparation.

Entertaining on the Run means planning a strategy and cooking in stages. Each recipe includes detailed information on how far ahead it can be made and how it can be reheated. And each menu includes a Game Plan to help you schedule your time. Many of the menu introductions include additional tips for saving time and steps as well.

Entertaining on the Run means slimmer, leaner foods with less fat, especially the saturated variety, and cholesterol. I am not a health expert or a nutritionist, but I try to eat sensibly. To that end, I have attempted to make most of the recipes as nutritious as possible, while still maintaining top-grade quality and taste. Several recipes offer leaner options for those who want to reduce the fat and cholesterol even further. But this is a special occasion book and, for those times we want to go all out and indulge and impress, I offer rich and luxurious desserts with no apologies.

Entertaining on the Run means foods that travel. If we don't have the time, means, or desire to cook an entire meal, we should get together with friends and plan co-op parties: I call them team cuisine. This book offers an array of ''no excuse'' gatherings, where the cooking is shared and the burden on the host is reduced.

Lastly, *Entertaining on the Run* emphasizes my belief that entertaining is a sport and, like any activity, takes practice. You may have a natural aptitude, but you aren't ready for the advanced slopes until you've conquered the bunny hills. When people are overly ambitious, they are usually disappointed with their efforts. Instead of using only time-proven recipes, or supplementing their own with storebought dishes, or enlisting friends' help, they run onto the court ready to become an instant champion, which is like playing tennis for the first time against Jimmy Connors. To ensure the recipes are explicit enough for a rookie, the book includes a special section describing basic techniques and ingredients. And to keep them creative enough for the veteran, it incorporates contemporary applications in new and upbeat combinations.

I have already reaped countless hours of enjoyable entertaining by using the ideas and menus that comprise this book. I hope the book provides you, too, with exciting alternatives to help increase the fun and enjoyment of entertaining and decrease the worry and hassle. If you love what you're doing, your guests will love it, too. It is my sincere wish that *Entertaining on the Run* entices you to take a detour off the treadmill of life, to pause and catch your breath, and in your own inimitable style, savor the happy adventures derived from getting together with friends and loved ones.

ABOUT *The* BOOK

I wish I could tell you that *Entertaining on the Run* will enable you to dash off a few recipes, toss them on a table, and sit back and be a guest at your own party. It will make entertaining easier, faster, and lots more fun, but no matter how casual the affair, being a host is never as carefree as being a guest. I believe that when we entertain, we are giving a gift, and although giving doesn't evoke the same emotions as receiving, it reaps its own rewards, which often are more fulfilling. *Entertaining on the Run* can help you host the events of your dreams, whether they are poised and posh or footloose and fancy-free—and it may even take you beyond them—but you will need to be organized and do some advance planning. Here's how to do it:

Formal?   *Casual? Outdoors?*
Birthday?   *Graduation?*

THE THEME

You are the architect with a blank page—you have full license to design the style, theme, time, and menu. Begin by defining the type of affair you want to have. If it's for a special occasion, a holiday, birthday, or shower, what time of day and type of food do you want to serve—an elegant midmorning Brunch on the Mediterranean or a festive Celebration Buffet Bash supper? For a business dinner or social evening at home, how formal do you want it? Do you lean toward a "kick up your heels" affair, where guests gather in your kitchen to top their own pizza, or the more traditional Chic Candlelight Chicken sit-down dinner? Plan the type of party that reflects you. Today anything goes, so forget past rules and do what feels comfortable. Some occasions dictate a sophisticated, sedate approach; others, a more high-spirited, let-loose one. This book offers suggestions and ideas to fit the many facets of our lives and personalities.

THE INVITATIONS

Once you have the blueprint—and before you have a change of heart—get the invites out. Depending on the occasion, your schedule, and the number of people, decide whether you want to telephone, send store-bought cards, or create your own. I enjoy awaiting my friends' reactions when they receive a unique and unexpected invitation through the mail—a balloon inscribed with IT'S A SURPRISE—DON'T BLOW IT, chopsticks tucked inside a paper-towel tube, a pizza box with a message on the top. Whatever you choose, be specific and include everything your guests need to know—not just when and where, but what type of meal, the dress, how to get there, and whether gifts are appropriate.

THE MENU

A well-thought-out menu is the foundation of the party. The number of guests, time of day, available space, budget and prep time, all are considerations in laying it. But a solid menu has many more angles. They are: 1) The dishes should be nutritionally balanced with complementary tastes and textures, without an overabundance of any one ingredient. 2) They should be color coordinated—a meal appeals to all our senses, but first to our eyes. 3) The recipes should be prepared at various stages, beginning several weeks ahead and freezing, if desired. If you are the sole cook, the menu should not include more than one last-minute dish. 4) They must fit in your oven, stove, refrigerator, or freezer. If you are baking several dishes before serving, make sure you have adequate oven space. If your refrigerator is crammed with hors d'oeuvres and salads, choose a frozen or room-temperature dessert. 5) The dishes should be easy to reheat and serve with a minimum of last-minute hassle. If you are cooking and saucing pasta, you don't want to be stir-frying vegetables and carving a roast. The menus in this book have been developed with all of these criteria in mind and are designed to be managed by one cook alone in the kitchen—but getting help never hurts. When you mix and match recipes to create your own menus, check that they fit these criteria.

Buffet? Sit Down? Family Style?

ABOUT SERVING

You have four different serving options: 1) Setting up a buffet and letting guests help themselves. This arrangement is especially suited for large groups and/or open kitchens. 2) Dishing up plates in the kitchen. An advantage here is that it eliminates serving pieces and dirty dishes. 3) Bringing platters to the table and dishing up family style. 4) Passing platters for guests to help themselves. Throw out past rules and choose whichever best fits your needs, space, schedule, help, and comfort level.

THE RECIPES

These are the building blocks that make up the foundation. I go to great lengths to ensure they are sturdy. When it comes to developing and testing, I'm compulsive (some people call it neurotic). Maybe making a recipe thirty times is excessive, but I want them to be so gratifying, healthful, clearly written, easy to prepare, and worth the effort that I try them willingly one more time. My favorite versions become the main recipes, and whenever practical, I offer variations to make them leaner and faster—and these are tested too. The recipes are then given to at least two testers—nonprofessional cooks, students, neighbors, and friends—who prepare them and complete a two-page questionnaire. To ensure you can make them on the run, I eliminate as many steps and dirty pots and pans as possible. And you won't be sprinting to various markets in search of exotic ingredients, because with very few exceptions (like Chinese chile sauce and unsweetened coconut milk in Mini Thai Crab Cakes, see page 158), you'll find the majority of the ingredients at any local supermarket.

ABOUT LEANER

This is not a diet book, but rather a compilation of contemporary recipes for special occasions, which reflect today's health concerns. If I had to choose between eliminating fat in a recipe that tasted fair and using some fat (but reduced) that tasted great, my choice was for the most flavorful. When we have friends over, we want to serve fantastic food, and because high taste can be attained with low fat, I have maximized its use. But great celebrations also deserve some splurging, so you'll find many of my desserts are decadent—but even they have been slimmed down. For example, when the original version of my Lemon Pineapple Trifle appeared on the cover of *Cook's Magazine* in 1989, the custard had five whole eggs, a quarter pound butter, and 1 cup whipping cream. My reduced fat version, which tastes every bit as spectacular, has two eggs, no butter, a half cup whipping cream, and a half cup light sour cream—not dietetic, but a substantial reduction. Some recipes in the book offer leaner options to reduce or eliminate fatty ingredients such as cheese, oil, cream, or nuts, while others, like the Baked Strawberry-stuffed French Toast (see page 16), suggest frozen liquid egg substitute for the fresh eggs. When a recipe offers a choice of regular, low-fat, or nonfat milk, yogurt, sour cream, or mayonnaise, always feel secure in choosing the one with the least fat. If the results were not as tasty, it wouldn't be offered as an option; it would be a leaner variation. You will find the serving portions substantial for the average eater. They are never reduced to benefit the nutritional analysis.

NUTRITIONAL ANALYSES

Each recipe includes a nutritional analysis because many of us want to know more about what we eat. When a recipe offers ingredient alternatives, such as regular, low-fat, or nonfat milk, yogurt, sour cream, cheese, or mayonnaise, the analysis was done on the ingredient with the lowest fat content. When a recipe calls for butter or margarine, butter was used. When a range in serving size is given, such as eight to ten servings, the analysis was done for the larger serving. When a range in amounts is given, such as three to four tablespoons olive oil, the smaller amount was used. Generally, optional ingredients and garnishes were not included. The leaner options, which obviously have less fat and cholesterol, were not included in the nutritional analysis.

ABOUT FASTER

Several recipes offer faster alternatives by substituting canned or frozen ingredients for the fresh, and packaged ones for homemade.

ABOUT PREP TIMES

Time in cooking is a relative factor. A recipe that is long and involved to a novice can be a quickie to an expert. I've observed students slowly and painstakingly chop onions into T-square precision cubes, while others pulsed them in a fraction of the time in a food processor. The Prep Times were calculated on an average and are not meant to be precise. They are only a guide to help you select the recipes that best fit your on-the-run schedule.

One month ahead... One week ahead... Day of the Party... 10 minutes before serving...

THE GAME PLAN

Even the simplest meal is easier to prepare when it's done in stages. Each menu in the book includes a Game Plan, indicating how far in advance the recipes can be made and what needs to be done before serving. You should supplement this with a working time frame of your own: 1) List each recipe and the date you plan to prepare it. 2) Make a grocery list. When you cook in stages, you won't need all the ingredients at the same time. You may prefer to purchase all the staples at once and the perishables as needed. Making lists early helps determine what needs to be ordered ahead or purchased from a specialty store. 3) Select serving pieces and utensils; if they need cleaning or polishing, do it early. 4) Make a Day of Party Time Plan. Write down each recipe with its garnish and what needs to be done before serving. If you are jotting down minutes and seconds and running on a stop-watch, your menu is too ambitious.

THE EXTRA POINTS

If the mere thought of cooking one or two dishes for company causes tremors, then you'll probably want to jog right on past the Extra Points. They are precisely what their name implies, the extras—themes, centerpieces, decorations, invitations, and entertainment—that lift the party above the ordinary. Some occasions, like a bridal shower or Thanksgiving feast, have a built-in motif, which you may want to enhance with favors and decorations, while others, like magically turning a Middle Eastern menu into an Aladdin's Night Party (see page 191), are strictly for fun and frolic.

Invitations Themes Games Place Cards Table Settings

About the Ingredients
and
Techniques

When several recipes call for the same ingredient or a specific technique that requires an explanation, rather than repeat it, I refer you to this section.

To Rise Bread: Choose a warm, draftfree spot, such as inside a gas oven with the pilot light on or in an electric oven warmed at 200°F. for 1 minute and then turned off. Or place a large shallow pan or roaster on the counter. Fill half full of boiling water. Place a baking sheet with the bowl of dough or shaped bread over the pan. Replenish the hot water as it cools. Put the water on to boil when you begin the recipe, so you won't have to wait for it. The microwave rising techniques suggested in the recipes are adapted from *Bread in Half the Time* by Linda West Eckhardt and Diane Collingwood Butts (Crown Publishers, Inc., 1991).

To Bake Bread: When you want a crisp crust, bake the bread on unglazed terra-cotta tiles or bread-baking stones that sit directly on oven racks. Tiles are available from cookware shops or more economically from tile and home supply stores, which will cut them to fit your oven. Use a small spray bottle filled with water to mist the bread once before and once during baking. Or, to create steam, throw several ice cubes onto the oven floor when you put the bread in.

To Reheat and Recrisp Bread: Preheat the oven to 400°F. Using your fingers or a spray bottle, sprinkle the crust with water. Place the loaf on a baking sheet and bake for 10 to 15 minutes, or until crisp.

To Make Bread Crumbs: Trim the crust off bread, tear into small pieces, and process in a food processor with the metal blade until crumbs form. If the bread is so fresh that it will become gummy when processed, or if the recipe calls for slightly stale bread, either leave the slices out on a work surface at room temperature for several hours, turning once, or bake at 250°F. until they dry out slightly. To make dry bread crumbs, bake bread crumbs at 250°F., stirring occasionally, until very dry and crisp, about 15 to 20 minutes. They are interchangeable with packaged dried bread crumbs. *1 slice bread makes about ½ cup crumbs.*

To Toast Bread Crumbs: Place bread crumbs on a baking sheet and bake at 350°F., stirring once or twice, until desired color is obtained, about 10 to 15 minutes.

Chinese Chile Sauce: This fiery condiment of chiles, garlic, salt, and oil is also labeled chile (or chili) paste, chile paste with garlic, or chile puree with garlic. Look for it in oriental markets or the oriental section of large supermarkets. After opening, store in the refrigerator.

To Cut Fresh Corn Off the Cob: Cut a small piece off the tip so the cob sits flat. Holding the stem end, stand the cob upright on a plate or sheet of wax paper. With a knife, cut downwards, removing 3 to 4 rows of kernels at a time.

Unsweetened Coconut Milk: Look for a Thai brand made only with coconut and water and without preservatives. Do not confuse this with sweetened cream of coconut used mainly for desserts and drinks. Once opened, it will keep for a week in the refrigerator. Do not freeze.

Flowers and Leaves for Garnishing: My favorite nonpoisonous leaves for garnishing are lemon, gardenia, and grape. Wash the leaves with warm water and dry well. For a shiny gloss, spray lightly with no-stick cooking spray. Some good choices for flowers include roses, pansies, lilacs, nasturtiums, violets, tulips, mums, and daisies. Check with your local poison control center to ensure the safety of using other varieties with food.

To Grate or Mince Ginger: Peel with a knife or vegetable peeler. If you are using a food processor for any part of the recipe, mince the ginger first in a clean bowl with the metal blade. Or, mince it with a sharp knife, grate on a hand grater or process in a mini processor. *1 ounce fresh ginger yields 3 tablespoons minced; a 1 × 1-inch piece yields 1 tablespoon minced.*

Jalapeño Chiles: All jalapeños are not created equal. Some are so hot that just one speck will set your mouth on fire, while others are so mild, they barely kindle a spark. Rather than sampling, I prefer using jarred or canned pickled jalapeños which have a consistent heat factor. Wear rubber gloves when handling chiles and clean your knife and work surface immediately. Mince pickled chiles by cutting off the core and putting them, seeds and all, in a food processor with the metal blade, or finely chop with a knife. Sliced pickled jalapeños may be substituted for the whole ones. *2 teaspoons of slices equal a 1-inch jalapeño.*

Fresh jalapeños should be seeded before dicing. To remove seeds, cut both ends off the chile, stand it on one end on the counter, and slice the flesh off in 4 or 5 strips; discard the seeds. The recipes in this book offer a range that will result in mild to moderate heat. I suggest you put in the minimum amount called for and add more at the end to taste. When using the processor, first mince the entire amount, remove part, and stir it into the completed dish for a spicier flavor. *A 1-inch jalapeño yields 1 packed teaspoon minced.*

To Clean Leeks: Rinse the outside of the leek, cut off all but 1 inch of the green top, and cut a thin slice from the root. Slice down from the top lengthwise almost to the root. Under cold running water, rinse the leek thoroughly between each layer to remove dirt and sand.

To Grate or Shred Lemon, Lime, and Orange Peel (also called rind and zest): Grated peel is finer than shredded, but unless a recipe specifies finely grated, they are interchangeable. Always grate the peel before cutting the fruit or juicing it. One way to grate peel is to use a standard metal grater. Hold the grater and the fruit over a sheet of wax paper, and rub the peel against the small round holes in the grater until the outer peel is removed. Do not grate the inner white pith or a bitter taste will result. To save time cleaning the particles of grated peel from the grater, cover the side you're using with a piece of parchment paper and rub the fruit back and forth over the paper. The grated peel will remain on the paper and can be easily scraped off. Another option is to remove the peel in large pieces with a vegetable peeler and mince them with a knife or in a food processor. For the finest grind, when the recipe calls for sugar, add a small amount of it to the processor with the peel. For small amounts of shredded peel, you can use a tool called a zester with 5 small holes on one end. Hold it in one hand and the fruit in the other over a sheet of wax paper. Scrape it along the peel of the fruit, making the strokes as long or short as desired. The shreds can be minced with a knife, if desired. *1 medium lemon yields 2 to 3 teaspoons grated peel. 1 medium lime yields 1 to 2 teaspoons grated peel. 1 medium orange yields 2 to 3 tablespoons grated peel.*

To Juice Lemons, Limes, Oranges, and Tangerines: To obtain the maximum amount of juice, microwave the whole fruit for 10 seconds on high (100%) power until softened slightly, and then roll it between your palm and the countertop. Cut in half and to obtain the maximum amount of juice, squeeze with a hand or electric juicer or reamer. *1 medium lemon yields 3 to 4 tablespoons juice. 1 medium lime yields 2 tablespoons juice. 1 medium orange yields 1/4 to 1/3 cup juice. 1 tangerine yields 3 to 4 tablespoons juice.*

To Grind or Finely Chop Nuts: Shelled nuts, especially chopped ones, become rancid very quickly, if they are not stored in vacuum-sealed bags in the freezer. Defrost before grinding or they will stick together. When a recipe specifies finely ground nuts, as in the Ebony, Ivory, and Milk Chocolate Torte (see page 122), grind a small amount at a time in a coffee grinder or mini processor. Or process a small amount at a time in a food processor. To ensure the nuts don't turn into nut butter, take 2 or more tablespoons of sugar from the recipe and add it to the nuts before processing. *4 ounces chopped walnuts, pecans, hazelnuts, or almonds make 1 cup; 5 1/4 ounces chopped shelled pistachios make 1 cup.*

To Toast Nuts, Coconut, and Sesame Seeds: Place shelled nuts, coconut, or sesame seeds on either the pan of a toaster oven or a baking sheet. Bake at 350°F. until light brown, about 10 to 15 minutes, depending on the variety, size, and amount, stirring every 3 to 4 minutes. Watch carefully; they burn easily. To brown in the microwave, spread 1 cup nuts, coconut, or seeds in a 9-inch microwavesafe pie plate. For nuts and seeds, microwave on high (100%) for 2 to 4 minutes, stirring occasionally. For coconut, microwave at 70% power for 2 to 4 minutes, stirring every minute.

To Pit Olives: You can purchase ripe olives pitted and even sliced, but those that are cured in brine, like kalamata and the tiny niçoise, are available only with the pits. To remove the pits, place the olives on a work surface and roll over them with a rolling pin or place in a plastic bag and smack with the side of a knife, cleaver, or meat pounder. The pits can be easily picked out.

To Peel Peaches: Peaches must be ripe or they will not peel. Plunge peaches into a saucepan of boiling water for 1 minute, or until the peel loosens. Plunge into cold water to stop cooking. Slip skin off.

Phyllo Dough (also spelled filo): From the Greek word for leaf, these paper-thin sheets of dough commonly used for strudel are, in fact, often referred to as leaves. They usually come in 12 × 16-inch sheets. Whenever possible, buy refrigerated phyllo that has not been frozen. They are available in Italian and Middle Eastern shops. Frozen phyllo often becomes brittle and dry when defrosted. Always bring phyllo to room temperature before using. The leaves dry out very quickly when exposed to the air, so when working, remove only what you need and keep the remainder covered with plastic wrap. Some cooks work on a lightly dampened towel, but I find it makes the dough soggy.

Sun-dried Tomatoes: Buying sun-dried tomatoes in bulk instead of packed in oil reduces the fat as well as the cost. Rehydrate them in boiling water to cover for 5 minutes or as directed in the recipe. Rehydrated tomatoes may be stored in olive oil in the refrigerator. To substitute oil-packed tomatoes, blot them with paper towels.

To Peel and Seed Tomatoes: Plunge ripe tomatoes into a saucepan of boiling water for 30 seconds, or until skin loosens. Run under cold water to stop cooking. Cut out core and peel off skin. To seed, cut tomato in half crosswise, not through the stem, to expose the seed pockets. Squeeze the tomato halves gently in your hand to force out the seeds.

MORNING GLORY

I've never understood why more entertaining isn't done around the breakfast table. It takes less food, less alcohol, less money, less hassle and there are fewer standards to worry about upholding. You can eat any time you want (who says you can't have breakfast at lunchtime?), serve as many dishes and/or courses as you're comfortable with (forget about hors d'oeuvres with this meal), and there are no preconceived rules of etiquette to follow. The only dilemma is what to serve, since we now know all our traditional dishes—eggs, bacon and sausage, home fries, hollandaise sauce and cheeses—are not good for us. This chapter offers a fresh approach with an abundance of vegetables and fruits and lower-fat morning extravaganzas like baked French toast sandwiches and savory stuffed baked potatoes, along with a few good reasons to make them. Whether it's for weekend guests, a bon voyage party, or parents and kids convening before Little League, you'll find selections here to meet every need.

BREAKFAST For WEEKEND GUESTS

You won't have to rise at the crack of dawn, or even before your guests, to get this lively morning menu on the table; you can prepare most of it in advance or enlist your guests' participation. Let team players join in the cooking, which then becomes a tournament in itself. Begin by blending up some frothy Cantaloupe Coolers (with or without the rum), offer a selection of newspapers, turn up the music, and let the games begin.

Two breakfast entrees—Baked Strawberry-stuffed French Toast and Gingerbread Oven Pancake—give guests a choice. The French toast can be served with strawberries in half the filling and bananas in the other half. The slices look captivating on plates with fresh Grand Marnier–tinged strawberries on one and bananas glimmering with maple syrup on the other. Gingerbread Oven Pancake is an adaptation of the popular Dutch baby or puffed oven pancake. The addition of sliced fruit sautéed in butter and brown sugar adds a substantial dimension to the pancake. While the fruit does keep the pancake from puffing up as high as a Dutch baby, the good news is that it won't collapse.

Although a wide variety of breakfast meats and sausages are commercially available, I prefer mixing my own Turkey Patties, which lets me give them unexpected twists. This way I also know there are no fillers and preservatives. Turkey Patties are an auspicious accompaniment for either the pancake or French toast and can be baked at 425° or 450°F., depending on which one you choose. Both baking times are included in the recipe. This menu serves five, if you double the pancake.

Menu

◆

CANTALOUPE COOLER

◆

BAKED STRAWBERRY-STUFFED
FRENCH TOAST
OR
GINGERBREAD OVEN PAN-
CAKE WITH
CARAMELIZED FRUIT

◆

CRUSTED TURKEY PATTIES
WITH
HONEY MUSTARD

GAME PLAN

Up to 2 Weeks Ahead	**Make and freeze turkey patties**
1 Day Ahead	**Make and soak French toast, if serving**
	Make strawberry sauce for toast
	Assemble ingredients for coolers and refrigerate
	Make batter for pancake, if serving
	Make Double Whipped Cream for pancake, if serving
	Defrost turkey patties
	Freeze evaporated milk for coolers

DAY OF PARTY

20 Minutes Ahead	**Bake French toast or pancake**
	Reheat strawberry sauce, if desired
6 to 10 Minutes Ahead	**Bake turkey patties**
Shortly Before Serving	**Blend Cantaloupe Coolers**

· 15 ·

Plus or minus the rum, this mix of cantaloupe and vanilla yogurt is so refreshing that friends have dubbed it "The Ultimate Eye-Opener." Quick, easy to make, and light on calories, it's tantalizing as a year-round cooler at any hour of the day.

PREP TIME: 10 minutes

FREEZE TIME: Evaporated milk, at least 4 hours

ADVANCE PREP: Assemble ingredients and refrigerate a day ahead. Blend just before serving.

NUTRITIONAL ANALYSIS

Per 6-ounce serving (with nonfat yogurt, without the rum)
114 calories
less than 1 g fat
1 mg cholesterol
48 mg sodium

Crisp and golden, these puffy pocketed toasts taste best when the bread soaks in the batter for several hours or overnight.

CANTALOUPE COOLER

½ cup evaporated skim milk, frozen in ice-cube tray or small shallow bowl
2 cups diced ripe cantaloupe (about 1 medium melon)
⅓ cup sugar
1 cup regular, low-fat, or nonfat vanilla yogurt

½ cup golden rum (optional)
1 cup ice cubes

Garnish (optional)
Cantaloupe slices or thin wedges
Lime twists
Mint leaves

Unmold frozen evaporated milk by running the bottom of the container under hot water. Place frozen milk in blender. Add cantaloupe, sugar, yogurt, rum, if using, and ice cubes. Blend on high until smooth and slushy, about 2 minutes, adding more ice if needed. Pour into wine glasses or goblets and garnish with fruit and mint, if desired.

Change of Pace: Substitute honeydew or casaba melons, papaya, or mango for the cantaloupe. Or, use peeled fresh, or frozen, peaches.

MAKES: 5 (6-ounce) servings, without the rum.

Faster: Eliminate frozen evaporated milk. Without the milk the recipe makes 4 (6-ounce) servings. Purchase cut-up cantaloupe from the supermarket salad bar.

BAKED STRAWBERRY-STUFFED FRENCH TOAST

Filling
1 package (8 ounces) regular or low-fat cream cheese, softened
1 tablespoon orange juice concentrate
1 cup thickly sliced strawberries, stems removed (½ pint)

Bread and Batter
1 loaf (16 ounces) Italian bread, about 4 inches wide
4 large eggs
½ cup regular, low-fat, or nonfat milk
2 teaspoons vanilla extract

Strawberry–Grand Marnier Sauce

2 cups plus 1 cup thickly sliced strawberries, divided (1½ pints)
⅓ cup sugar

1 tablespoon cornstarch
3 tablespoons orange juice concentrate
¼ cup plus 1 tablespoon Grand Marnier, divided

To Make Filling: In a medium bowl, stir cream cheese until smooth. Stir in concentrate. Gently stir in berries; they do not need to be completely incorporated.

To Prepare Bread: Cut a small diagonal slice off each end of the bread and discard. Slice bread diagonally into 1- to 1½-inch-thick slices. Holding the knife parallel to the counter, cut each slice almost in half, leaving 1 side attached, to make a pocket. Divide the filling among the pockets, pressing closed around edges. Place on rimmed baking sheet.

To Make Batter: In a shallow bowl, whisk together the eggs, milk, and vanilla. Slowly pour over bread, turning to coat completely. (Bread may be baked immediately, or refrigerated up to 24 hours covered with plastic wrap, or transferred to plastic bags.)

To Make Sauce: In a medium saucepan off the heat, stir together 2 cups berries, sugar, cornstarch, orange juice, ⅔ cup water, and ¼ cup Grand Marnier until cornstarch is dissolved. Cook over moderately low heat, stirring often, until mixture comes to a boil, turns clear, and thickens. Remove from heat and cool. Stir in remaining 1 cup berries and 1 tablespoon Grand Marnier and set aside to serve warm or at room temperature. (Sauce may be refrigerated overnight.)

To Bake: Before serving, preheat oven to 450°F. Generously grease or spray a clean baking sheet (not the cushioned variety because they don't facilitate browning).

Place bread on baking sheet about 2 inches apart. Bake for 6 to 9 minutes, or until bottoms are golden. Turn and bake for 6 to 9 minutes longer, or until both sides are golden. Transfer to plates, top with some of the sauce, and pass remainder.

MAKES: 5 servings, 2 slices each.

Leaner: Substitute 1 carton (8 ounces) frozen egg substitute, thawed, for the 4 eggs.

Change of Pace: To make Banana-stuffed French Toast, substitute 2 small bananas, sliced, for the strawberries in the filling. Omit sauce and top with 2 sliced bananas and maple syrup.

PREP TIME: Toast, 20 minutes; sauce, 10 minutes

BAKE TIME: 16 to 20 minutes

ADVANCE PREP: Bread may be stuffed and soaked in the batter overnight and baked before serving. Sauce may be refrigerated overnight.

NUTRITIONAL ANALYSIS

Per slice toast (with low-fat cream cheese and nonfat milk)
221 calories
6 g fat
97 mg cholesterol
389 mg sodium

Per 2 tablespoons sauce
21 calories
0 g fat
0 mg cholesterol
less than 1 mg sodium

Taste buds will rise and shine with this baked pancake similar in texture to a Yorkshire pudding. Gingerbread spices pep up the molasses and enliven the slices of fresh peaches or nectarines. The recipe makes four average servings, but because everyone always wants seconds, it can be doubled and baked in a 12-inch skillet for the same length of time.

PREP TIME: 15 minutes

BAKE TIME: 18 to 20 minutes

ADVANCE PREP: Batter may be refrigerated overnight.

NUTRITIONAL ANALYSIS

Per serving (with nonfat milk)
305 calories
10 g fat
176 mg cholesterol
129 mg sodium

GINGERBREAD OVEN PANCAKE WITH CARAMELIZED FRUIT

½ cup regular, low-fat or nonfat milk
3 large eggs
2 tablespoons molasses
1½ teaspoons ground ginger
1 teaspoon ground cinnamon
½ teaspoon ground nutmeg
½ cup all-purpose flour
¼ cup plus 2 tablespoons packed light brown sugar, divided

3 medium or 2 large, firm, ripe peaches, peeled (see page 12), or unpeeled nectarines, sliced ¾ inch thick (about 2 cups)
2 tablespoons butter or margarine
Sliced peaches, nectarines, and/or berries, for garnish (optional)
Confectioners' sugar for topping (optional)
Double Whipped Cream (see page 266) (optional)

Place oven rack on bottom rung and preheat oven to 425°F.

To Make Batter: In a food processor with the metal blade or a large bowl with whisk, process or whisk milk, eggs, molasses, ginger, cinnamon, and nutmeg until blended. Mix in flour and ¼ cup brown sugar until blended. If using a whisk, the batter will remain slightly lumpy. Let stand while preparing the fruit. (Batter may be refrigerated, covered, overnight.)

To Bake: In a 10-inch nonstick skillet with ovenproof handle (or wrap handle in double thickness of foil), melt butter or margarine over moderate heat; swirl to coat bottom. Add 2 tablespoons brown sugar and cook, stirring, until sugar melts and bubbles. Add peaches or nectarines and stir to coat, about 30 seconds. Whisk or process batter to blend and pour over hot fruit. Immediately transfer skillet to oven and bake for 18 to 20 minutes or until puffed and crisp around edges. If desired, sprinkle with confectioners' sugar. Cut into wedges and serve with a dollop of Double Whipped Cream and additional fruit, if desired.

MAKES: 4 servings.

Faster: Substitute 1 cup (half a 1-pound package) frozen sliced peaches, thawed and well drained on paper towels, for the fresh.

Leaner: For a lighter, less custardlike pancake, replace the 3 whole eggs with 1 whole egg and 3 egg whites. Baking time remains the same. Top with peach yogurt instead of Double Whipped Cream.

Change of Pace: Substitute 2 large Golden or Red Delicious apples, peeled, cored, and thinly sliced for the peaches.

CRUSTED TURKEY PATTIES WITH HONEY MUSTARD

Coating
½ cup chopped pecans
3 cups Corn Chex or Crispix
   cereal
¼ cup regular, low-fat, or nonfat
   mayonnaise
1 tablespoon honey
2 tablespoons Dijon mustard
½ teaspoon dry mustard

Turkey Patties
2 medium garlic cloves, peeled
5 large green onions, cut into
   1-inch pieces (about 1 cup)

2 ounces lean Canadian bacon,
   cut into chunks (½ cup)
1 pound turkey breast cutlets,
   cut into chunks
2 tablespoons regular, low-fat,
   or nonfat mayonnaise
1 teaspoon honey
2 tablespoons Dijon mustard
1¼ teaspoons dried tarragon
½ teaspoon salt, or to taste
½ teaspoon freshly ground black
   pepper, or to taste

To Make Coating: In a food processor with the metal blade, chop pecans into small pieces. Add cereal and pulse until mixture is finely chopped. Remove to a shallow bowl. In another shallow bowl, stir together mayonnaise, honey, and mustards.

To Make Patties: In same processor bowl, mince garlic. Add green onions and pulse to chop. Add bacon and turkey and process until chopped. Add mayonnaise, honey, mustard, tarragon, salt, and pepper. Pulse to combine. Shape into ten 2½-inch patties, about ¾ inch thick. Dip both sides and edges into the mustard mixture and then into the crumbs, pressing to adhere. (Patties may be refrigerated, covered, overnight, or frozen up to 2 weeks. Defrost before baking.)

To Bake: Before serving, place rack on top rung of oven and preheat oven to either 425°F. or 450°F.

Place patties on greased baking sheet and bake either at 425°F. for 8 to 10 minutes or 450°F. for 6 to 8 minutes, or until tops are golden and meat is cooked through. Do not overcook or patties will be dry.

MAKES: 10 patties.

Leaner: Substitute ½ cup Grape Nuts cereal for the pecans.

Change of Pace: To make Chicken Patties, substitute 1 pound boneless, skinless chicken breasts for the turkey.

These baked patties are made with white-meat turkey breast, green onions, and the tangy sweetness of Dijon mustard and honey, then encrusted with a coating of breakfast cereal and pecans. They are important enough to be a casual dinner entree—try them sandwiched on a bun with lettuce and tomatoes.

PREP TIME: 25 minutes

BAKE TIME: 6 to 10 minutes.

ADVANCE PREP: May be refrigerated overnight or frozen.

NUTRITIONAL ANALYSIS

Per patty (with nonfat mayonnaise)
150 calories
5 g fat
22 mg cholesterol
548 mg sodium

BRUNCH
On The
MEDITERRANEAN

When I was faced with the challenge of co-hosting a brunch for twenty-five guests at a friend's home with only one oven, I developed these flexible dishes that taste terrific at room temperature and can be balanced on a lap and eaten with a fork. Another benefit is the menu spans the seasons, utilizing fruits and vegetables available year round. These dishes are sturdy enough to tote to a beach house or on a boat, yet festive enough for a shower, birthday, or anniversary party.

Frosty Melon Soup with Champagne provides a celebratory start and is easy to multiply for any size crowd.

The Eggplant, Two-Tomato, and Pesto Torte features all the advantages of a casserole. It is assembled, refrigerated or frozen, and reheated in the same springform pan. The recipe involves preparing several different layers—baking eggplant, cooking tomato sauce, and making pesto—but it actually improves in flavor and texture when frozen and reheated, and is just as tasty at room temperature as hot. Since the bitterness in eggplant comes with age, look for smaller ones that have no soft spots or wrinkles; large ones tend to have overdeveloped seeds that add to the bitter flavor. This torte is much lighter than other recipes I've seen, as well as being more robust and virtually indestructible.

Double Mushroom–Sausage Strudel with its substantial filling is another candidate for serving at room temperature.

Corn Custard Strata, a cross between custard and cornbread, has a puddinglike texture and replaces the usual egg dishes. The original recipe called for a stick of butter and one and a half cups of heavy cream. My updated version uses two tablespoons of butter or margarine, milk, and buttermilk (nonfat works great) and still tastes incredibly rich. This is the only recipe in the menu that benefits from being baked immediately before serving. When making it for a crowd, do not attempt to double the recipe and bake it in a larger pan. It needs to bake in a square or round pan, so you'll need to make two or more. You may question whether one recipe really serves twelve people. I've made this many times and if you serve it as a side dish, it really does.

When you sit down to eat, put the Amaretti Streusel Apple Squares into the preheated oven, turn off the heat and leave the dessert in the oven until ready to serve. It can be either baked and served from the same dish or cut into squares, transferred to a platter, and garnished with fresh leaves and flowers. This menu serves eight, allowing for seconds of everything but the soup.

GAME PLAN

1 Month Ahead	**Make and freeze eggplant torte** **Make and freeze strudel** **Make and freeze apple squares**
2 Days Ahead	**Defrost eggplant torte**
1 Day Ahead	**Make soup** **Defrost strudel** **Defrost apple squares** **Bake eggplant torte** **Assemble dry ingredients for corn custard**

DAY OF PARTY

1 Hour Ahead	**Reheat eggplant torte**
30 to 45 Minutes Ahead	**Bake Corn Custard Strata** **Rewarm apple squares** **Bake strudel**
Before Serving	**Pour Champagne into soup**

EXTRA POINTS

THE TABLE

Decorate with wicker baskets, terra-cotta pots, or flower boxes brimming with Provençale vegetable groupings such as white, Japanese, and baby eggplants; golden, plum, and cherry tomatoes; purple and yellow onions, scallions, leeks, and garlic bulbs; bunches of fresh herbs. Drape your table like a canvas awning—purchase striped fabric and lay it out with stripes going diagonally across. Use a variety of different color napkins tied with raffia. (See color photo, page 13.)

THE PLACE CARDS/ FAVORS

Write guests' names on seed packets and insert them into small terra-cotta pots (or paint names on the pots) and fill with fresh herbs or geraniums. (See color photo, page 13.)

A splash of the bubbly in each guest's soup wakes up the palate as well as the guest. To obtain the smoothest texture, grate the ginger on a hand grater and puree the ingredients in a blender instead of a food processor. For a pretty presentation, serve the soup in small cantaloupe halves.

PREP TIME: 15 minutes

CHILL TIME: May be served immediately if the ingredients are chilled

ADVANCE PREP: May be refrigerated overnight.

NUTRITIONAL ANALYSIS

Per 6-ounce serving (with low-fat yogurt, not including berry garnish)
108 calories
1 g fat
2 mg cholesterol
37 mg sodium

FROSTY MELON SOUP WITH CHAMPAGNE

1 ripe honeydew, Persian, or casaba melon, or 2 cantaloupes (5 to 6 pounds total)
2 tablespoons peeled and grated fresh ginger (see page 10)
¼ cup fresh lime juice (about 2 limes) (see page 11)
1 cup regular or low-fat vanilla yogurt

Fresh small berries, such as raspberries, black or boysenberries, or strawberries, for garnish
Grated nutmeg, preferably freshly grated, for garnish
About ¼ bottle Champagne

To Make Soup: Quarter melons, remove seeds, and peel. Chop fruit into small pieces; you should have about 8 cups. Puree in batches in a blender. Add ginger, lime juice, and yogurt and blend until smooth. Refrigerate until chilled. (Soup may be refrigerated overnight.)

To Serve: Serve in soup bowls, small cantaloupe halves, or goblets. Garnish with fresh berries and sprinkling of nutmeg. At each guest's place, pour a splash of Champagne into soup.

MAKES: 8 (¾-cup) servings.

Leaner: Although regular or low-fat yogurt are preferred because they are thicker, nonfat yogurt may be substituted.

Change of Pace: To make Pineapple-Melon Soup, substitute ½ fresh pineapple (4 cups chopped) for half the melon.

DOUBLE MUSHROOM–SAUSAGE STRUDEL

Filling
1 ounce dried shiitake
  mushrooms (about 1 cup)
1 pound hot Italian sausage,
  casing removed
2 teaspoons olive oil
1½ pounds fresh mushrooms,
  thinly sliced
1 tablespoon Dijon mustard
½ cup regular or light sour
  cream

1 teaspoon dried thyme
Freshly ground black pepper

No-stick cooking spray or 5 to 6
  tablespoons olive oil
8 sheets phyllo dough, at room
  temperature (see page 12)
  (half a 1-pound package)

To Make Filling: Place dried mushrooms and 1½ cups water in a 4-cup microwavesafe glass measure. Microwave, covered, on high (100%) for 2 to 4 minutes, or until very hot. Remove and steep mushrooms at least 20 minutes. Squeeze mushrooms, discarding broth.

Meanwhile, in a large skillet over high heat, sauté sausage, breaking up with spoon until brown, about 15 minutes; drain in colander. Wipe grease from pan, add olive oil and sauté fresh mushrooms over high heat until very brown, about 6 to 8 minutes. Cut tough stems from soaked shiitakes and slice mushrooms into ¼-inch strips. In a large bowl, stir together sausage, fresh and dried mushrooms, mustard, sour cream, thyme, and pepper to taste.

To Assemble: For each strudel, place 4 sheets phyllo on work surface. Spray or brush each sheet lightly with cooking spray or olive oil. Spoon half the filling in a log along 1 long edge of phyllo, leaving a 2-inch border. Fold phyllo over filling, tuck in ends and roll up. Spray or brush tops with oil. If not baking immediately, wrap in foil. (Unbaked strudels may be refrigerated overnight or frozen. Defrost in the refrigerator or at room temperature.)

To Bake: Preheat oven to 400°F.

Place strudels, seam side down, on a greased or sprayed rimmed baking sheet at least 2 inches apart. Slice into 1½-inch pieces, cutting only halfway to the bottom. Bake for 25 to 30 minutes or until golden. (Strudels may also be frozen after baking. Bring to room temperature and reheat at 400°F. for 10 minutes, or until hot.) Before serving, cut through slices.

MAKES: 24 slices.

resh and dried mushrooms, mixed with spicy sausage, bound with sour cream, and wrapped in strudel leaves, make an elegant brunch dish or appetizer. In taste tests, it was impossible to tell the strudels sprayed with no-stick cooking spray from those brushed with olive oil. After freezing, however, the sprayed strudels became so crisp and brittle that the leaves shattered. So, if freezing, brush phyllo with olive oil instead of cooking spray.

PREP TIME: 40 minutes

BAKE TIME: 25 to 30 minutes

ADVANCE PREP: May be refrigerated overnight or frozen before or after baking.

NUTRITIONAL ANALYSIS

Per serving (with light
sour cream and cooking
spray)
95 calories
5 g fat
2 mg cholesterol
25 mg sodium

My daughter Margi, a novice cook, says this dish has improved her culinary reputation so much that she is no longer embarrassed to admit she's my daughter. The assembled torte benefits from being refrigerated or frozen and baked a day before serving. (See color photo, page 13.)

PREP TIME: 60 minutes

BAKE TIME: 50 to 60 minutes

ADVANCE PREP: May be refrigerated up to 2 days or frozen. Best baked a day before serving and reheated.

EGGPLANT, TWO-TOMATO, AND PESTO TORTE

3 medium eggplants (3 to 3½ pounds)
About ¼ cup olive oil

Two-Tomato Sauce
1 tablespoon olive oil
1 large onion, chopped
⅓ cup sun-dried tomatoes, cut with scissors into small pieces (see page 12)
1 can (28 ounces) Italian-style plum tomatoes, drained
2 small zucchini, very thinly sliced (about ½ pound)
1 teaspoon dried oregano or 1 tablespoon chopped fresh oregano leaves
1 tablespoon raspberry vinegar
Salt and freshly ground black pepper

Pesto Sauce
3 large garlic cloves, peeled
2 cups (lightly packed) fresh basil leaves (about 1½ ounces)
¼ cup shredded parmesan cheese

1 cup dry bread crumbs, packaged or fresh (see page 10)
6 ounces sliced regular or low-fat jack or mozzarella cheese
3 tablespoons shredded parmesan cheese
Fresh basil leaves, for garnish (optional)

To Bake Eggplant: Preheat oven to 400°F.

Cut ends off eggplant, peel and slice crosswise into ¼- to ⅜-inch slices. Cover 2 baking sheets with heavy foil. Generously brush with olive oil. Arrange eggplant slices close together in 1 layer. Brush tops with olive oil. Bake for 12 minutes. Rotate baking sheets and bake 12 to 15 minutes longer or until eggplant is very soft and bottoms are lightly browned. Remove from oven and loosen from baking sheet with a spatula; leave on baking sheets until cool enough to handle.

To Make Tomato Sauce: While eggplant bakes, in a large skillet over moderately high heat, heat olive oil. Add onion and sauté, stirring, for 2 minutes. Cover pan with a sheet of wax paper and a lid and cook over low heat, stirring occasionally, until onion is soft but not brown, about 10 minutes. Meanwhile, place sun-dried tomatoes in 2-cup microwavesafe measure with 1 cup water. Cover with plastic wrap and microwave on high (100%) for 3 to 4 minutes, or until very soft. Remove tomatoes to a food processor with the metal blade, add ¼ cup of the liquid, and process until pureed. Cut canned tomatoes in half, squeeze out seeds, and remove any hard stems. Add to food processor and pulse until chunky. Stir into onions. Add zucchini, oregano, vinegar, and salt and pepper to taste. Cook, uncovered, over moderate heat, stirring occasionally, until zucchini is soft, about 5 to 7 minutes.

To Make Pesto Sauce: In a food processor with the metal blade, mince garlic. Add basil and parmesan. Process until ground. Add 3 tablespoons water and pulse to incorporate.

To Assemble: Grease or spray a 9-inch springform pan. Sprinkle bread crumbs over bottom. Spoon 1 cup tomato sauce over crumbs; it will not cover them. Arrange a third of the eggplant over sauce. Spread with 1 cup tomato sauce, layer with half the sliced cheese, half the pesto, a third of the eggplant, 1 cup tomato sauce, the remaining cheese, pesto, eggplant, and tomato sauce. (Torte may be refrigerated, covered, up to 2 days or frozen up to 1 month. Defrost on rimmed plate in refrigerator for 2 days or at room temperature for 8 hours. Juices will leak out as it defrosts. The torte is best baked one day before serving and reheated.)

To Bake: Preheat the oven to 400°F.

Wrap springform bottom in heavy foil (if it has been frozen, it will leak) and place on baking sheet. Bake, covered with foil, in center of oven until heated through, 40 minutes if at room temperature, 50 to 60 minutes if cold. Sprinkle with parmesan cheese and bake, uncovered, for 10 minutes. Let stand 15 minutes before serving or bring to room temperature and refrigerate, covered, overnight. To reheat, bring to room temperature and bake, uncovered, at 400°F. for 15 to 20 minutes or until heated through.

Before serving, remove sides of springform and place torte on serving platter. Garnish with fresh basil leaves, if desired.

MAKES: 10 servings.

Remember those magical puddings that separated into layers of custard and bread while baking? This updated version is surprisingly creamy and satisfying, even when made with nonfat milk and buttermilk. The blue cheese topping is optional, but its tang has a real affinity for sweet corn.

PREP TIME: 12 minutes

BAKE TIME: 26 minutes

ADVANCE PREP: Combine dry ingredients 1 day ahead. Make and bake before serving.

NUTRITIONAL ANALYSIS

Per serving (with nonfat buttermilk and nonfat milk)
154 calories
6 g fat
48 mg cholesterol
447 mg sodium

CORN CUSTARD STRATA

1 cup yellow cornmeal
½ cup all-purpose flour
1 tablespoon sugar
1 teaspoon baking soda
1 teaspoon salt, or to taste
1 cup regular, low-fat, or nonfat buttermilk
2 large eggs, beaten lightly
1 cup plus ½ cup regular, low-fat, or nonfat milk, divided

¾ cup fresh or frozen corn kernels
2 tablespoons butter or margarine
½ cup gorgonzola or blue cheese, frozen and crumbled (optional)

Preheat the oven to 400°F.

To Make the Batter: In a large bowl, stir together cornmeal, flour, sugar, baking soda, and salt. Whisk in buttermilk, eggs, and 1 cup of the milk until blended. Stir in corn. Put butter or margarine in 9-inch square baking dish. Place in center of oven and heat until melted and sizzling, about 3 minutes. Remove from oven and swirl to coat bottom and sides. Pour excess butter into batter and stir to combine. Immediately pour batter into pan. Sprinkle remaining ½ cup milk over the top.

To Bake: Bake for 20 minutes. If desired, sprinkle top with cheese. Bake for 6 to 8 more minutes, or until the sides and top are brown and crusty, but the center still jiggles when the pan is shaken. Cut into squares to serve.

MAKES: 12 side-dish servings.

Leaner: One whole egg and 2 egg whites may be substituted for the 2 whole eggs. Do not use frozen egg substitutes; they will not set up.

AMARETTI STREUSEL APPLE SQUARES

Pastry
1½ cups all-purpose flour
2 tablespoons sugar
Dash salt
1¼ teaspoons baking powder
¼ pound (1 stick) butter or
    margarine
¼ cup regular, low-fat or nonfat
    milk
1 large egg
1 teaspoon vanilla extract

Amaretti Streusel
½ cup all-purpose flour
¾ cup sugar
¼ teaspoon cinnamon
¾ cup coarsely crushed amaretti
    cookies (place cookies in
    plastic bag and crush with
    hands) (2½ ounces)
½ cup sliced almonds
4 tablespoons (½ stick) butter or
    margarine, melted

3 pounds tart green apples,
    peeled, halved, cored, and
    sliced ¼ inch thick
Double Whipped Cream, for
    serving (see page 266)
    (optional)

To Make Pastry: Place rack in lower third of oven and preheat oven to 375°F. In a medium bowl, stir together flour, sugar, salt, and baking powder. In a 4-cup microwavesafe measure, microwave butter or margarine, covered with a paper towel, on high (100%) until melted. Whisk in milk, egg, and vanilla. Stir into flour mixture until incorporated. Press into bottom of prepared pan. (If difficult to press, let rest 10 minutes.)

To Make Streusel: In a medium bowl, stir together flour, sugar, cinnamon, cookies, and almonds. Add melted butter and stir until distributed. Arrange apples over pastry. Sprinkle streusel over apples.

To Bake: Bake for 40 to 45 minutes, or until pastry is golden and apples are soft. (Dessert may be cooled, covered with heavy foil, and refrigerated up to 2 days or frozen up to 1 month. Defrost at room temperature. Reheat, uncovered, at 400°F. until warm, about 10 minutes.) Cut into squares and serve warm with whipped cream, if desired.

MAKES: 12 to 15 servings.

Faster: To peel, core, and slice apples quickly, use an apple peeler-corer-slicer gadget, available at cookware shops.

Layers of soft, juicy apples baked on a cakelike pastry crust under a crunchy almond streusel topping is not really a pie, nor a cake, nor a coffeecake. It's a true hybrid. Baked in a casserole to serve a crowd, it's as welcome for dessert after a casual dinner as it is for a brunch or a tea. I like to serve it warm (it reheats fine), topped with a dollop of whipped cream.

PREP TIME: 30 minutes

BAKE TIME: 40 to 45 minutes

ADVANCE PREP: May be refrigerated up to 2 days or frozen.

NUTRITIONAL ANALYSIS

Per serving (with nonfat milk)
285 calories
13 g fat
39 mg cholesterol
159 mg sodium

MERRY WINTER MORNING MENU

W hether this menu is served before the living room becomes a sea of wrapping paper prior to breakfast, or after the calm for brunch, this is another gift for your loved ones on Christmas morning. It's also great for New Year's, or for that matter any time or any season when you want a memorable morning meal. By varying the fruit in the palettes according to what's in season, and substituting fresh berries for the cranberries in the coffee cake, the menu spans the year.

The craze for baked potatoes inspired the Spud Boats. They're a one-dish meal in a potato shell, with a filling of vegetables, meat, and eggs. If you double the potato recipe, the menu will serve ten. My Smoked Salmon Napoleon is a star, especially when decorated with smoked salmon flowers.

To round out this celebratory menu, the Crowned Cran-Apple Coffee-cake Wreath, dotted with the holiday colors of red and green apples and scarlet cranberries, can also double as a centerpiece for the table.

Menu

◆

FRESH FRUIT PALETTES

◆

BRUNCH SPUD BOATS

◆

SMOKED SALMON NAPOLEON

◆

CROWNED CRAN-APPLE COFFEECAKE WREATH

G A M E   P L A N

Up to 1 Month Ahead	**Make coffeecake** **Bake and freeze puff pastry layers for the Napoleon**
2 Weeks Ahead	**Make yogurt cheese for Fruit Palettes**
1 Day Ahead	**Bake potatoes and chop ingredients for Spud Boats** **Defrost coffeecake** **Defrost puff pastry for Napoleon**

DAY OF PARTY

Up to 8 Hours Ahead	**Prepare fruit for palettes**
Up to 2 Hours Ahead	**Make topping and spoon fruit over coffeecake** **Reheat puff pastry and assemble the Napoleon** **Assemble Fruit Palettes** **Bring potato shells to room temperature**
15 Minutes Before Serving	**Fill and bake Spud Boats** **Spoon caramel over fruit on coffeecake**

EXTRA ◆ POINTS ◆

THE TABLE

Place a two-inch round candle in the center of the coffeecake, or mix and match a grouping of candles in various sizes and tie them together with a ribbon. (See color photo, page 16.)

For a holiday table decoration, stack graduated sizes of grapevine wreaths (spray painted, if you like) around a potted plant. Hide the dirt with a blanket of Spanish moss. Garnish the wreaths or the plant with small pears, apples, cranberry garlands, ornaments or little packages. (See color photo, page 16.)

Treat your eyes as well as your palate to artistically arranged stacks of fresh fruit topped with a thick dollop of drained lemon yogurt. These also make a terrific light dessert. Don't feel limited by my suggestions—use any fruits in season. (See color photo, page 16.)

PREP TIME: 20 minutes

DRAIN TIME: Yogurt cheese, at least 4 hours

ADVANCE PREP: Yogurt cheese may be refrigerated up to 2 weeks. Fruit may be prepared 8 hours before serving.

FRESH FRUIT PALETTES

For Each Serving
1 to 2 tablespoons lemon yogurt cheese (see page 43)
1 slice fresh pineapple
1 slice melon, such as honeydew, cantaloupe, or Crenshaw, or papaya
2 slices firm but ripe kiwi

2 slices starfruit (carambola), unpeeled (optional)
Small sprig red or green seedless grapes
2 small mint sprigs

At least 4 hours before serving, make yogurt cheese.

To Prepare Fruit: Peel and core pineapple and slice horizontally into ⅜-inch rings. Peel melon or papaya, cut in half, remove seeds and slice into ⅜-inch half-moon slices. Peel kiwi and slice into ⅜-inch rounds. (Fruits may be refrigerated up to 8 hours. Layer fruit with paper towels and cover with plastic wrap.)

To Assemble Each Serving: Place a round of pineapple on each plate. Top with 2 slices of melon, 2 rounds of kiwi, starfruit, if using, and a dollop of yogurt cheese. Garnish the top with grapes and sprigs of fresh mint.

BRUNCH SPUD BOATS

3 medium baking potatoes,
    scrubbed
No-stick cooking spray
1 to 2 tablespoons olive oil
⅔ cup chopped lean ham or
    Canadian bacon (3 ounces)
⅓ cup diced zucchini
⅓ cup diced red bell pepper
3 green onions, with tops, sliced

6 eggs, beaten
2 tablespoons grated parmesan
    cheese (optional)
Guacamole and Corn Salsa (see
    page 170), Pineapple-Papaya
    Salsa (see page 79), or
    storebought salsa for serving
    (optional)

To Make Potato Shells: Prick potatoes with a fork and bake in a micro-wave oven on a plate on high (100%) for 7 to 11 minutes, rotating after 3 minutes, until tender when pierced with a knife. Or bake in a conventional oven at 450°F. for 50 to 60 minutes. They should be soft but firm enough to dice.

Preheat oven to broil. Cut potatoes in half lengthwise and scoop out pulp, leaving a ½-inch shell. Dice scooped-out potato. Spray both sides of potato shells with cooking spray. Place on baking sheet and broil until edges are browned and top is slightly crisped but not dry, about 3 to 4 minutes. (Shells may be refrigerated overnight. Refrigerate cooked potato separately. Bring both to room temperature before filling.)

To Make Filling: Preheat oven to 500°F. In a large skillet, preferably nonstick, over high heat, heat 1 tablespoon oil until hot. Sauté potatoes, turning with a spatula until they begin to turn golden, about 5 minutes, adding more oil if needed. Stir in ham, zucchini, and red pepper and sauté, stirring, until vegetables soften slightly, about 3 minutes. Add eggs, reduce heat to medium-low, and cook, stirring lightly, until very loosely set. Stir in green onions. Fill potato shells and sprinkle tops with cheese, if desired. Place potatoes on baking sheet and bake for 5 minutes, or until eggs are set and cheese melts. Serve with salsa, if desired.

MAKES: 6 servings.

Leaner: Substitute 1½ cups frozen egg substitute, thawed, for the 6 eggs. Decrease ham to ⅓ cup or substitute smoked chicken or turkey.

Sail the wave of a contemporary breakfast with this scrambled Denver omelet cresting in a baked potato shell.

PREP TIME: 30 minutes

COOK TIME: To microwave potatoes, 7 to 11 minutes; to bake, 50 to 60 minutes

ADVANCE PREP: Potato shells and cooked potatoes may be refrigerated overnight. Vegetables and ham may be chopped a day ahead.

NUTRITIONAL ANALYSIS

Per serving (with lean ham)
202 calories
9 g fat
219 mg cholesterol
281 mg sodium

Layering flaky puff pastry with creamy cheese, sliced onions, cucumbers, dill, and smoked salmon is like spiffing up a lox and cream cheese platter for a soiree. This Napoleon is also great for a cocktail party. Cut it into squares and garnish each one with a small salmon ''flower'' and sprig of dill. (See color photo, page 16.)

PREP TIME: 30 minutes

BAKE TIME: 20 minutes

ADVANCE PREP: Pastry may be baked a day ahead or frozen. Assemble up to 2 hours before serving.

NUTRITIONAL ANALYSIS

Per serving (with low-fat cheese)
304 calories
19 g fat
39 mg cholesterol
638 mg sodium

SMOKED SALMON NAPOLEON

Pastry
1 package (17¼ ounces) puff pastry, defrosted if frozen but still very cold
1 egg, lightly mixed with 1 tablespoon water

Filling
About 2 teaspoons Dijon mustard
½ pound regular or low-fat garden vegetable or herb soft cheese, such as Rondelé or Boursin, at room temperature
½ hothouse or seedless cucumber or 1 small regular cucumber, peeled and very thinly sliced

2 tablespoons chopped fresh dill or 1 tablespoon dried dillweed
½ red onion, peeled and very thinly sliced
8 to 10 ounces thinly sliced smoked salmon

Garnish (optional)
2 to 3 slices smoked salmon
Dill sprigs

To Bake Pastry: Preheat oven to 350°F.

On a lightly floured board, roll 1 sheet (or half) of pastry into a rectangle about 15 × 12 inches. Cut rectangle in half lengthwise, making two 15 × 6-inch pieces. Place on lightly greased baking sheet. Roll and cut second sheet in same manner. Place one of the pastry rectangles on a second baking sheet. (Reserve fourth rectangle for another use.) Prick the three sheets with a fork at about 1-inch intervals. Brush tops with beaten egg, making sure it doesn't drip down the sides. Bake for 20 minutes, or until golden, rotating if necessary to ensure even browning. Remove to racks to cool. (Pastry may be covered with foil and held at room temperature overnight, or frozen in an airtight container so they don't get crushed. Defrost at room temperature and reheat at 400°F. for 5 to 10 minutes before assembling.)

To Assemble: Up to 2 hours before serving, trim pastry to even the edges, if necessary. Place 1 sheet on a platter. Spread with a thin layer of mustard (it goes only on this layer) and a third of the cheese. (If the cheese is difficult to spread, warm slightly in the microwave.) Top with half the cucumber slices, overlapping them slightly, sprinkle with half the dill, top with half the onions, and cover with half the salmon. Place second pastry on top and spread with a third of the cheese. Repeat layering remaining cucumber, dill, onion, and salmon. Spread underside of third pastry layer with remaining cheese (this will help it adhere) and place on top of the loaf, cheese side down.

To Garnish: If desired, make smoked salmon roses or cut salmon into flowers with canape cutters. Arrange with dill sprigs on top of Napoleon. Cover with plastic wrap and place in a cool place at room temperature until ready to serve, but no longer than 2 hours. With a serrated knife, cut into thin slices or squares.

MAKES: 10 servings.

SMOKED SALMON ROSES

For each rose, roll 1 slice of salmon up tightly for the center of the rose, fanning it out for petals as you wind around. Overlap second slice loosely around center to form outer petals. Squeeze base to hold slices together, fanning out edges to make ruffled petals.

This moist, pound cake–textured apple cake is decked out for Christmas with red and green apples, crimson cranberries, and a caramel glaze. If you omit the nuts and use nonfat yogurt in the topping, there is only one gram of fat in the entire recipe. But, pretend I didn't tell you—it tastes fattening. (See color photo, page 16.)

PREP TIME: Cake, 25 minutes; topping, 15 minutes

BAKE TIME: 45 to 55 minutes

ADVANCE PREP: Cake may be refrigerated up to 2 days or frozen. Topping may be put on up to 2 hours ahead.

NUTRITIONAL ANALYSIS

Per serving (with egg whites and pecans)
364 calories
10 g fat
0 cholesterol
208 mg sodium

Per serving (without pecans)
274 calories
1 g fat
0 cholesterol
208 mg sodium

CROWNED CRAN-APPLE COFFEECAKE WREATH

Coffeecake
3 large tart apples, such as Pippin or Granny Smith, peeled, cored, and cut into chunks (about 3 cups)
1 cup fresh or frozen cranberries
1⅓ cups all-purpose flour
1 cup whole wheat flour
2 teaspoons baking soda
2 teaspoons ground cinnamon
1½ cups sugar
¼ teaspoon salt
4 egg whites or ⅓ cup frozen egg substitute, thawed
½ cup applesauce, preferably chunky

Cran-Apple Topping
¼ cup sugar
½ cup (packed) light brown sugar
Dash salt
¼ cup regular, low-fat, or nonfat plain yogurt
1½ cups pecan halves
1 small red apple, unpeeled and cut into ⅜-inch slices
1 small green apple, unpeeled and cut into ⅜-inch slices
⅓ cup fresh or frozen cranberries

Grease or spray a 12-cup tube pan with a removable bottom, such as an angel food cake pan. Preheat oven to 350°F.

To Make Coffeecake: In a food processor fitted with the metal blade, pulse apples until coarsely chopped; remove to a bowl. Pulse cranberries until coarsely chopped; remove to apples. In same food processor bowl, pulse both flours, baking soda, cinnamon, sugar, and salt. Add egg whites or egg substitute and applesauce and pulse until batter is moistened. Add chopped apples and cranberries and pulse until incorporated.

To Bake: Pour batter into prepared pan; it will fill only a third of the pan. Bake for 45 to 55 minutes, or until toothpick inserted in center comes out clean. Cool in pan 10 minutes. Cake will fall as it cools. Go around edges with a knife and remove sides of pan. Cut away from bottom and invert onto rack. Cool completely. (Cake may be refrigerated up to 2 days or frozen. Defrost at room temperature.)

To Make Topping: Up to 2 hours before serving, in a 3-quart (12-cup) microwavesafe bowl, stir both sugars, salt, and yogurt together until blended. Microwave, uncovered, on high (100%) for 5 to 7 minutes without stirring, until caramel color. Stir in pecans, apple slices, and cranberries. Microwave on high (100%) for 1 to 3 minutes, or until caramel is melted and syrupy. Stir fruit to coat. With a slotted spoon, remove fruit and nuts and spoon on top of cake. Set caramel aside until it thickens enough to coat. Spoon over fruit. (If caramel gets too thick, microwave for 10 seconds.)

MAKES: 12 servings.

Change of Pace: To make Cran-Apple-Fig Cake, stir ½ cup diced dried figs into cake batter with the apples and cranberries.

POWER-PACKED BREAKFAST BUFFET

When my fit friend Phyllis hit fifty, she sent visors through the mail inviting sports nuts to meet Grape Nuts by joining her for a jog around the park with breakfast to follow. At the starting line, a group of marathon runners took off like gusts of wind, while the social strutters kept up a chatting pace. Back at her house, she gave us T-shirts to change into with ''Fit and Fifty'' printed on them (but they could also say something like Thirtysomething, Sporty at Forty, Sexy at Sixty, etc.) and, as an additional favor, she supplemented us with individual packets of vitamins.

Although this memorable party took place nearly ten years ago, I still remember that she served a variety of omelets, cheeses, and assorted breads and muffins, the health food of the eighties. With an updated, lower-fat menu, this theme is ideal for today's on-the-go, exercise-conscious society. The theme is sporty; it incorporates the workout right into the party—cycling, tennis, racquetball, or whatever—it's inexpensive, and the food is so casual and simple to prepare that even insecure cooks can get it on the table without breaking into a sweat.

Begin with a yogurt bar that packs enough nourishment to jump-start any sluggish body or mind. Set up Yogurt-Granola Parfaits in either individual goblets or a large glass bowl or put out the ingredients and let guests assemble their own.

Then offer a selection of cereals—homemade granola and storebought varieties—with low-fat or nonfat milk. For a leaner twist on muffins, bake them in miniature muffin tins instead of the usual three-inch size. A recipe for twelve large ones will make twenty-four to thirty smaller ones and will bake about five minutes faster.

◆

YOGURT-GRANOLA PARFAITS

◆

MULTICRUNCH MAPLE GRANOLA

◆

TRIPLE CHERRY MUFFINS

◆

CARROT BRAN-ANA MUFFINS

◆

CORNMEAL BREAKFAST BARS WITH APRICOTS AND DATES

◆

PLAIN AND FLAVORED YOGURT CHEESES

◆

FRESH AND DRIED PEAR PRESERVES

You may also wish to serve some mini bagels, as well as a new take on a muffin/coffeecake, Cornmeal Breakfast Bars.

And of course you'll need some spreads. To keep calories to a minimum but take taste to the max, make some Fresh and Dried Pear Preserves in the microwave. Replace cream cheese with nonfat cheeselike yogurt spreads, made by draining the liquid from plain or fruit-flavored yogurts. Fill sports coolers with Gatorade, sports tea, and/or high-powered fruit drinks. This menu can be adapted for any size crowd. Plan on 1½ muffins per person.

GAME PLAN

Up to 1 Month Ahead	**Make and freeze Carrot Bran-ana Muffins** **Make and freeze Triple Cherry Muffins** **Make and freeze Cornmeal Breakfast Bars** **Make granola**
2 Weeks Ahead	**Make yogurt cheese** **Make Fresh and Dried Pear Preserves**
1 Day Ahead	**Purchase bagels** **Defrost muffins and cornmeal bars** **Cut fruit for parfaits and layer in paper towels**
DAY OF PARTY 30 Minutes Ahead	**Assemble parfaits or put out ingredients for guests** **to assemble their own** **Rewarm muffins and cornmeal bars, if desired** **Toast bagels, if serving**

It's great when something that looks this alluring can be so nutritious. Assemble these parfaits in individual stemmed goblets or layer them in a large glass bowl and serve as a breakfast entree, first course, or dessert for any meal.

PREP TIME: 30 minutes for 6 parfaits (not including making granola)

ADVANCE PREP: Fruit may be cut and refrigerated overnight. Assemble parfaits before serving.

YOGURT-GRANOLA PARFAITS

For Each Serving
About 1 cup assorted fresh fruits, such as melons, oranges, pineapple, kiwi, berries, or seedless grapes, cut into ½-inch chunks
¼ cup (4 tablespoons) fruit-flavored or lemon-flavored regular, low-fat, or nonfat yogurt

2 tablespoons Multicrunch Maple Granola (recipe follows) or storebought granola

As close to serving as possible, place a third of the fruit in bottom of a parfait glass or goblet. Top with 2 tablespoons yogurt, 1 tablespoon granola, a third of the fruit, remaining yogurt, and granola. Arrange remaining fruit on top. Serve immediately so granola does not get soggy.

Or, multiply the recipe as desired and layer in a glass bowl.

NUTRITIONAL ANALYSIS

Per serving
192 calories
4 g fat
3 mg cholesterol
68 mg sodium

MULTICRUNCH MAPLE GRANOLA

½ cup maple syrup
3 tablespoons orange juice
2 tablespoons (packed) light
  brown sugar
¼ teaspoon salt, or to taste
1½ teaspoons ground cinnamon
1½ cups regular or quick rolled
  oats

½ cup wheat germ
⅓ cup sesame seeds
⅓ cup dry-roasted sunflower
  seeds
½ cup chopped walnuts
½ cup shredded coconut

Preheat oven to 300°F. Line a baking sheet with heavy-duty foil and grease or spray with cooking spray.

In a small bowl, stir together maple syrup, orange juice, brown sugar, salt, and cinnamon. Stir oats, wheat germ, sesame and sunflower seeds, walnuts, and coconut together on the baking sheet. Pour syrup mixture over and stir and toss until well coated. Spread out evenly in pan. Bake for 30 to 40 minutes, stirring well after 15 minutes, until mixture is golden brown. It will be slightly soft but will firm up as it cools. Remove from oven, cool, and store in an airtight container. (May be stored at room temperature for several weeks or refrigerated for several months.)

MAKES: about 4 cups.

Leaner: Substitute 1 cup packaged mixed dried fruit bits for the nuts and coconut. Reserve 6 tablespoons of the maple syrup mixture and stir it into the fruit in a microwavesafe bowl. Microwave, covered, on high (100%) for 2 to 3 minutes, or until hot. Let steep while granola bakes. Stir softened fruit into granola for the last 5 minutes of baking.

Keep this crackly crunchy cereal on hand to sprinkle on fruit or yogurt or just for snacking.

PREP TIME: 10 minutes

BAKE TIME: 35 minutes

ADVANCE PREP: May be stored airtight for several weeks or refrigerated for several months.

NUTRITIONAL ANALYSIS

Per ¼ cup
148 calories
7 g fat
0 cholesterol
46 mg sodium

TRIPLE CHERRY MUFFINS

These are jam-packed with cherries—dried and canned in the batter with a dollop of preserves in the center.

PREP TIME: 20 minutes

BAKE TIME: 15 to 20 minutes

ADVANCE PREP: May be refrigerated up to 2 days or frozen.

Streusel Topping
¼ cup (packed) light brown sugar
2 tablespoons all-purpose flour
1½ teaspoons ground cinnamon
3 tablespoons regular or quick rolled oats
1 tablespoon vegetable oil

Cherry Muffins
1 can (16 ounces) tart cherries
⅔ cup (packed) light brown sugar
1¼ cups all-purpose flour
¼ cup oat bran high-fiber hot cereal

2 teaspoons baking powder
½ teaspoon baking soda
½ teaspoon ground cinnamon
¼ teaspoon salt
⅓ cup orange juice concentrate, thawed
2 egg whites
2 tablespoons vegetable oil
½ cup dried cherries or cranberries
2 tablespoons cherry preserves

Preheat oven to 375°F. Spray or grease 12 muffin cups.

To Make Topping: In a small bowl, stir together brown sugar, flour, cinnamon, and oats. Add oil and toss with fingers until blended; set aside.

To Make Muffins: Drain cherries, reserving ¼ cup juice; discard remaining juice. In a food processor with the metal blade, pulse brown sugar, flour, oat bran, baking powder, baking soda, cinnamon, and salt until mixed. Add orange juice concentrate, egg whites, oil, and ¼ cup cherry juice. Pulse until blended. Add 1 cup of the tart cherries (reserve the remainder for another use) and dried cherries, and pulse 6 to 8 times or until incorporated. Spoon into muffin cups, filling to the top. Spoon ½ teaspoon preserves into the center of each. Sprinkle streusel over tops.

To Bake: Bake for 15 to 20 minutes or until toothpick comes out clean. Cool 10 minutes, go around edges with a sharp knife, and lift the muffins to cooling racks. Serve warm or at room temperature. (Muffins may be refrigerated up to 2 days or frozen. Reheat at 375°F. for 5 minutes or until warm.)

MAKES: 12 muffins.

NUTRITIONAL ANALYSIS

Per muffin
215 calories
4 g fat
0 cholesterol
151 mg sodium

CARROT BRAN-ANA MUFFINS

½ cup raisins
¾ cup all-purpose flour
½ cup oat bran high-fiber hot cereal
½ cup (packed) light brown sugar
½ cup regular or quick rolled oats
1 teaspoon baking powder
1½ teaspoons ground cinnamon
½ teaspoon baking soda
¼ teaspoon salt

1 medium banana, mashed (about ⅓ cup)
¼ cup regular, low-fat, or nonfat milk
2 egg whites, lightly beaten, or ¼ cup frozen egg substitute, thawed
2 tablespoons vegetable oil
1 teaspoon vanilla extract
½ cup shredded carrots
½ cup walnuts (optional)

Preheat oven to 400°F. Grease 12 muffin cups or fill with paper cupcake liners and spray with cooking spray.

To Make Muffins: Pour enough boiling water over raisins to cover and let stand 5 minutes. Drain well and set aside. In a large bowl, stir together flour, oat bran, brown sugar, oatmeal, baking powder, cinnamon, baking soda, and salt. Stir in banana, milk, egg whites, oil, and vanilla until mixture is thoroughly moistened. Do not overmix; the batter should be lumpy. Stir in raisins, carrots, and nuts, if using. Spoon into muffin cups, filling two thirds full.

To Bake: Bake for 18 to 20 minutes, or until toothpick inserted in center comes out clean. Remove from pans and serve warm. (Muffins may be stored at room temperature up to 2 days or frozen. Reheat at 375°F. for 5 minutes or until warm.)

MAKES: 12 muffins.

This unique combination of fruit, vegetable, and cereal produces a moist, cholesterol-free muffin.

PREP TIME: 20 minutes

BAKE TIME: 18 to 20 minutes

ADVANCE PREP: May be stored at room temperature up to 2 days or frozen.

NUTRITIONAL ANALYSIS

Per muffin (with egg whites and nonfat milk)
144 calories
3 g fat
less than 1 mg cholesterol
125 mg sodium

Pastry chef, cookbook author, and friend Jim Dodge gets the credit for turning cornbread into breakfast bars. My reduced-fat version still showcases the coarse texture and buttery essence of the cornmeal. Chock-full of dried fruit, these make a nice addition to a muffin basket, a coffeecake platter, or a nutritious breakfast on the run.

PREP TIME: 20 minutes

BAKE TIME: 20 minutes

ADVANCE PREP: May be refrigerated up to 3 days or frozen.

NUTRITIONAL ANALYSIS

Per bar (with nonfat milk)
99 calories
2 g fat
20 mg cholesterol
107 mg sodium

CORNMEAL BREAKFAST BARS WITH APRICOTS AND DATES

1 cup dried apricots, coarsely chopped
1¾ cups regular, low-fat, or nonfat milk
¾ cup yellow cornmeal
4 tablespoons (½ stick) unsalted butter or margarine
½ cup sugar

1 teaspoon vanilla extract
2 large eggs
1 cup all-purpose flour
¼ cup wheat germ, preferably honey crunch
1 tablespoon baking powder
¾ teaspoon salt, or to taste
1 cup pitted chopped dates

Preheat the oven to 400°F. Grease or spray a 9 × 13-inch baking dish.

To Make Batter: Place apricots and milk in a 4-cup microwavesafe measuring cup. Microwave, covered, on high (100%) for 3 to 4 minutes, or until very hot. Stir in the cornmeal until smooth. Cool to room temperature, stirring occasionally.

In a food processor with the metal blade, process butter, sugar, and vanilla until creamy, about 1 minute. Add eggs and process until blended. Add the flour, wheat germ, baking powder, and salt and pulse until incorporated; do not overmix. Add the apricot mixture and dates and pulse 3 or 4 times until incorporated, leaving fruit in chunky pieces. Spread the batter in the prepared pan.

To Bake: Bake for 20 minutes, or until the top begins to brown and the edges begin to pull away. Cool completely in the pan. Cut into 2¾ × 1¼-inch bars. (Bars may be refrigerated up to 3 days or frozen.) Serve warm or at room temperature.

MAKES: 28 bars.

Leaner: Substitute 3 egg whites for the 2 whole eggs.

Change of Pace: Substitute 1 to 2 cups chopped dried apples, pears, peaches, figs, or prunes for the apricots and/or dates.

PLAIN AND FLAVORED YOGURT CHEESES

3 cups regular, low-fat, or nonfat plain or flavored yogurt

Place a funnel or strainer over a medium bowl. Line it with a double thickness of cheesecloth or a paper coffee filter. Spoon in yogurt and cover with plastic wrap. Place in a cool place up to 4 hours or refrigerate overnight. Transfer the cheese to a covered container, discard the liquid, and refrigerate. Make as much or as little as you like. (Cheese may be refrigerated up to 2 weeks.)

MAKES: 1 to 1½ cups.

Cream cheese contains about sixty times the amount of fat per cup as nonfat yogurt cheese, which is one good reason to make it. Another is the variety of flavors to choose from.

PREP TIME: 5 minutes

DRAIN TIME: 4 hours at room temperature; overnight in refrigerator

ADVANCE PREP: May be refrigerated up to 2 weeks.

NUTRITIONAL ANALYSIS

Per tablespoon (with nonfat yogurt)
24 calories
less than 1 g fat
1 mg cholesterol
33 mg sodium

Falling somewhere between chutney and jam, this easy microwave spread features the pleasing taste and texture of soft fresh pears with the concentrated intensity and chewiness of dried ones.

PREP TIME: 20 minutes

COOK TIME: 20 to 25 minutes

ADVANCE PREP: May be refrigerated up to 4 weeks.

NUTRITIONAL ANALYSIS

Per tablespoon
54 calories
less than 1 g fat
0 cholesterol
6 mg sodium

FRESH AND DRIED PEAR PRESERVES

½ cup finely chopped dried pears, cores removed
4 fresh pears, peeled, halved, cored, and cut into ¼-inch dice
Grated peel and juice of 1 lemon (see page 11)
1 teaspoon minced fresh ginger (see page 10)
¼ cup maple syrup

Place all ingredients in a 2-quart (8-cup) microwavesafe bowl. Microwave, uncovered, on high (100%) for 20 to 25 minutes, stirring after 10 minutes, until mixture is as thick as jam. Cool completely, cover, and refrigerate.

MAKES: 1 cup.

MIDDAY MEALS

oast the bride or mother-to-be. Honor the birthday child. Celebrate with co-workers. Watch a game. Casual or elegant, luncheons are usually planned around events. Whatever the mood, here you'll find sophisticated salads for those times that call for linens and lace, sturdy sandwiches for toting on a picnic or for munching while cheering in front of the TV, Mexican madness to liven up a charity event or office meeting, plus all the trappings for your kids' own three-ring circus.

SANDWICHES
For
SUPER SPORTS

Whether you're huddling around the TV or tailgating at a game, tackling a menu for a sporting event can be as challenging as strategizing maneuvers on the field. I've watched hot-blooded fans catapult out of their seats, tossing food from their laps onto the floor like an incomplete pass. The edibles should be as sturdy as a linebacker, as durable as a goal post, and as manageable as the coolest of quarterbacks.

Here are some unique, great-tasting handheld edibles with fillings almost too sophisticated for mere sandwiches. Both the Southwestern Chicken Bread Bowl and Basque Tuna Baguette are stuffed creations made by hollowing out and filling bread loaves. To compress the bread and make the sandwiches easier to eat, the loaves are weighted down and refrigerated for an hour. Once the weight is removed, the sandwich can be consumed immediately or refrigerated for several hours or overnight. The Vegetarian Hye Roller, with its smooth/warm and cool/crunchy tastes and textures goes together quickly, especially if you chop the vegetables in a food processor. Another stuffed sandwich, one made from a homemade loaf, is the White, Red, and Green Italian Braid (see page 142).

My deli salads are made without mayonnaise to allow their crisp, clean flavors to shine through. Although both salads serve six, they can be easily multiplied. Supply bowls of popcorn and pretzels, a platter of homemade and/or storebought cookies, sit back, relax, and enjoy the cheers from your fans. If you serve all the sandwiches and double the salads, this menu serves twelve.

GAME PLAN

1 Month Ahead	**Make and freeze NCL All-Star Cookies** **Make and freeze Biscotti with Dried Fruits**
1 Day Ahead	**Prepare vegetables and dressing for slaw** **Make Red-Skin Potato Salad and Crisp Garlic Green Beans** **Make Basque Tuna Baguette** **Make Hye Rollers on tortillas, if using** **Make Southwestern Chicken Bread Bowl** **Defrost cookies**

DAY OF PARTY

4 Hours Ahead	**Toss slaw with dressing** **Assemble Hye Rollers on pita bread, if using**
1 Hour Ahead	**Crisp Chicken Bread Bowl and Tuna Baguette, if desired**
Shortly Before Serving	**Toss green beans into potato salad**

EXTRA ◆ POINTS

THE INVITATIONS

Write your message on rubber or plastic footballs or yellow fabric to resemble penalty flags, for example, "Don't get a penalty—be sure to show up."

THE TABLE

Cover your table with a lap blanket, decorate with pom-poms and pennants in team colors.

THE KICKER

Organize betting pools with winners announced at half-time (or even at the end of each quarter) as well as at the game's end.

The only similarity be-tween this sandwich and the humble mayonnaise-drenched ones of my childhood is the canned tuna fish. Basil, spinach, cheese, and olives lift this one to new heights.

PREP TIME: 20 minutes

CHILL TIME: 1 hour

ADVANCE PREP: May be refrigerated overnight.

BASQUE TUNA BAGUETTE

Basil Dressing
1 garlic clove, peeled
1 cup (lightly packed) fresh basil
  leaves
¼ cup olive oil
1 tablespoon capers, drained
1 tablespoon balsamic vinegar
2 teaspoons Dijon mustard

Sandwich
1 baguette (10 to 12 ounces),
  about 15 × 2½ inches
3 thin slices regular or low-fat
  provolone or mozzarella
  cheese (3 ounces)

2 cups torn fresh spinach
1 can (6¼ ounces) tuna fish
  packed in water, drained
2 large plum tomatoes, thinly
  sliced
3 large radishes, sliced
6 black olives, preferably
  kalamata, pitted and sliced
  (see page 12)
Freshly ground black pepper

To Make Dressing: In a food processor with the metal blade, process all the ingredients until well blended.

To Assemble Sandwich: Cut the bread in half horizontally. Hollow out the top and bottom, leaving a ½-inch shell. (It may be easier if you also cut the bread crosswise in two.) Spread the dressing over the inside of the top and bottom. Layer the cheese, spinach, tuna, tomatoes, rad-ishes, and olives into the bottom. Sprinkle with pepper. Cover with bread top. Wrap in plastic wrap or foil and place on a baking sheet. Top with another baking sheet and weigh down heavily with cans or weights for 1 hour. Remove weights and serve immediately or refrig-erate until serving. (Sandwich may be refrigerated overnight.)

If desired, crisp the bread before serving by baking the loaf at 450°F. for 5 to 10 minutes. To serve, cut the loaf crosswise into 2-inch slices.

MAKES: 4 to 6 servings.

NUTRITIONAL ANALYSIS

Per serving (with low-fat provolone)
320 calories
15 g fat
21 mg cholesterol
638 mg sodium

SANDWICHES FOR SUPER SPORTS

VEGETARIAN HYE ROLLERS

¾ cup chopped cucumber,
    preferably hothouse or
    seedless
Salt

Tahini Dressing
5 tablespoons tahini, stirred well
3 tablespoons fresh lemon juice
2 large garlic cloves, minced
Salt

6 green onions with tops,
    chopped (about ¾ cup)
8 large radishes, chopped (about
    1 cup)

3 plum tomatoes, seeded and
    finely chopped (see page 12)
2 large (10-inch) sturdy pita
    breads, Sahara brand
    preferred, or 4 large (10-inch)
    flour tortillas
8 jarred peperoncini, drained and
    sliced lengthwise into quarters
¼ pound string cheese, torn into
    ¼-inch strings (about 1¼
    cups)

Place chopped cucumber in colander in sink and sprinkle lightly with salt. Let drain for 20 minutes. Meanwhile, prepare dressing and vegetables.

To Make Dressing: In a small bowl, stir together tahini, 3 tablespoons water, lemon juice, garlic, and salt to taste. It will be as thick as mayonnaise. (Dressing may be refrigerated up to 1 week.)

To Prepare Vegetables: Squeeze cucumbers dry in a clean towel. Add green onions, radishes, and tomatoes and squeeze gently to remove excess liquid. If not using immediately, refrigerate in towel until ready to assemble sandwiches or up to 6 hours. Transfer to a bowl and toss together.

To Make Pita Sandwiches: Cut pita bread in half crosswise to make 2 flat rounds. If they are not soft and pliable, place on a plate, cover with plastic wrap, and microwave on high (100%) for 30 to 50 seconds. Spread each round with 2 tablespoons dressing. Spread a layer of vegetables and peperoncini down the center. Sprinkle with cheese and roll up tightly. Repeat with remaining ingredients. Wrap in plastic wrap and refrigerate at least 1 hour or up to 4 hours before serving. Cut each sandwich in half to serve.

To Make Tortilla Sandwiches: Follow directions for assembling pita sandwiches. (Tortilla sandwiches may be refrigerated overnight.)

MAKES: 4 servings.

I discovered this roll-up sandwich in a little hole-in-the-wall Middle Eastern deli in Los Angeles. The word Hye means Armenian and the alluring flavors of this sandwich exemplify that country's cuisine. The exotic flavor of the secret sauce originates from tahini, a canned puree of sesame seeds found in the gourmet section of many supermarkets. The filling is enough for two split 10-inch pita pockets or four 10-inch tortillas.

PREP TIME: 20 minutes

CHILL TIME: 1 hour

ADVANCE PREP: Dressing may be refrigerated up to 1 week. Tortilla sandwiches may be refrigerated overnight, pita sandwiches, up to 4 hours.

NUTRITIONAL ANALYSIS

Per sandwich (with pita bread)
387 calories
16 g fat
0 cholesterol
774 mg sodium

Layers of glazed grilled chicken, crunchy corn-jícama salsa, and spicy sun-dried tomato puree form a festive filling in an edible bread shell. If you can't find jícama, substitute chunks of cucumber, salted, drained, and patted dry.

PREP TIME: 50 minutes

GRILL OR BROIL TIME: 6 minutes

CHILL TIME: 1 hour

ADVANCE PREP: May be refrigerated overnight.

NUTRITIONAL ANALYSIS

Per serving
342 calories
9 g fat
51 mg cholesterol
353 mg sodium

SOUTHWESTERN CHICKEN BREAD BOWL

1 pound boneless, skinless chicken breasts
⅓ cup hot jalapeño jelly, melted

Sun-dried Tomato and Jalapeño Puree
½ cup sun-dried tomatoes (see page 12)
1 pickled or fresh seeded jalapeño (1 to 1½ inches) (see page 10)

Corn-Jícama Salsa
2 garlic cloves, peeled
1 pickled or fresh seeded jalapeño (1 to 1½ inches) (see page 10)
4 green onions, quartered (about ½ cup)

⅓ cup chopped cilantro
1 cup very coarsely chopped jícama
1 cup fresh or frozen corn, thawed and blotted dry on paper towels
¼ cup regular or light sour cream
2 tablespoons fresh lime juice
¼ teaspoon salt, or to taste

1 round loaf sourdough bread, about 7 inches
6 cups napa cabbage, finely shredded (about 6 ounces)
1 avocado, peeled, halved, pitted, and thinly sliced

To Cook Chicken: Preheat coals or broiler. Generously brush 1 side of chicken with jelly. Grill, jelly side down, 3 to 4 inches from coals or broil as close to unit as possible for about 3 minutes. Brush with jelly, turn, and cook for 3 to 5 minutes, or until cooked through. Cool and cut into ⅜-inch strips.

To Make Puree: Place the tomatoes in a medium microwavesafe bowl and cover with water. Microwave on high (100%) for 3 to 4 minutes, or until soft. Remove from water, place in food processor with metal blade and process with jalapeño until finely minced, scraping sides as needed. Puree will not be smooth.

To Make Salsa: In a food processor with the metal blade, process garlic and jalapeño until minced. Add green onions and cilantro; pulse until finely chopped. Add jícama and pulse until coarsely chopped. Remove to a bowl and stir in corn, sour cream, lime juice, and salt. (Salsa may be refrigerated overnight and drained before using.)

To Assemble Sandwich: Cut a slice off top of bread for a lid. Cut out bread from bottom and sides, leaving a ½-inch shell. Spread bottom, sides, and underside of lid with the puree. Layer half the chicken, cabbage, salsa, and avocado into bread bowl. Repeat with second layer of each. Cover with bread lid and wrap loaf in foil. Refrigerate weighted down with a baking sheet and tin cans or bricks for 1 hour. Remove weights and serve immediately or refrigerate until serving. (Sandwich may be refrigerated overnight.)

If desired, crisp the bread before serving by baking the loaf at 450°F. for 5 to 10 minutes. Cut into wedges to serve.

MAKES: 6 to 8 servings.

GREEN, GOLD, AND ORANGE SLAW WITH LIMA GRANDS

Slaw
½ pound napa cabbage (4 cups shredded)
1 medium yellow crookneck squash (about 4 ounces)
3 large green onions, cut into thirds and then into thin strips
½ red bell pepper, seeded, halved, and cut into thin strips
1 can (16 ounces) lima grands (also called butter beans and California large limas), rinsed and drained

Dressing
2 garlic cloves, peeled
3 anchovy fillets, rinsed
1 medium orange, peeled, seeded, and separated into segments
1 tablespoon Dijon mustard
1 teaspoon Worcestershire sauce
2 tablespoons fresh lemon juice
1½ teaspoons ground cumin
1 tablespoon olive oil

Salt

To Prepare Slaw: In a food processor with ¼-inch (4 mm) slicing blade or with a sharp knife, slice cabbage into shreds. Place in large bowl. Cut stem ends off squash and shred with shredding disk or hand shredder; add to cabbage. Mix in green onions, red pepper strips, and lima grands.

To Make Dressing: In same food processor bowl (no need to wash it), process garlic and anchovies until minced. Add orange segments and process until pureed, about 30 seconds; it will not be smooth. Add mustard, Worcestershire sauce, lemon juice, cumin, and oil. Process until blended. (Dressing may be refrigerated overnight.)

To Assemble: At least 1 hour before serving, pour dressing over vegetables; toss well. Add salt to taste. Refrigerate for at least 1 hour or up to 4 hours.

MAKES: 6 to 8 servings.

My brand new slaw is high in flavor, low in fat, and long on pizzazz. Shreds of napa cabbage, yellow squash, and red bell peppers bound with a zesty orange vinaigrette have converted a large number of reluctant cumin and anchovy eaters.

PREP TIME: 20 minutes

CHILL TIME: 1 hour

ADVANCE PREP: Vegetables and dressing may be refrigerated, separately, overnight. Tossed salad may be refrigerated up to 4 hours.

NUTRITIONAL ANALYSIS

Per serving
82 calories
2 g fat
1 mg cholesterol
347 mg sodium

RED-SKIN POTATO SALAD WITH CRISP GARLIC GREEN BEANS

Two mustards, plus a dollop of chutney, lend a sweet spicy tang to this oil-free salad. Sports moms and kids will welcome having this waiting in the fridge for a family on the go.

PREP TIME: 25 minutes

COOK TIME: 5 to 6 minutes

ADVANCE PREP: Salad may be refrigerated overnight. Stir in beans before serving.

1½ pounds small red potatoes (about 6)

Dressing
3 tablespoons fruity chutney, such as Major Grey mango chutney
2 tablespoons fresh lemon juice
¼ cup grainy mustard, such as Moutarde de Meaux

1 tablespoon Dijon mustard

1 small red onion, thinly sliced
3 tablespoons fresh dill or
   1 tablespoon dried dillweed
Salt
Freshly ground black pepper

¼ recipe (½ pound) Crisp Garlic Green Beans (see page 121)

To Cook Potatoes: Fill a medium saucepan with water and bring it to a boil. Scrub potatoes and slice ¼ inch thick by hand or in a food processor with the ¼-inch (4 mm) slicing blade. Boil until tender, but slightly crisp when pierced with the tip of a sharp knife, about 5 to 6 minutes.

To Make Dressing: While potatoes cook, in a small bowl, stir together chutney, lemon juice, and mustards. Drain potatoes and place in a medium bowl. Stir in onion, dressing, and dill and toss until coated. Season to taste with salt and pepper. Cover and refrigerate. (Salad may be refrigerated overnight.)

Prepare Crisp Garlic Green Beans as recipe directs. Before serving, toss beans into salad. Serve chilled or at room temperature.

MAKES: 6 servings.

NUTRITIONAL ANALYSIS

Per serving
169 calories
2 g fat
0 cholesterol
635 mg sodium

NCL ALL-STAR COOKIES

½ pound (2 sticks) butter or
    margarine, melted
1 cup sugar
1 cup (packed) light brown sugar
2 large eggs
1 teaspoon vanilla extract
2 cups all-purpose flour
1 teaspoon baking powder
1 teaspoon baking soda

1 teaspoon ground cinnamon
1 teaspoon ground ginger
2½ cups regular or quick rolled
    oats
1½ cups chocolate chips (about
    ½ pound)
½ cup raisins
¾ cup coarsely chopped walnuts
    or pecans (3 ounces)

Preheat oven to 375°F. Line 2 baking sheets with parchment paper or grease them.

In a large mixing bowl with electric mixer, mix butter and sugars on low speed until blended, about 1 minute. Mix in eggs and vanilla until well mixed, about 1 minute. Add flour, baking powder, baking soda, cinnamon and ginger. Mix on low speed until combined, about 1 minute. Add oats, chips, raisins, and nuts and mix on low until incorporated. (If the mixture is stiff, you may need to stir them in by hand.)

Drop batter from 2-ounce (2-inch) ice cream scoop or by rounded tablespoons about 1½ inches apart onto prepared baking sheets. Bake for 12 to 15 minutes only. The edges will be crisp, but the centers will be soft. They will look underdone but will firm up considerably as they cool. If baking on 2 oven racks, rotate the sheets halfway through the baking time. Immediately remove to wire racks to cool. (Cookies may be stored airtight for several days or frozen.)

MAKES: about 26 cookies.

When recipe tester Sue Vohrer tossed together two all-American favorite cookie batters, oatmeal-raisin and chocolate chip, she won one for the National Cookie League.

PREP TIME: 20 minutes

BAKE TIME: 12 to 15 minutes

ADVANCE PREP: May be stored airtight for several days or frozen.

NUTRITIONAL ANALYSIS

Per cookie
265 calories
12 g fat
35 mg cholesterol
131 mg sodium

To dunk or not to dunk? That is the question. Unlike traditional unadorned dry biscotti, these are imbued with anise and Marsala and are chock-full of nuts and dried figs, apricots, raisins, and currants.

PREP TIME: 20 minutes

CHILL TIME: 1 hour

BAKE TIME: 30 to 35 minutes plus 5 minutes standing

ADVANCE PREP: May be stored at room temperature up to 2 weeks or frozen.

NUTRITIONAL ANALYSIS

Per biscotti
110 calories
5 g fat
19 mg cholesterol
82 mg sodium

BISCOTTI WITH DRIED FRUITS

¼ cup dried apricots
¼ cup dried figs
¼ cup golden raisins
¼ cup currants
¼ cup Marsala
¼ cup hazelnuts, almonds,
    walnuts, or pecans
¼ cup walnuts
¼ pound (1 stick) unsalted
    butter or margarine, cut into
    8 pieces

1 cup sugar
2 large eggs
2 cups all-purpose flour
3 teaspoons baking powder
¼ teaspoon salt
2 teaspoons anise seeds
1 tablespoon anise-flavored
    liquor, such as Pernod
    (optional)

To Make Dough: In a food processor with the metal blade, pulse apricots and figs until chopped. Transfer to an 8-cup (2-quart) microwavesafe bowl and stir in raisins, currants, and Marsala. Microwave, covered, on high (100%) for 2 to 4 minutes, or until hot and fruits are soft. Cool to room temperature.

In same food processor bowl, pulse nuts until coarsely chopped. Remove to small bowl. Add butter and sugar to processor and process until creamed. Add eggs and process until blended; the mixture will look curdled. Add flour, baking powder, salt, and anise seeds and pulse until incorporated. Pulse in liquor, if using. Remove to bowl with dried fruit. Stir in nuts until well blended. Cover and refrigerate for 1 hour or longer.

To Shape: Preheat oven to 350°F. Grease or spray 2 baking sheets.

Pat dough into 4 logs, 2 per sheet, about 1 inch high, 1 inch wide, and 15 inches long, spacing at least 4 inches apart.

To Bake: Bake for 15 to 20 minutes, or until lightly browned, rotating the positions of the sheets halfway through the baking time. Logs will flatten and spread as they bake. Remove from oven and reduce temperature to 325°F. With a spatula, loosen bottoms from the baking sheet and let cool 5 minutes. Transfer to a cutting board. With a sharp knife, cut diagonally into ¾-inch slices. Return the slices to a baking sheet cut side down and bake for 8 to 10 minutes, or until cut surfaces dry out slightly but interiors remain soft. Remove to racks and cool to room temperature. (Biscotti may be stored in an airtight container at room temperature for 2 weeks or frozen.)

MAKES: about 52 biscotti.

Faster: Substitute 1 cup packaged mixed dried fruit bits for the apricots, figs, raisins, and currants.

Menu

◆

CHAM CHAM BUBBLES

◆

YOGURT PRALINE NUTS

◆

A TRIO OF SALADS:
TWO-RICE SALAD WITH
SHIITAKES, LEEKS, AND
ORANGES

•

JADE CHICKEN SALAD WITH
PEANUT DRESSING

•

SEAFOOD TORTELLONI SALAD
WITH JALAPEÑO-LIME
VINAIGRETTE

◆

PESTO BISCUITS

◆

FROZEN CHOCOLATE CHUNK
MERINGUE MOUSSE

JOYFUL SHOWER

When a Dutch maiden's father forbade her to marry a poor miller, her friends showered her with gifts to enable her to marry without the traditional dowry to help set up housekeeping. Several years later, an Englishwoman, remembering the Dutch girl's plight, gathered a group of friends to bring small gifts to an impoverished bride. Thus, legend tells us, bridal showers began centuries ago.

Today we shower the new mom as well as the new bride and although brunches, afternoon teas, dinners, dessert and couples parties are gaining in popularity, luncheons are still the most common.

Besides the built-in motifs of love and romance or storks, it's fun to plan a theme that can be carried out with colorful decorations, centerpieces and favors. Adults love letting their hair down and have as much fun playing games as children, so you may wish to include some special activities to ensure your shower is an unforgettable one (see page 57).

Fortunately, with all the decorations and excitement of opening gifts and playing games, the food need not be expensive or elaborate. In planning a luncheon menu, I strive for variety and simplicity, choosing dishes that are pleasing to look at and tempting to eat. The trio of salads—Two-Rice Salad with Shiitakes, Leeks, and Oranges, Jade Chicken Salad with Peanut Dressing, and Seafood Tortelloni with Jalapeño-Lime Vinaigrette—meet all these criteria. Besides, they easily expand for any size crowd and can be prepared ahead. Each is substantial enough to be a complete meal when accompanied with Pesto Biscuits, Gorgonzola Puffovers (see page 105), or storebought rolls.

For a small gathering of eight to ten guests, choose one or two of the salads and dish up the plates in the kitchen. For larger groups, it's simplest to set up a buffet and let guests sit around tables or eat off their laps. If there's more than one hostess, divide the recipes and let each one make a salad.

Finish with Frozen Chocolate Chunk Meringue Mousse, ready and waiting in the freezer; it's guaranteed to bring a deluge of praise. Then sit back and enjoy the fun. When showers reign, happiness pours. This menu serves twenty-four if you serve all three salads and double the recipes for the nuts, biscuits, and dessert.

GAME PLAN

1 Month Ahead	**Make and freeze Yogurt Praline Nuts** **Make and freeze Chocolate Chunk Meringue** **Mousse** **Make and refrigerate fudge sauce** **Make and freeze Chocolate Hearts, if using**
2 Weeks Ahead	**Make and freeze Pesto Biscuits** **Make dressing for Jade Chicken Salad**
1 Day Ahead	**Make Seafood Tortelloni Salad** **Prepare vegetables and noodles for chicken salad** **Marinate and grill or broil chicken for salad** **Make Two-Rice Salad** **Defrost biscuits and nuts**
DAY OF PARTY 1 Hour Ahead	**Bring Seafood Tortelloni Salad to room temperature** **Remove springform sides from mousse, decorate, if** **desired, and return to freezer**
15 Minutes Ahead	**Rewarm biscuits** **Toss chicken salad** **Toss oranges and reserved dressing into rice salad** **Heat fudge sauce** **Pour Chambord into glasses for Cham Cham** **Bubbles** **Remove mousse from freezer**
Shortly Before Serving	**Pour champagne** **Reheat fudge sauce**

EXTRA POINTS

THE THEME

• Often the tone of a bridal shower is set by the bride, who requests a certain type, such as kitchen, linen, honeymoon, or lingerie, and the guests bring appropriate gifts. Other gift-related themes might include a "Round the Clock" or "All Year Round" shower where a specific hour of the day or night or month of the year is written on each guest's invitation and a suitable gift is brought for that particular hour or month.

• For a rainbow motif, tie a profusion of rainbow-colored ribbons around the napkins. For the centerpiece, use spray paint or glitter to make a large Styrofoam rainbow. Insert the ends into pots filled with floral foam and covered with gold foil–wrapped chocolate coins and flowers. Or purchase rainbow-decorated coffee mugs and fill them with flowers and balloons.

- A theme of candy kisses can be carried out by strewing large and small kisses wrapped in silver and gold foil around the table along with silver and gold confetti. Attach some kisses to sticks and insert them into a floral centerpiece with silver and gold Mylar balloons and ribbons. For a place card/favor, write each guest's name on a ribbon and tie it around a small jar filled with kisses.

THE INVITATIONS

For a baby shower invitation, write a card and paste it on the back of a box of baby cereal and mail it in a padded envelope. Or write a note and insert it into a plastic toy baby bottle and mail it in a padded envelope.

FUN AND GAMES

SAFETY PIN GAME

Good for a bridal or baby shower. You will need enough ribbon to tie around each guest's wrist, plus 5 small gold safety pins per person. Pin 5 safety pins onto each ribbon bracelet. As each guest arrives, tie a ribbon around her wrist. Choose three words no one is allowed to say during the shower, such as the groom's name, wedding, dress, baby, mom, etc. Whenever a guest hears another guest say one of these words, she can take a safety pin from that person. The one with the most pins at the end wins. Reward the winner with an inexpensive but fitting prize.

GUESS THE BABY

For a baby shower, ask guests to bring baby pictures of themselves and let the other guests guess who's who.

FILL IN THE BLANKS

Purchase a variety of common household products. Wrap and number each one. Write a life story about the bride and groom or new mom and dad, leaving blank spaces numbered to correspond with the gift-wrapped items. Give each guest one of the wrapped items. The honoree stands up and reads the narrative. When she comes to a blank, the guest with the corresponding number opens that gift and fills in the blank. Make copies of the narrative for each guest to fill in and take home. For example:

It all began on July 28 when Cindy walked into a party and saw 1. She immediately felt great 2 and soon they were giving each other 3 and 4. Both of them, seeking a 5 commitment and 6 for each other, agreed that they would never go 7 again.

1. Mr. Clean; 2. Joy;
3. Huggies; 4. Kisses;
5. Total; 6. Intensive Care;
7. Solo

CHAM CHAM BUBBLES

Pour a small amount (about 1 teaspoon) Chambord into each champagne glass. Fill with Champagne.

YOGURT PRALINE NUTS

¼ cup sugar
½ cup (packed) light brown
    sugar
¼ cup regular, low-fat, or nonfat
    plain yogurt

Salt
½ teaspoon vanilla extract
2 cups unsalted nuts, such as
    pecan or walnut halves or
    whole blanched almonds

To Make in Microwave: Do not double the recipe. If you don't have a microwavesafe candy thermometer, fill a small bowl with ice water. In a 3-quart microwavesafe bowl, stir together sugars, yogurt, and a dash of salt until smooth and brown sugar is free of lumps. Insert thermometer and microwave, uncovered, on high (100%) for 5 to 8 minutes, without stirring, until mixture is caramel colored and boiling with large bubbles. The thermometer should read 235°F. Or, spoon a drop of syrup into ice water. In one minute it should be firm enough to snap but still slightly soft when chewed. Stir in vanilla and nuts until coated. Mixture will be very sticky and stiff. Microwave on high (100%) for 1 to 2 minutes more, or until caramel has melted and nuts are coated.

To Make on Stove: In a medium saucepan, stir together sugars, yogurt, and a dash of salt. Cook over moderate heat, without stirring, until the mixture reaches the soft ball stage, 235°F. on a candy thermometer, 8 to 10 minutes. Remove from heat and stir in vanilla. Quickly stir in nuts to coat.

Spread on a greased baking sheet, separating the nuts as much as possible. They will become opaque as they cool. When cool, break into pieces; you'll have some individual nuts and some clusters. Store in covered container. (Nuts may be refrigerated up to 1 month or frozen.)

MAKES: 2 cups.

A kick of raspberry-flavored Chambord liqueur in a glass of Champagne trips the light fantastic.

When I hosted a radio show in Los Angeles, one of my listeners sent me this incredible recipe for candied nuts made on top of the stove. I love the recipe, and now that I've adapted it to the microwave, I make it all the time. These nuts are a perfect party snack, a welcome gift, and a great nibble with Champagne or with an after-dinner liqueur.

PREP TIME: 5 minutes

COOK TIME: Microwave, 6 to 11 minutes; stovetop, 8 to 10 minutes

ADVANCE PREP: May be refrigerated up to 1 month or frozen.

NUTRITIONAL ANALYSIS

Per 2 tablespoons (with pecans and nonfat yogurt)
129 calories
9 g fat
0 cholesterol
5 mg sodium

This vegetarian salad is proof that light and delicate need not be synonymous with pale and bland. It is refreshingly bold with the nutty accents of wild rice and walnut oil, the sweetness of oranges, and a profusion of vegetables.

PREP TIME: 20 minutes

COOK TIME: About 50 minutes

ADVANCE PREP: May be refrigerated overnight.

NUTRITIONAL ANALYSIS

Per serving
313 calories
8 g fat
0 cholesterol
670 mg sodium

TWO-RICE SALAD WITH SHIITAKES, LEEKS, AND ORANGES

¾ ounce dried shiitakes (about ¾ cup)
1¼ cups uncooked wild rice (about 6 ounces)
1 teaspoon salt
¾ cup uncooked long-grain white rice
3 medium leeks, cleaned, quartered, and sliced (see page 11) (about 2 cups)
1½ cups fresh or frozen corn kernels (see page 10)
1 medium red bell pepper, halved, seeded, and sliced into ¾- × ¼-inch strips
3 tablespoons soy sauce

Walnut-Orange Vinaigrette
¾ cup fresh orange or tangerine juice (see page 11)
⅓ cup red wine vinegar
¼ cup walnut oil
1 tablespoon chopped fresh tarragon leaves or 1 teaspoon dried tarragon, crumbled
Salt and freshly ground black pepper

2 small oranges or tangerines, peeled, quartered, and sliced
Boston or butter lettuce, for garnish (optional)

To Soak Mushrooms: Place shiitakes and 1 cup water in a 4-cup microwavesafe glass measure. Microwave, covered, on high (100%) for 2 to 3 minutes, or until very hot. Remove and steep mushrooms for at least 20 minutes. Squeeze mushrooms, reserving broth. Discard stems and slice thin.

To Cook Rice and Vegetables: Pour reserved mushroom broth, 3¾ cups water, and salt into a deep saucepan. Rinse and drain wild rice. Add to saucepan and bring to a boil. Cover, reduce heat to medium-low, and simmer for 30 minutes. Add white rice, cover, and continue simmering for 15 minutes, or until rice is almost tender and most of the water is absorbed. Stir in leeks, corn, pepper strips, and shiitakes and simmer 5 to 10 minutes more. The wild rice should be crunchy, the white rice tender, and the vegetables crisp. Remove to a bowl and stir in soy sauce.

To Make Vinaigrette: In a medium bowl or jar, mix together juice, vinegar, walnut oil, and tarragon; season to taste with salt and pepper. Pour 1 cup over rice mixture and toss well. (Rice may be refrigerated covered overnight. Refrigerate remaining vinaigrette separately.)

Before Serving: Toss remaining dressing and oranges into rice. Serve the salad chilled or at room temperature. Serve on salad plates or platter lined with lettuce leaves.

MAKES: 8 main-dish servings.

Faster: Substitute 2 packages (5 to 6 ounces each) white and wild rice mix for the wild and white rice. Cook according to package directions, substituting mushroom broth for some of the water. Add leeks, corn, red pepper, and shiitakes the last 10 minutes of cooking time.

Change of Pace: Before serving, toss in ½ pound thin asparagus spears, cooked (see page 149) and cut into thirds; or ½ pound cooked snow peas; or ½ pound cooked fresh Sugar Snap Peas (see page 98) or ½ pound thawed frozen sugar snap peas, uncooked and blotted dry, cut in half crosswise. Do not marinate any of these or they will lose their bright green color.

JADE CHICKEN SALAD WITH PEANUT DRESSING

Peanut Dressing
1½ tablespoons finely minced fresh ginger (see page 10)
¾ cup soy sauce
6 tablespoons sugar
6 tablespoons distilled white vinegar
9 tablespoons vegetable oil
¼ cup chunky peanut butter

Salad
6 boneless, skinless chicken breast halves (about 3 pounds)
1 package (3 ounces) Ramen noodles, crumbled with fingers (discard seasoning packet or reserve for another use)

1 head romaine lettuce, cut into bite-size pieces (about 8 cups)
½ head napa cabbage, cut into bite-size pieces (about 4 cups)
6 green onions, sliced (about ¾ cup)
1 can (8 ounces) water chestnuts, drained and coarsely chopped
1 small hothouse or seedless cucumber, chopped into ½-inch pieces (about 1½ cups)
4 plum tomatoes, chopped into ½-inch pieces
Napa cabbage leaves, for serving

To Make Dressing: In a glass jar or medium bowl, mix ginger, soy sauce, sugar, vinegar, oil, and peanut butter until blended. (Dressing may be refrigerated for 1 week. Bring to room temperature before using.)

To Make Salad: Cut off all fat from chicken and place breasts in a large

(continued)

Here you use the same gingery peanut sauce to marinate the chicken and dress the salad. For small gatherings, you may wish to serve the sliced chicken hot over the chilled greens. For large groups, though, it's easier to grill or broil it ahead and serve it at room temperature.

PREP TIME: 30 minutes

MARINADE TIME: 4 to 6 hours in refrigerator

GRILL OR BROIL TIME: 6 to 12 minutes

ADVANCE PREP: Dressing may be refrigerated up to 1 week. Chicken may be cooked, Ramen noodles toasted, and vegetables prepared a day ahead.

plastic zipper bag. Pour over ½ cup of the dressing. Marinate chicken in the refrigerator for 4 to 6 hours, turning once.

Meanwhile, crumble noodles and bake at 350°F. in toaster oven or regular oven until golden, about 10 minutes. (Noodles may be stored airtight at room temperature for 2 days.) Prepare lettuce and cabbage, wrap in paper towels and a plastic bag, and refrigerate. (Greens and chopped vegetables may be refrigerated overnight.)

Remove chicken from marinade and blot dry with paper towels. Grill over hot coals or broil in shallow roasting pan lined with heavy foil, 3 to 4 inches from flame, for 3 to 6 minutes per side or until browned and cooked through. The timing will vary with the size of the breasts. (Chicken may be cooled and refrigerated overnight.)

To Assemble: Up to 1 hour before serving, slice chicken into thin strips. In a large bowl, combine chicken, lettuce, cabbage, green onions, water chestnuts, cucumber, and tomatoes. Refrigerate until ready to serve. Line salad plates or platter with napa cabbage leaves. Add as much dressing as needed and toss well. Spoon salad onto cabbage leaves and sprinkle with noodles.

MAKES: 8 to 10 main-dish servings.

Faster: Substitute storebought cooked chicken for the chicken breasts. Shred the chicken, but do not marinate it. You will have dressing left over.

NUTRITIONAL ANALYSIS

Per serving
487 calories
23 g fat
116 mg cholesterol
1415 mg sodium

SEAFOOD TORTELLONI SALAD WITH JALAPEÑO-LIME VINAIGRETTE

Salad
1 cup dry white wine or
  imported dry vermouth
¾ to 1 pound scallops, Eastern
  or bay scallops if available
¾ to 1 pound medium raw
  shrimp, peeled and deveined
6 medium plum tomatoes,
  seeded and chopped (see
  page 12) (about 1½ cups)
6 green onions, sliced (about
  ¾ cup)
About 2 pounds fresh spinach or
  cheese-filled tortelloni

Jalapeño-Lime Vinaigrette
2 large garlic cloves, peeled
1 pickled or fresh seeded
  jalapeño, about ¾ to 1 inch
  (see page 10)
6 tablespoons fresh lime juice
  (see page 11)
⅓ cup olive oil
½ cup reduced poaching liquid
Salt and freshly ground black
  pepper

½ cup (lightly packed) chopped
  cilantro
Red cabbage or radicchio leaves,
  for garnish

To Make Salad: In a medium skillet over high heat, bring wine to a boil. Add scallops and cook, turning, 1 to 2 minutes, until opaque; do not overcook. Remove with slotted spoon to large bowl. Add shrimp and simmer, turning, until they turn pink; remove to scallops. If scallops are large, cut them into quarters. Boil poaching liquid until reduced to ½ cup. Set aside. Stir tomatoes and green onions into seafood. Bring a large pot of salted water to a boil. Add tortelloni and cook as directed on package until tender to the bite. Drain well and add to seafood.

To Make Vinaigrette: In a food processor with the metal blade, process garlic and jalapeño until minced. Add lime juice, olive oil, and reserved poaching liquid; process to blend. Season with salt and pepper to taste. If you desire a spicier vinaigrette, mince another jalapeño and add to dressing. (Dressing may be refrigerated up to 2 days.)

Pour vinaigrette over salad, add cilantro and toss well. Cover and refrigerate at least 1 hour or preferably overnight. Bring to room temperature 1 hour before serving.

To Serve: Line salad plates or a large platter with cabbage or radicchio leaves and spoon salad onto leaves.

MAKES: 8 main-dish servings.

Fresh tortelloni, large stuffed tortellini, can be found in the refrigerator section of most supermarkets. (Large pastas are usually spelled with an ''o''; smaller ones with an ''i.'') Tossed with scallops and shrimp and marinated for several hours or preferably overnight in a zesty lime vinaigrette, they make a splendid main-dish salad. To reduce fat, the seafood poaching liquid replaces much of the oil in the dressing.

PREP TIME: 30 minutes

CHILL TIME: 1 hour

COOK TIME: About 15 minutes

ADVANCE PREP: May be refrigerated overnight.

NUTRITIONAL ANALYSIS

Per serving (with cheese tortelloni)
476 calories
14 g fat
140 mg cholesterol
618 mg sodium

Pesto is commonly used to flavor pasta, salads, and sauces. Here I incorporate it into simple biscuits. Patting dough into a round and dividing it into pie-shaped wedges is the fastest way I know of shaping tender, crumbly biscuits.

PREP TIME: 15 minutes

BAKE TIME: 15 to 18 minutes

ADVANCE PREP: May be stored at room temperature overnight or frozen up to 2 weeks.

NUTRITIONAL ANALYSIS

Per biscuit (with nonfat milk)
152 calories
7 g fat
19 mg cholesterol
175 mg sodium

PESTO BISCUITS

2 garlic cloves, peeled
2 cups all-purpose flour
2 teaspoons baking powder
½ teaspoon baking soda
¼ teaspoon salt
⅓ cup (lightly packed) basil leaves
2 tablespoons plus 1 tablespoon grated parmesan cheese, divided

⅓ cup shortening, butter, or margarine
⅔ cup regular, low-fat, or nonfat milk
1 tablespoon plus 1 tablespoon pine nuts, toasted (see page 12), divided
1 egg, mixed with 1 teaspoon water for glaze
Butter, for serving (optional)

Place rack in upper third of oven and preheat to 425°F.

To Make Dough: In a food processor with the metal blade, process garlic until minced. Add flour, baking powder, baking soda, salt, and basil. Pulse until well combined and basil leaves are coarsely chopped. Add 2 tablespoons of the parmesan cheese and shortening. Pulse until mixture resembles coarse meal. Add milk and 1 tablespoon of the pine nuts and pulse until dough clings together. Remove to a lightly floured board and knead gently about 6 times.

To Shape: On a lightly greased baking sheet, shape the dough into a 7-inch round, ½ inch thick. With a knife, cut it into 12 equal wedges, not quite through to the bottom. Brush top with egg and sprinkle with the remaining 1 tablespoon cheese and 1 tablespoon pine nuts, pressing them into dough.

To Bake: Bake for 15 to 18 minutes, or until golden. Serve warm, breaking or cutting along scores. Serve with butter, if desired. (Biscuits may be stored airtight overnight or frozen up to 2 weeks. Rewarm at 400°F. before serving.)

MAKES: 12 biscuits.

Leaner: Omit pine nuts. Brush top with 1 tablespoon liquid egg substitute or egg white mixed with 1 teaspoon water.

Faster: Substitute 3 tablespoons prepared pesto for the garlic, basil, and cheese in the batter.

FROZEN CHOCOLATE CHUNK MERINGUE MOUSSE

Meringue Cookies
2 bars (1.4 ounces each) chocolate-covered toffee (Heath or Skor bars), broken into small pieces
10 chocolate sandwich fudge or Oreo cookies, broken up
5 large egg whites, at room temperature
1½ cups confectioners' sugar
1 cup chopped almonds, toasted (see page 11)

Mousse
2 cups whipping cream

2 tablespoons confectioners' sugar
2 tablespoons Amaretto or golden rum
1 teaspoon vanilla extract

Garnish
Whipped cream for garnish (optional)
Chocolate Hearts (see page 67) or chocolate-covered toffee bars
Fatless Fudge Sauce (see page 66)

To Make Meringue Cookies: Preheat oven to 325°F. Line 2 large baking sheets with parchment paper or foil and grease the paper. In a food processor with the metal blade, chop toffee and cookies into small pieces. In a large mixing bowl with electric mixer, beat egg whites to soft peaks. Gradually add 1½ cups confectioners' sugar, 1 tablespoon at a time, until stiff, glossy peaks form. Fold in toffee mixture and toasted nuts. Using a soup spoon, drop mounds of the meringue batter onto the prepared baking sheets and spread into 3- to 4-inch circles, about ½ inch thick. Bake for 30 to 35 minutes or until tops are crisp, rotating the sheets halfway through the baking time. Turn off oven and leave in oven for 30 minutes. Transfer baking sheets to cooling racks and cool completely before removing.

To Make Mousse: Cut meringue cookies into about ¾-inch pieces. Beat the cream until soft peaks form. Beat in 2 tablespoons confectioners' sugar, Amaretto, and vanilla. Fold in cookie pieces. Pour into a lightly oiled 9-inch springform pan; smooth the top. Cover with foil and freeze overnight. (Mousse may be frozen up to 1 month. It may be removed from springform and wrapped in heavy foil, if desired.)

To Serve: Remove springform and if desired, garnish top with rosettes of whipped cream and Chocolate Hearts or toffee candy cut into triangular pieces. Return to freezer until serving. Cut into wedges and serve with fudge sauce.

MAKES: 10 to 12 servings.

Once, after I took this springform dessert out of the freezer for a dinner party, a guest had a mishap and the mousse was forgotten until it was too soft to cut. Left no choice, I spooned it into dessert dishes. It wasn't until my guests asked for the recipe that they learned that it was meant to be a frozen dessert. This proves that some recipes are so sensational, no matter how you treat them, they still get raves.

PREP TIME: 25 minutes

BAKE TIME: 30 minutes plus 30 minutes with oven turned off

CHILL TIME: At least 24 hours

ADVANCE PREP: Mousse may be frozen up to 1 month. Chocolate hearts may be frozen.

NUTRITIONAL ANALYSIS

Per serving (without sauce)
343 calories
25 g fat
58 mg cholesterol
107 mg sodium

It's hard to believe this rich, fudgy sauce has less than ½ gram of fat per serving (the amount the FDA considers fat free).

PREP TIME: 5 minutes

MICROWAVE TIME: 10 to 14 minutes

ADVANCE PREP: May be refrigerated up to 1 month.

FATLESS FUDGE SAUCE

¾ **cup granulated sugar**
1½ **cups (packed) light brown sugar**
⅓ **cup unsweetened cocoa powder**

1¼ **cups plain nonfat yogurt**
Dash salt
1 **tablespoon vanilla extract**

In a 12-cup (3-quart) microwavesafe bowl, stir sugars, cocoa, yogurt, and salt together until thoroughly moistened. Microwave, uncovered, on high (100%) for 10 to 14 minutes, without stirring, until bubbly, thickened, and syrupy. Sauce will continue to thicken as it cools. Remove from microwave and stir in vanilla. (Sauce may be refrigerated in a widemouth container up to 1 month.) Reheat on top of stove or in microwave before serving.

MAKES: 2 cups sauce.

NUTRITIONAL ANALYSIS

Per tablespoon
63 calories
½ g fat
0 cholesterol
10 mg sodium

CHOCOLATE HEARTS

**12 ounces (2 cups) semisweet
   chocolate chips or candy
   coating chocolate chips from
   cake decorating or cookware
   shops**

Heat chocolate in microwavesafe bowl or on top of stove in double boiler until melted and smooth. Line the back of a baking sheet with wax paper. Spread the chocolate into a ¼-inch-thick rectangle. Freeze 2 to 5 minutes or refrigerate until it begins to set but is soft enough to cut. Using a heart-shape cookie cutter, cut out hearts. Or purchase chocolate heart molds from a cake-decorating or cookware shop, fill with melted chocolate, freeze until firm, and pop out. Store in cool place or freeze. (Hearts may be frozen for 1 month.)

Menu

◆

DIZZY DINOSAUR DIP

◆

FUNNY-FACE PIZZAS

◆

ICE CREAM CONE CLOWNS

◆

CLOWN CAKE

THREE-RING CIRCUS BIRTHDAY PARTY

*H*aving four kids in six years entitles me to a gold medal in birthday party hosting. By the time my youngest child, Kenny, turned sixteen, I'd given more than sixty parties, which makes me an authority on the subject. At best, children's birthday parties are exhausting. Just as you're ready to feed the hungry hordes, one child has to go to the bathroom (or already has), another one has fallen in the mud, and another is crying. It's important to be flexible and keep the activities simple, the time short, and the food easy.

Because every child has a secret desire to swing from a trapeze, walk a tightrope, and tame the lions, a party "under the big top" is an ideal theme for children between the ages of three and seven. Like the circus, every family has a clown, so why not ask him or her to dress up and help entertain the children? The busier you keep the little ones, the happier they—and you—will be.

Allow the kids to decorate their own Funny-Face Pizzas. I offer several options for pizza crusts, from refrigerated ones in the tube to pita breads. If cost is not a factor, you can even buy prebaked shells. Of course my topping suggestions are just that; you might discuss other options with the birthday child. To bake several pizzas at one time, place each on a piece of heavy foil directly on the oven rack.

Pizza is such a popular entree that some vegetables and dip make a complete meal. Dizzy Dinosaur holds enough dip for about six to eight children, so for larger groups you would want to make several.

Since the Clown Cake is the main attraction, it deserves center stage on the table. Surround it with strips of brightly colored cellophane strewn with peanuts in the shell. Although you might be tempted to substitute a cake mix for my made-from-scratch batter, don't. I've already tried it—a mix does not get cooked through when baked in a bowl. You may, however, use storebought frosting instead of my cream cheese version. You will find colored candy-coating chips for decorating at cake-decorating shops and some cookware shops. It takes only a little advance planning and organization to make a very special circus party. Take it from an Olympian—the extra touches that go into making an afternoon of fantasy fun will create memories to last a lifetime. This menu is designed to be multiplied. It is written to serve six.

GAME PLAN

1 Month Ahead	**Make and freeze pizza crusts**
2 Weeks Ahead	**Make, decorate, and freeze Clown Cake**
3 Days Ahead	**Make and freeze Ice Cream Cone Clowns** **Make dip**
1 Day Ahead	**Make dinosaur(s)** **Cut vegetables for dip** **Prepare toppings for pizza** **Defrost Clown Cake**
DAY OF PARTY	
4 Hours Ahead	**Finish decorating cake** **Fill dinosaur with dip** **Assemble ingredients for pizza**

EXTRA POINTS

THE INVITATIONS

Write a colorful note with the party's details and tie it around a paper clown hat or party blower, or slip it into a Cracker Jack box.

THE TABLE

Make a circus wagon centerpiece by cutting the top off a box or carton that fits your table and is about eight inches high. Cover the sides with circus or animal wrapping paper. Place it on two narrow Styrofoam rectangles about two inches high. Glue or staple two paper plates on each side for wheels. Glue on cookies for hubcaps. Fill box with cellophane and popcorn or peanuts and decorate with curly ribbon. (See color photo, page 7.)

FUN AND GAMES

- Make a poster of Dumbo, cut out the mouth and have a bean bag or ball toss. Or simply decorate a plastic garbage bag and cut a hole in it.

- Hide peanuts around the yard or playroom and have a peanut hunt.

- Let the kids make finger puppets by breaking peanuts in half crosswise and removing the nuts. They can decorate the shells with markers or glue on small scraps of material to resemble animals and put the shells on their fingers.

P repare to hear giggles when you present a scooped-out acorn squash dinosaur filled with a creamy dip. (See color photo, page 7.)

PREP TIME: 10 minutes

ADVANCE PREP: Dip may be refrigerated up to 3 days. Dinosaur may be refrigerated overnight.

NUTRITIONAL ANALYSIS

Per tablespoon (with light sour cream)
27 calories
2 g fat
7 mg cholesterol
43 mg sodium

DIZZY DINOSAUR DIP

Dinosaur
1 acorn squash
Sturdy wooden toothpicks
4 large brussels sprouts
1 small zucchini, with a curved stem end, if possible
2 cloves

Vegetable Dip
1 package (4 ounces) low-fat garlic-herb cheese
1 cup regular or light sour cream
Assorted raw vegetables, potato chips, and/or pretzels, for dipping

To Make Dinosaur: Slice about a third off top of acorn squash. Scoop out all seeds and fiber from large section to make a bowl for the dip. Turn over. Insert toothpicks through stem end of sprouts and attach to rounded bottom for legs. To make neck and head, cut the end of the zucchini opposite the stem at an angle leaving about 2½ inches for the neck and attach with toothpicks to rim of acorn squash. Insert cloves on each side of head for the eyes. (Dinosaur may be wrapped in plastic wrap and refrigerated overnight.)

To Make Dip: In a medium bowl, stir together cheese and sour cream until blended. (Dip may be refrigerated up to 3 days.) This makes 1⅓ cups.

To Serve: Fill the body of the dinosaur with dip and cover with squash top. Serve with desired vegetables, chips, and/or pretzels.

MAKES: 6 to 8 servings.

FUNNY-FACE PIZZAS

2 tubes (10 ounces each)
   refrigerated pizza crust, or 1
   bag (24 ounces) frozen dinner
   rolls, or 3 large pita breads

Topping
1 jar (14 to 15 ounces) pizza
   sauce (the squeeze variety is
   fun for kids to use)
1 cup shredded low-fat
   mozzarella cheese (4 ounces)

¼ pound peperoni, thinly sliced
1 can (5¾ ounces) colossal or
   jumbo pitted ripe olives,
   drained and sliced
1 small red or green pepper,
   seeded and sliced
Sautéed sliced mushrooms,
   onions, cooked sausage,
   cooked ground beef, sautéed
   sliced zucchini for topping
   (optional)

To Make Individual Pizza Crusts: If using refrigerated pizza crust, unroll each package onto flat surface and roll each ¼ inch thick. Cut each into three 5½-inch rounds and use remainder plus scraps to form hats and decorations. Transfer to greased baking sheet and prick with fork to keep from puffing up. Bake at 400°F. for 5 to 7 minutes, or until set and beginning to color, repricking if necessary.

If using frozen dinner rolls, defrost and separate rolls. Press 2 together and roll into 6-inch flat rounds, reserving some rolls for hats and decorations. Bake on greased baking sheet at 450°F. for 5 to 7 minutes, or until set and beginning to color. (Crusts may be wrapped in foil and stored at room temperature overnight or frozen up to 1 month. Defrost at room temperature.)

If using pita bread, divide each in half and lightly toast halves.

To Assemble: Either put out an assortment of toppings and allow each child to design his/her own pizza or assemble the pizzas yourself by spreading them with sauce, cheese, and desired toppings.

Final Baking: Place on baking sheets or heavy-duty foil and bake at 450°F. for 4 to 6 minutes, or until cheese is melted and crusts are golden.

MAKES: enough toppings for 6 (5-inch) pizzas. Crust amounts vary with type.

Here are several options for making pizza crusts. If space permits, allow each little Rembrandt to top his/her own prebaked crust with a clown face or free-form mosaic. (See color photo, page 7.)

PREP TIME: Varies with type of crust

BAKE TIME: To prebake crusts, 5 to 7 minutes; completed pizzas, 4 to 6 minutes

ADVANCE PREP: Partially baked crusts may be stored at room temperature overnight or frozen.

NUTRITIONAL ANALYSIS

Per 5-inch pizza (with low-fat mozzarella)
477 calories
18 g fat
20 mg cholesterol
1120 mg sodium

There's no such thing as too many clowns at a birthday party. This one is a dense, fudgy, smiling cake baked in an ovenproof bowl and decorated with candy, toys, and lots of love. The low oven temperature and long baking time assure that the cake cooks all the way through without the sides drying out. (See color photo, page 7.)

PREP TIME: 15 minutes, plus frosting and decorating

BAKE TIME: 1 hour and 35 to 55 minutes

ADVANCE PREP: Undecorated cake may be stored at room temperature overnight or frozen. Decorated cake may be refrigerated overnight or frozen up to 2 weeks.

NUTRITIONAL ANALYSIS

Per serving (with low-fat milk, low-fat cream cheese)
382 calories
19 g fat
28 mg cholesterol
207 mg sodium

CLOWN CAKE

Chocolate Cake
2 cups sugar
2 large eggs
1 cup regular or low-fat milk
1 cup unsweetened cocoa powder
1 cup shortening
½ teaspoon salt
2 teaspoons baking powder
1 teaspoon baking soda
2 teaspoons vanilla extract
3 cups all-purpose flour
1 cup boiling water

Cream Cheese Frosting
1 package (8 ounces) regular or low-fat cream cheese, at room temperature
½ cup shortening
3 cups confectioners' sugar
1 teaspoon vanilla extract

Decorations
1 rubber ball or jaw breaker, about 1½ inches in diameter
Red licorice laces
2 pink candy-coating chips (optional)
2 blue candy-coating chips (optional)
Red decorating icing in tubes
Chocolate decorating icing in tube
Wooden skewer
Paper clown hat
Doily and ribbon for collar

To Make Cake: Preheat oven to 325°F. Grease an ovenproof mixing bowl about 9 inches across the top and 3 inches deep that holds about 10 cups of water with shortening and line it with heavy foil, leaving about 2 inches extended over the sides. Grease the foil and set aside.

Measure sugar, eggs, milk, cocoa, shortening, salt, baking powder, baking soda, vanilla, and flour into large mixing bowl. Add boiling water. Mix with electric mixer until smooth and blended, about 2 minutes. Pour batter into prepared bowl, spreading the top evenly.

To Bake: Bake for 1 hour and 35 to 55 minutes or until a toothpick inserted into the center comes out clean. The top will be cracked and crusty. Remove from oven and cool completely in bowl. To remove cake, pull up on foil. (Cake may be wrapped in foil and stored at room temperature overnight or frozen.)

To Make Frosting: In mixing bowl with electric mixer, cream cheese, shortening, confectioners' sugar, and vanilla until well blended and smooth. If too thin to spread, refrigerate until desired consistency.

To Frost and Decorate: Place cake, dome side up, on a small plate or cardboard round cut to fit the bottom of the cake. Drop frosting in small mounds over cake and spread to cover it completely. Spread smooth.

Place rubber ball or jaw breaker in center for nose. Cut licorice into two 6-inch strips for the eye loops and two 2½-inch strips for bottom of eyes. Place on cake. Cut a 2-inch licorice strip for top lip and a 4-inch strip for bottom lip. Place on cake, using toothpick to help move into place. Place a pink chip on each side of face for cheeks and 1 blue chip in each eye for eye balls. Or pipe cheeks and eyes with frosting. Pipe tongue with red icing. For hair, cover top and sides of cake with red licorice laces. Finish eyes with squiggles of chocolate icing. (See color photo, page 7.) (Cake may be refrigerated overnight, loosely covered with foil, or frozen up to 2 weeks. Defrost in refrigerator overnight.)

Before Serving: Place skewer into hat and place on clown's head. Pleat doily into a ruffle and place on platter. Place cake in center. Ruffle ribbon around bottom edge of cake for collar.

MAKES: about 20 servings.

ICE CREAM CONE CLOWNS

1 quart ice cream, any flavor
Chocolate sprinkles
6 storebought pointed waffle cones

Chocolate chips
Gum drops
Decorating icing tubes

Line a baking sheet with foil or wax paper. Scoop ice cream into 6 balls. Roll half of each ball in sprinkles for hair. Place on baking sheet. Press cone into top on a slant for the hat. Decorate face with chocolate chip eyes, gum drop nose, and piped icing for mouth, collar, buttons, and decorations on hat.

Cover well with heavy foil and freeze until serving. Place on plates, hat side up. (Clowns may be frozen, well covered, up to 3 days.)

MAKES: 6 cone clowns.

With the kids both devouring this treat and playing with it, you'll want to have plenty of napkins—even towels—on hand.

PREP TIME: 30 minutes

CHILL TIME: At least 1 hour

ADVANCE PREP: May be frozen up to 3 days.

NUTRITIONAL ANALYSIS
Per cone
229 calories
10 g fat
39 mg cholesterol
117 mg sodium

Menu

◆

**SANGRIA BLANCO WITH
FRESH FRUIT**

◆

**BLACK BEANS WITH ONIONS
AND BALSAMIC VINEGAR**

◆

**PORK PICADILLO IN BAKED
TOSTADA CUPS**

◆

PINEAPPLE-PAPAYA SALSA

◆

**MARGARITA ICE CREAM
TORTE**

MUCHO FEISTY FIESTA

s catchy as the strains of strolling mariachis are the bold aromas of my South-of-the-Border fete. Casually festive is the description for this Mexi-fare, which can be multiplied for large crowds at an afternoon or evening buffet of grand proportions or suffice for an intimate sit-down luncheon. Since everything on the menu can be prepared in advance, you can loosen up with your amigos over a glass of frosty Sangria Blanco.

The tostada cups are just the right size for a luncheon portion. To make them for dinner, offer two per person or use ten-inch tortillas and bake them in larger bowls. Or omit the cups and serve the picadillo over rice and then include tortillas in Garden Salad with Tortilla Strings and Grainy Mustard Vinaigrette (see page 172). The tortilla cups also make terrific holders for salads, salsa, or other saucy dishes.

Hearty, piquant Mexican food calls for a refreshing dessert and the Margarita Ice Cream Torte cools the palate. For a dessert that won't melt, substitute Lime Mousse in a Seafoam Shell (see page 187) or Light and Lush Lemon Cake (see page 233). This menu serves ten, but can be multiplied for larger groups.

GAME PLAN

1 Month Ahead	**Make and freeze pork**
	Make and freeze torte
	Make and freeze black beans
	Bake and freeze Tostada Cups
3 Days Ahead	**Make Pineapple-Papaya Salsa**
1 Day Ahead	**Defrost pork**
	Defrost beans
	Defrost Tostada Cups
	Make Sangria Blanco

DAY OF PARTY

4 Hours Ahead	**Prepare condiments for pork**
15 Minutes Before Serving	**Heat pork**
	Rewarm Tostada Cups
	Reheat beans
	Add sparkling water and fruit to sangria

EXTRA POINTS

THE TABLE

Be big, be bold, be bright. Lay multicolored runners across your table and wrap cactus in intensely colored tissue or paper bags tied with raffia. Intersperse or substitute paper flowers in hot tones. Bring in additional color with crepe paper streamers and/or scarves. Stack bricks or tiles pyramid fashion and top them with platters of food, Mexican artifacts, piñatas, and cactus. For a centerpiece, surround the brim of a sombrero with small terracotta or colored pots filled with chili peppers and/or flowers. (See color photo, page 1.)

THE KICKER

Visit your local import store for specialty items like drinking straws with pleated paper fruits and flowers.

Serve this sparkling wine cooler to lift your guests' spirits when they arrive or as a re- fresher with the meal. (See color photo, page 1.)

PREP TIME: 10 minutes

CHILL TIME: At least 30 minutes

ADVANCE PREP: May be refrigerated overnight.

SANGRIA BLANCO WITH FRESH FRUIT

½ cup sugar
2 bottles (750ml each) Chablis wine
½ cup orange liqueur, such as Triple Sec or Cointreau
1 lemon, halved and sliced

2 limes, halved and sliced
2 oranges, halved and sliced
2 cups sparkling mineral water, chilled
Strawberries (optional)
Sliced kiwi (optional)

In a small saucepan over moderate heat, bring 1 cup water and sugar to a boil. Simmer 5 minutes, or until the sugar is dissolved. Cool to room temperature. Stir sugar syrup, wine, liqueur, lemon, lime and or- ange slices together. Cover and refrigerate until chilled. (Mixture may be refrigerated overnight.)

Just Before Serving: Pour wine mixture into a large pitcher or punch bowl. Stir in sparkling water. Serve over ice in wine goblets, adding a few citrus slices and strawberries and/or kiwi, if desired, to each glass.

MAKES: 12 (6-ounce) servings.

NUTRITIONAL ANALYSIS

Per 6-ounce serving
137 calories
0 fat
0 cholesterol
5 mg sodium

BLACK BEANS WITH ONIONS AND BALSAMIC VINEGAR

1 tablespoon olive oil
1 medium red onion, chopped
2 garlic cloves, minced
1½ teaspoons ground cumin
1½ teaspoons hot chile powder

2 cans (16 ounces each) black
    beans, rinsed and drained
1 tablespoon plus 2 teaspoons
    balsamic vinegar
¼ teaspoon salt, or to taste

To Make in Microwave: In a 6- to 8-cup microwavesafe bowl, stir together oil, onion, and garlic. Cover with plastic wrap and microwave on high (100%) for 2 minutes. Stir and microwave for 2 to 3 minutes more, or until translucent. Stir in cumin, chile powder, beans, vinegar, and salt. Cover and microwave for 5 minutes, or until heated through.

To Make on Stove: In a medium saucepan, heat olive oil over moderate heat until hot. Add onion and cook until translucent, about 8 minutes. Add garlic, cumin, and chile powder. Cook, stirring, until mixed, about 30 seconds. Add beans, vinegar, and salt to taste. Cook, stirring often, until heated through.

(Beans may be refrigerated up to 2 days or frozen. Reheat before serving.)

MAKES: 12 servings.

W hy go to the trouble of soaking and cooking dried black beans for hours when this speedy version tastes just as good?

PREP TIME: 10 minutes

COOK TIME: 10 minutes

ADVANCE PREP: May be refrigerated up to 2 days or frozen.

NUTRITIONAL ANALYSIS

Per serving
67 calories
2 g fat
0 cholesterol
49 mg sodium

In Mexico you would expect to find picadillo, a spicy shredded meat mixture sweetened with raisins and cinnamon, stuffed into turnovers or chiles. My version fills muffin cup–size tortilla shells. For dinner, double the recipe and offer two tortilla cups per person. Serve with a choice of cooling condiments. (See color photo, page 1.)

PREP TIME: 30 minutes

BAKE TIME: 1 hour 30 minutes

ADVANCE PREP: May be refrigerated up to 2 days or frozen. Tostada cups may be stored at room temperature up to 2 days or frozen.

NUTRITIONAL ANALYSIS

Per serving (not including condiments)
235 calories
10 g fat
59 mg cholesterol
427 mg sodium

PORK PICADILLO

No-stick cooking spray
2 pounds lean pork stew meat (shoulder or leg), cut into 2-inch cubes
2 large onions, chopped
2 cans (28 ounces each) whole tomatoes
4 large garlic cloves, minced
½ cup golden raisins
¼ cup cider vinegar
4 teaspoons hot chile powder
¼ teaspoon ground cinnamon
¼ teaspoon cayenne, or more to taste

1 tablespoon dried oregano
1 tablespoon ground cumin
½ teaspoon salt, or to taste

Baked Tostada Cups, for serving (see page 79)

Condiments
Pineapple-Papaya Salsa (see page 79)
1 cup shredded lettuce
3 medium tomatoes, chopped
1 cup sour cream

Preheat oven to 350°F.

Spray bottom of ovenproof Dutch oven or heavy, wide saucepan with cooking spray and heat over high heat until hot. Add pork and sauté, stirring often, until browned, about 10 minutes. Add onions and sauté, stirring occasionally, until soft, about 8 to 10 minutes. Break up tomatoes (or chop in food processor) and add them with the liquid from 1 of the cans to the pork. Discard remaining liquid. Stir garlic, raisins, vinegar, and spices into pork and bring to a boil.

Cover and bake for 1½ hours, stirring every 30 minutes, until meat is very tender and shreds easily. When cool, shred pork with 2 forks. (Pork may be refrigerated up to 2 days or frozen up to one month. Reheat on top of stove or in microwave.)

To serve, spoon pork into tostada cups. Pass salsa and other condiments.

MAKES: 10 servings.

BAKED TOSTADA CUPS

10 (regular, not light) flour tortillas, 6 to 8 inches in diameter

Place oven rack on bottom rung. Preheat oven to 300°F.

Place 5 tortillas in a plastic bag or on a plate covered with plastic wrap. Microwave on high (100%) for 30 to 40 seconds, or until soft enough to bend. While warm, press into 3½-inch custard cups, soufflé dishes, or 2½- to 3-inch muffin cups to form fluted cups. Repeat with remaining tortillas. Bake for 25 to 30 minutes, or until very crisp and lightly browned. Remove tortillas from tins. (Cups may be stored in an airtight container at room temperature up to 2 days or frozen. Before filling, reheat at 350°F.)

MAKES: 10 tostada cups.

NUTRITIONAL ANALYSIS

Per tostada
95 calories
2 g fat
0 cholesterol
110 mg sodium

PINEAPPLE-PAPAYA SALSA

1 pickled or fresh seeded jalapeño, about ¾ to 1 inch (see page 10)
1 garlic clove, peeled
1 large or 2 small green onions, cut into 1-inch pieces
1¼ cups peeled, seeded, and coarsely chopped papaya
2½ cups fresh pineapple, cut into ¾-inch chunks
3 tablespoons fresh lime juice
¼ teaspoon salt, or to taste

In a food processor with the metal blade, process jalapeño and garlic until minced. Add green onion and pulse until chopped. Add papaya, pineapple, lime juice, and salt and pulse until chopped into small pieces. Be careful not to process too fine; salsa should be chunky. Remove to a bowl and refrigerate until chilled. (Salsa may be refrigerated up to 3 days.)

MAKES: 3 cups

Change of Pace: To make Pineapple-Mango Salsa, substitute 1 mango for the papaya.

To make Pineapple-Orange Salsa, substitute 1¼ cups peeled, seeded, and chopped oranges for the papaya.

Sweet fruit and spicy jalapeño bring symmetry to the cinnamon-scented, chile-spiked picadillo. This salsa is also great with grilled fish, pork, and poultry. (See color photo, page 1.)

PREP TIME: 10 minutes

CHILL TIME: 30 minutes

ADVANCE PREP: May be refrigerated up to 3 days.

NUTRITIONAL ANALYSIS

Per 2 tablespoons
12 calories
less than 1 g fat
0 cholesterol
23 mg sodium

MARGARITA ICE CREAM TORTE

Oreo Crust
30 Oreo sandwich cookies
  (2½ cups crumbs)
4 tablespoons (½ stick) butter or
  margarine, melted

Margarita Filling
½ cup frozen lemonade
  concentrate, thawed
6 tablespoons tequila
Grated peel of 1 lime
  (see page 11)

2 tablespoons plus 2 teaspoons
  fresh lime juice (2 small limes)
2 tablespoons orange liqueur,
  such as Triple Sec or curaçao
5 to 6 drops green food coloring
  (optional)
2 quarts good quality vanilla ice
  cream, softened slightly

To Make Crust: Preheat oven to 350°F. Oil an 8½- or 9-inch springform pan. In a food processor with the metal blade, process cookies into crumbs. Add butter and pulse until incorporated. Set aside 2 tablespoons for garnish and press remainder into bottom and halfway up sides of prepared pan. Bake for 10 minutes. Remove and cool to room temperature.

To Make Filling: In a large bowl, stir lemonade, tequila, lime peel and juice, orange liqueur, and food coloring, if using, together. Add ice cream and stir until blended, but do not let the ice cream melt. Spoon into crust. Sprinkle reserved crumbs around top edge. Cover with foil and freeze overnight or until firm. (Torte may be frozen up to 2 weeks.)

Before Serving: Remove sides of springform and, if desired, insert a knife between crust and bottom and remove torte to platter. Cut into wedges. Leftovers may be refrozen.

MAKES: 10 to 12 servings.

Leaner: Reduce crumbs in crust to 12 cookies (1 cup crumbs) and butter or margarine to 2 tablespoons. Spread on bottom of pan only. To make Margarita Yogurt Torte, substitute vanilla low-fat or nonfat frozen yogurt for the ice cream.

Stir a margarita cocktail into vanilla ice cream, pile it into a crisp chocolate cookie crust, and enjoy an invigorating dessert. When greasing the springform be sure to use oil, not shortening or butter, which harden when chilled.

PREP TIME: 30 minutes

FREEZE TIME: 24 hours

ADVANCE PREP: May be frozen up to 2 weeks.

NUTRITIONAL ANALYSIS

Per serving
438 calories
25 g fat
69 mg cholesterol
269 mg sodium

DRESS-UP DINNERS

These are dressed-up menus for exquisite dining, but you can wear whatever you please. When the occasion calls for your fanciest offerings—the boss is coming to dinner, you're celebrating an engagement or reciprocating a ''gourmet'' friend's invitation—your biggest dilemma will be deciding between chicken, fish, or beef. Each menu is designed for candlelight, roses, and six to eight persons, but when the occasion calls for greater numbers, the recipes can be multiplied to serve as many as you wish. And when it's an interlude only for two, be that Valentine's Day, an anniversary, or kindling passion, I've included a romantic repast to strum the heart strings.

Menu

◆

OYSTER SAMPLER:
BAKED OYSTERS FLORENTINE

•

CREOLE-BAKED OYSTERS

•

OYSTERS WITH FRESH
TOMATO COULIS

◆

BUTTER LETTUCE AND
TOMATOES WITH V-8
VINAIGRETTE

◆

VERMOUTH-GLAZED
SCALLOPS WITH JULIENNED
VEGETABLES

◆

HOMINY OR POLENTA
HEARTS

◆

PUFF PASTRY APPLE TARTLETS
WITH CONTEMPO CARAMEL
SAUCE

A ROMANTIC DINNER à DEUX

When an intimate sentimental occasion arises, or when you feel the need to create one, consider this menu. Through the ages certain foods have been said to have aphrodisiac qualities—chocolate, onions, garlic, cheese, and the epitome, the oyster. It was, after all, the Greek goddess of love, Aphrodite, whom the Romans renamed Venus, who sprang fully formed from the sea, giving birth to the idea that bivalves can enhance amorous occasions. Who am I to argue with tradition? I've included recipes that blend myth with reality, and rather than take chances on missing the passion boat by limiting oysters to only one dish, there are three. Plus, I offer a delighted scallop entree served over hominy or polenta, which is shaped into hearts.

Once oysters are shucked, they are extremely easy to prepare. If you haven't mastered the technique, ask your fishmonger to do it, or steam the oysters briefly until they open just a crack. Don't throw the shells away, scrub them and dry them by leaving them out or putting them in the oven. They are then ready to be filled with jarred shucked oysters.

The idea of shaping grits into hearts comes from my assistant, Rita Calvert, who hails from North Carolina and is more familiar with this Southern staple than I. The results are spectacular and I have since become a hominy convert, even preferring them to their Italian cousin, polenta.

A fitting partner for this substantial main dish is a simple salad of crisp greens and tomatoes heightened with a refreshing splash of V-8 vinaigrette. If that doesn't appeal, you might serve Tomato Relish in Plum Tomato Shells (see page 109).

For many, chocolate is the ultimate fantasy dessert, but you may remember it was the apple that aroused Adam's ardor in the Garden of Eden. With that in mind, I've included individual apple-shaped apple tarts to complete the romantic repast.

Should you choose to share this feast with another couple, the scallops may be doubled and cooked in one large skillet. Be sure to sear them in batches, though; if you crowd them, they will steam instead of brown. The other recipes can all be easily doubled.

GAME PLAN

1 Month Ahead	**Make and freeze Hominy Hearts**
2 Days Ahead	**Cook bacon and spinach and prepare dressing for Oysters Florentine** **Make sauce and crumb topping for Creole Oysters** **Make tomato coulis for oysters** **Make V-8 Vinaigrette**
DAY OF PARTY 8 Hours Ahead	**Cook scallops and vegetables** **Prepare lettuce and tomatoes**
4 Hours Ahead	**Bake puff pastry apples and prepare filling** **Bake Hominy Hearts**
Before Serving	**Assemble and bake Oysters Florentine** **Assemble and bake Creole Oysters** **Cook and top Oysters with Fresh Tomato Coulis** **Bake or reheat Hominy Hearts** **Make sauce and finish scallops** **Assemble salad** **Reheat puff pastry** **Reheat apples and caramel sauce**

EXTRA POINTS

THE SETTING

Move your romantic meal from where you customarily dine to a new and cozy spot—a small table in the living room, cushions in front of the fire, or trays in the bedroom.

THE TABLE

Make a centerpiece pertinent to your sweetheart's hobbies or interests—CDs and musical score sheets for the symphony lover; TV guides and snacks for the couch potato; pliers and hammers for Mr. Fix-it; weights or golf or tennis balls for the sports enthusiast. Arrange in a basket with moss or flowers and add a few balloons on a stick.

Write the menu on a card and place it in a small picture frame. (See color photo, page 8.)

Irst in the oyster sampling come oysters cloaked in creamy Russian dressing with crisp bacon and wilted emerald spinach. (See color photo, page 8.)

PREP TIME: 15 minutes

BAKE TIME: 10 minutes

ADVANCE PREP: Dressing, bacon, and spinach may be prepared up to 2 days ahead.

BAKED OYSTERS FLORENTINE

Russian Dressing
¼ cup regular, low-fat, or nonfat mayonnaise
1 tablespoon bottled red chile sauce
1 teaspoon Dijon mustard
1 teaspoon lemon juice
¼ teaspoon Tabasco sauce, or to taste

3 slices regular or reduced-fat bacon
1 cup (packed) coarsely chopped fresh spinach, large stems removed
4 large oysters on the half shell, drained and blotted very dry
2 teaspoons grated parmesan cheese

To Make Dressing: Stir mayonnaise, chile sauce, mustard, lemon juice, and Tabasco sauce in small bowl. (Dressing may be refrigerated up to 2 days.)

Chop bacon and cook in microwave or on top of stove until crisp. Drain well on paper towels. Place spinach in microwavesafe pie plate, cover with plastic wrap, and microwave on high (100%) for 30 seconds to 2 minutes, or until wilted. Chop fine. Set aside. (Bacon and spinach may be refrigerated up to 2 days.)

To Bake: Preheat oven to 425°F. Before serving, spoon dressing over oysters and top with spinach, bacon, and parmesan cheese. Place on baking sheet and bake for 10 minutes, or until cheese begins to brown and bubble.

MAKES: 4 oysters.

NUTRITIONAL ANALYSIS

Per oyster (with reduced-fat bacon, nonfat mayonnaise)
90 calories
4 g fat
42 mg cholesterol
443 mg sodium

CREOLE-BAKED OYSTERS

Red Creole Sauce
1 garlic clove, peeled
2 green onions, cut into 1-inch pieces
½ cup thick tomato pasta sauce, homemade or storebought
A-1 Sauce
⅛ teaspoon crushed red pepper flakes

Crumb Topping
2 tablespoons chopped pecans, toasted (see page 11)
3 tablespoons packaged cornbread stuffing mix
1 teaspoon honey
2 teaspoons Dijon mustard

4 large oysters on the half shell, drained and patted very dry
2 teaspoons fresh lemon juice

To Make Sauce: In food processor with metal blade, mince garlic. Add green onions and pulse until chopped. Add pasta sauce, a dash of A-1 Sauce, and red pepper flakes. Pulse until combined. (Sauce may be refrigerated up to 2 days.)

To Make Crumb Topping: Stir all ingredients together in a small bowl. (Crumbs may be refrigerated up to 2 days.)

To Assemble and Bake: Preheat oven to 425°F. Before serving, place oysters on baking sheet. Drizzle with lemon juice. Top each with 1 to 2 tablespoons creole sauce and sprinkle with crumbs. Bake for 10 minutes, or until crumbs are golden and sauce is bubbling.

MAKES: 4 oysters.

A sprinkling of crumbled cornbread stuffing with pecans and honey mustard lends Southern flair to baked oysters in a zippy tomato sauce. (See color photo, page 8.)

PREP TIME: 15 minutes

BAKE TIME: 10 minutes

ADVANCE PREP: Sauce and topping may be refrigerated up to 2 days.

NUTRITIONAL ANALYSIS

Per oyster
139 calories
5 g fat
34 mg cholesterol
538 mg sodium

In this version, cooked oysters are topped with a relish of swiftly sautéed tomato bits seasoned with basil and garlic. (See color photo, page 8.)

PREP TIME: 15 minutes

COOK TIME: 3 to 10 minutes

ADVANCE PREP: Coulis may be refrigerated up to 2 days. Cook oysters and top them as close to serving as possible.

OYSTERS WITH FRESH TOMATO COULIS

Tomato Coulis
1 teaspoon olive oil
1 garlic clove, minced
1 teaspoon minced shallot
3 medium plum tomatoes, seeded and chopped into ⅜-inch dice (see page 12)

1 teaspoon raspberry vinegar
1 teaspoon finely chopped fresh basil leaves or ¼ teaspoon dried basil
¼ teaspoon sugar

8 oysters in the shell

To Make Coulis: Heat olive oil in a small sauté pan over medium high heat. Sauté garlic and shallot until soft, 3 to 4 minutes. Add tomatoes and cook, stirring often, until they come to a boil and begin to wilt but still retain their fresh color, about 3 minutes. Stir in vinegar, basil, and sugar. Remove from heat. (Coulis may be refrigerated up to 2 days. Bring to room temperature before using.)

To Cook Oysters: Scrub shells. In a skillet, bring ½ inch water to a boil. Add oysters, cover, and steam until the shells open, about 3 to 10 minutes. Discard any that don't open. (Timing will vary with different oysters.) Remove from heat and remove half the shell. Drain off any liquid.

To Assemble: Place oysters in the half shell on a platter and spoon 2 to 3 teaspoons coulis over each.

MAKES: 8 oysters.

Faster: If you have reserved oyster shells, purchase jarred oysters, place one in each half shell and bake, covered with foil, at 450°F. for 10 minutes. Top with coulis and serve.

BUTTER LETTUCE AND TOMATOES WITH V-8 VINAIGRETTE

1 small head butter or Boston
   lettuce
2 medium tomatoes

V-8 Vinaigrette
2 teaspoons balsamic vinegar
1 tablespoon plus 1 teaspoon
   V-8 juice or tomato juice

2 tablespoons olive oil
1 garlic clove, minced
Salt
Freshly ground rainbow
   peppercorns or black pepper

Separate lettuce into leaves, rinse, and pat dry. Refrigerate, wrapped in paper towels, until ready to assemble the salad. Cut out core from tomatoes and slice ¼ inch thick.

To Make Vinaigrette: In a small bowl or jar, whisk or shake vinegar, V-8 juice, oil, garlic, and salt and pepper to taste until blended. (Dressing may be refrigerated up to 3 days.)

To Assemble: Line each salad plate with a whole lettuce leaf. Slice remaining lettuce into ½-inch shreds, alternate with tomato slices, and drizzle with dressing.

MAKES: 2 servings.

Choose only the smallest lettuce leaves to alternate with bright ripe tomato slices for a very simple, very fresh salad.

PREP TIME: 10 minutes

ADVANCE PREP: Vinaigrette may be refrigerated up to 3 days.

NUTRITIONAL ANALYSIS

Per serving
174 calories
14 g fat
0 cholesterol
56 mg sodium

Toss scallops with a kaleidoscope of matchstick vegetables and a glimmer of sauce, and mound them onto Hominy or Polenta Hearts. The secret to obtaining golden crusted scallops with a soft and juicy interior is to sear them quickly over very high heat. Be sure to heat the skillet until it's almost smoking before adding the scallops. (See color photo, page 9.)

PREP TIME: 25 minutes

COOK TIME: About 10 minutes

ADVANCE PREP: Sautéed scallops and vegetables may be refrigerated up to 8 hours.

VERMOUTH-GLAZED SCALLOPS WITH JULIENNED VEGETABLES

1 medium leek, cleaned (see page 11)
1 medium carrot, peeled
1 small zucchini
¼ cup flour, for dredging
¾ pound sea scallops, rinsed and patted very dry
1 to 2 tablespoons olive oil, divided
1 large garlic clove, minced
1 cup (tightly packed) fresh spinach leaves, large stems removed and cut into ½-inch strips

Vermouth Sauce
½ cup dry vermouth or dry white wine
¾ cup chicken or vegetable broth
1 teaspoon fresh lime juice
1 teaspoon cornstarch
2 tablespoons heavy cream
Salt and freshly ground black pepper

1 recipe Hominy or Polenta Hearts (recipe follows)

To Prepare Vegetables: Cut leek, carrot, and zucchini in 2-inch lengths and then into matchstick strips by hand or with julienne blade of food processor.

To Cook Scallops: Place flour in a shallow dish, add scallops, toss to coat, and pat off excess. In a large skillet (preferably nonstick) over high heat, heat 2 teaspoons olive oil until very hot and almost smoking. Test heat by adding 1 scallop; the oil should bubble furiously and the bottom brown in 1 minute. Sauté scallops until golden, about 1 to 2 minutes per side. (If pan is not hot enough, juices will come out of scallops before they brown. Remove them from heat anyway.) Place on plate and set aside.

To Cook Vegetables: In same skillet over moderate heat, heat 1 teaspoon oil. Add leeks and carrots and sauté, stirring, for 1 minute, scraping up any brown bits from bottom of pan. Add zucchini and garlic and sauté for 1 to 2 minutes, or until vegetables are almost tender. If too dry, add additional oil as needed. Add spinach and cook just until wilted. Remove vegetables to scallops. (Scallops and vegetables may be refrigerated, covered, up to 8 hours.)

To Make Sauce: Before serving stir vermouth or wine, broth, and lime juice into skillet. Cook over moderate heat until reduced to about half, 4 to 6 minutes. Remove from heat. Stir cornstarch into cream and whisk into sauce. Return to heat and cook, stirring, until mixture comes to a

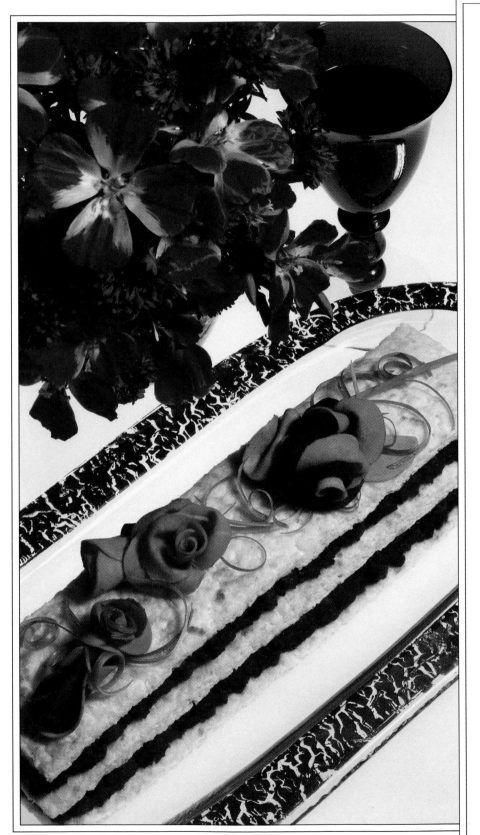

CEREMONIAL PASSOVER SEDER

◆

To modernize gefilte fish, it's layered in a torte to look as dazzling as a showy dessert.

◆

GEFILTE FISH TORTE GARNISHED WITH CARROT AND BEET ROSES
(page 238)

FANCIED-UP FILLET OF BEEF

◆

This glamorous salad makes an outstanding first course or entree for an important luncheon.

◆

FACING PAGE

SALAD GREENS WITH PASTA PINWHEELS AND WARM TOMATO VINAIGRETTE
(page 116)

Firecracker Invitation (page 257)

Rolled Stuffed Flank Steak Santa Fe (page 258)
Tex-Mex Baked Beans (page 260) • Cornbread Pudding (page 262)

Red, White, and Blueberry Shortcake with Chocolate Biscuits
(page 264)

SOUTHWESTERN
FOURTH OF JULY

◆

In celebration of our
country's independence
and barbecue history,
here is a menu with
Southwestern flair and
guaranteed gusto.

◆

FACING PAGE
Clockwise from right:

RED-SPANGLED SLAW WITH
DRIED CRANBERRIES
(page 261)

◆

CORNBREAD PUDDING
(page 262)

◆

ROLLED STUFFED FLANK STEAK
SANTA FE
(page 258)

◆

TEX-MEX BAKED BEANS
(page 260)

Oyster Sampler: Creole-Baked Oysters (page 85)
Baked Oysters Florentine (page 84) • Oysters with Fresh
Tomato Coulis (page 86)

Romantic centerpiece and menu for the music lover (page 83)

Puff Pastry Apple Tartlets with Contempo Caramel Sauce
(page 90)

ROMANTIC DINNER
À DEUX

◆

When an intimate sen-
timental occasion arises,
or you want to create
one, consider this
romantic repast.

◆

FACING PAGE

VERMOUTH-GLAZED SCALLOPS
WITH JULIENNED VEGETABLES
ON HOMINY HEARTS
(pages 88 and 89)

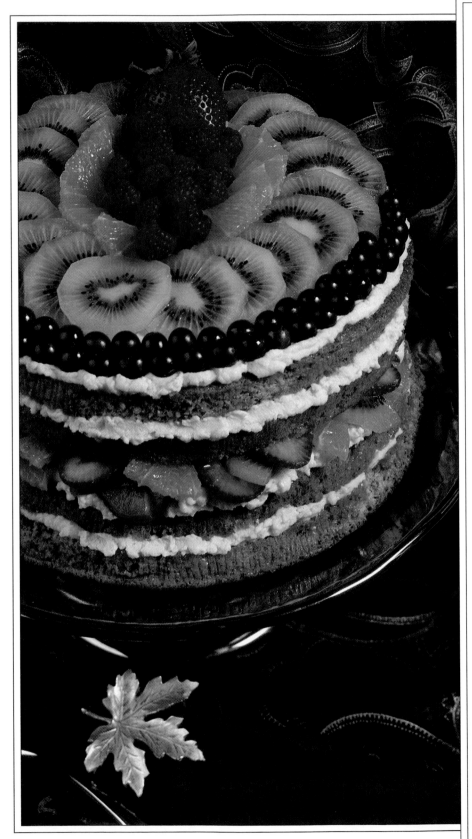

GRILLED MAGIC OF THE MIDDLE EAST DINNER

◆

Framed with a jewellike crown of fresh fruit, this elegant dessert is as pretty as a still life.

◆

ORANGE-PISTACHIO TORTE WITH RICOTTA AND FRESH FRUIT
(page 197)

PEKING CHICKEN ON THE PATIO

◆

From stir-frys to sombreros, chiles to chopsticks, this is a fiesta where anything goes.

◆

FACING PAGE
Clockwise from left:

CRUDITÉS WITH PEANUT DIPPING SAUCE
(page 212)

◆

PEKING CHICKEN IN TORTILLAS
(page 213)

◆

CRISPY CHINESE SALAD WITH KIWI VINAIGRETTE
(page 215)

◆

SWEET PEA GUACAMOLE
(page 214)

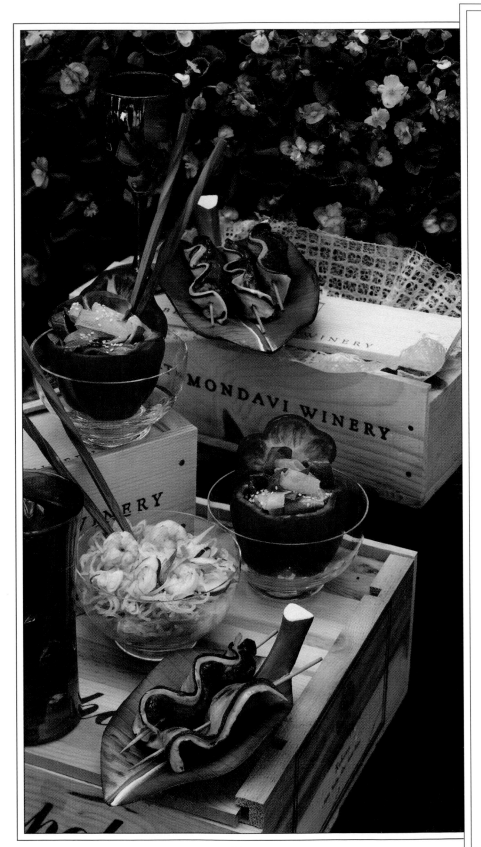

ROUND MOON
JAPANESE
BOX SUPPER

ROUND MOON JAPANESE BOX SUPPER

◆

Here's a Japanese in-
spired picnic that travels
from sandy beaches to
moonlight on the bay.

◆

Clockwise from top:

**PORK YAKIMONO WITH GREEN
AND YELLOW SQUASH RIBBONS**
(page 204)

◆

**SPINACH AND CUCUMBER
SHREDS IN SWEET PEPPER CUPS**
(page 205)

◆

**SHRIMP SALAD WITH CELLO-
PHANE NOODLES**
(page 206)

BRUNCH ON THE MEDITERRANEAN

◆

Give your guests a
taste of Provence with
this colorful garden-
fresh vegetarian entree.

◆

FACING PAGE

**EGGPLANT, TWO-TOMATO, AND
PESTO TORTE**
(page 24)

· 12 ·

Fall harvest centerpiece (page 269)

Thanksgiving place cards (page 269)

Harvest Patchwork Cake (page 276)

THANKSGIVING FEAST

◆

You won't need to be up at daybreak to prepare this elegant, lighter menu. Guests will applaud the unique combination of traditional ingredients.

◆

FACING PAGE
Clockwise from right:

HONEY GRAHAM–SWEET POTATO ROLLS
(page 274)

◆

ROAST BREAST OF TURKEY WITH CORNBREAD, SPINACH, AND PECANS
(page 270)

◆

CRANBERRY-GLAZED BABY CARROTS
(page 272)

◆

WILD RICE PILAF WITH LEEKS AND DRIED PEARS
(page 273)

MERRY WINTER MORNING

◆

This joyful breakfast is a gift for your loved ones on Christmas morning or any day of the year.

◆

Clockwise from top:

GRAPEVINE WREATH CENTERPIECE
(page 29)

◆

SMOKED SALMON NAPOLEON
(page 32)

◆

CROWNED CRAN-APPLE COFFEECAKE WREATH
(page 34)

◆

FRESH FRUIT PALETTES
(page 30)

boil. Increase heat to high and cook for 1 minute. Add scallops and vegetables and cook, stirring, until heated through and sauce thickens, 1 to 3 minutes. Season with salt and pepper to taste. With a spatula, place a warm Hominy or Polenta Heart on each plate and spoon scallops and vegetables into the center.

MAKES: 2 generous servings.

HOMINY HEARTS

½ cup white or yellow old-fashioned grits, not quick cooking or instant
¾ cup chicken or vegetable broth

2 tablespoons plus 1 tablespoon grated parmesan cheese, divided
No-stick cooking spray

To Cook Hominy: Cover a flat baking sheet with heavy foil, and grease or spray the foil. In a 4-cup microwavesafe bowl, stir together grits, ½ cup water, and broth. Microwave, covered, on high (100%) for 4 to 6 minutes, stirring every 2 minutes, until mixture is as thick as mashed potatoes, but not dry. Whisk smooth and stir in 2 tablespoons cheese.

To Shape Hearts: Divide the hot mixture in half on prepared baking sheet and shape into 2 hearts, each about ½ inch thick, 6 inches long, and 5½ inches across at the widest part, pushing up the sides to form a 1-inch raised edge. Spray tops with cooking spray. (Hearts may be covered and refrigerated up to 2 days or frozen. Bring to room temperature before baking.)

To Bake: Place rack in upper third of oven and preheat to 500°F. Sprinkle tops of hearts with remaining 1 tablespoon cheese. Bake for 13 to 18 minutes, or until heated through and edges begin to turn golden. (Hearts may be baked several hours ahead and reheated at 500°F. for 2 minutes.) Remove to plates with spatula.

MAKES: 2 servings.

Leaner: Omit 2 tablespoons parmesan cheese from the batter and sprinkle 1 tablespoon cheese over the tops. If serving with a saucy entree, omit all the cheese and, if desired, add a little salt to the batter.

Change of Pace: To make Polenta Hearts, substitute ¾ cup yellow cornmeal for the ½ cup grits.

In the South they might call these gussied-up grits. You Northerners who are tempted to turn the page—don't! You'll be missing a unique side dish that is a great trade for pasta. These are wonderfully creamy with a crisp exterior and are especially good with a saucy entree. (See color photo, page 9.)

PREP TIME: 15 minutes

BAKE TIME: 13 to 18 minutes

ADVANCE PREP: Unbaked hearts may be refrigerated up to 2 days or frozen. They may be baked several hours ahead and reheated before serving.

NUTRITIONAL ANALYSIS

Per serving
352 calories
4 g fat
8 mg cholesterol
572 mg sodium

You may be surprised to learn that nonfat yogurt can replace butter and cream in caramel sauce. Making the sauce and cooking the apples right in it in the microwave, instead of on top of the stove, eliminates steps and dirty dishes and reduces the chances of burning the sugar. Store-bought puff pastry, cut and baked in apple shapes, makes a flaky sandwich for the caramel-soaked apples. (See color photo, page 8.)

PREP TIME: 30 minutes

BAKE TIME: Pastry, 16 to 20 minutes; filling, 9 to 14 minutes in the microwave

ADVANCE PREP: Pastry may be baked up to 4 hours ahead. Filling may be cooked up to 4 hours ahead.

NUTRITIONAL ANALYSIS

Per serving
968 calories
37 g fat
108 mg cholesterol
650 mg sodium

PUFF PASTRY APPLE TARTLETS WITH CONTEMPO CARAMEL SAUCE

Pastry
1 sheet frozen puff pastry, thawed until pliable but still very cold (half a 17¼-ounce package)
1 egg, mixed with 1 teaspoon water for wash

Caramel Apple Filling
½ cup (packed) light brown sugar
¼ cup granulated sugar

¼ cup plain nonfat yogurt
Salt
2 large or 3 small tart green apples, peeled, halved, cored, and sliced ½ inch thick
1 tablespoon cornstarch
¼ teaspoon ground cinnamon

Garden leaves for garnish (see page 10) (optional)
Vanilla or cinnamon ice cream or frozen yogurt for serving (optional)

To Prepare Pastry: Preheat oven to 375°F. If puff pastry is folded in thirds, to eliminate the creases, fold it in half and on a lightly floured board, roll to ¼-inch thickness. Cut out 2 apple shapes about 6 inches wide and 5 inches long. Cut out 4 leaves and 2 stems, about 4 to 5 inches long. (They may look large, but will shrink.) Place pastry on lightly greased baking sheet. Brush tops with egg wash; do not let it drip down the sides or the pastry won't puff up. If time permits, refrigerate at least 15 minutes to reduce shrinkage. Bake for 16 to 20 minutes, or until golden brown. Remove to racks and cool completely. (Pastry may be kept at room temperature, covered with foil, up to 4 hours. Recrisp at 375°F. in toaster oven or conventional oven for 3 to 4 minutes.)

To Make Filling: In an 8-cup (2-quart) microwavesafe measuring cup or bowl, stir together brown and white sugars, yogurt, and a dash of salt until thoroughly moistened. Microwave, uncovered, on high (100%) for 5 to 8 minutes, without stirring, until golden caramel color. The mixture should be as thick as honey but not so stiff you can't stir it.

Meanwhile, in a large plastic bag toss apple slices with cornstarch and cinnamon until coated. As soon as caramel is ready, stir in apples. Microwave on high (100%), uncovered, for 2 minutes, stir, and microwave for 2 to 4 minutes more, or until tender to the bite. With a slotted spoon, remove apples to a small bowl. (Apples and caramel may be held at room temperature up to 4 hours. Before serving, reheat each separately in microwave until warm.)

To Assemble: With a serrated knife, slice puff pastry apples in half horizontally and remove any uncooked pastry. Before serving, divide warm caramel sauce between 2 dessert plates, swirling to coat bottom. Place bottom half of pastry on each plate. Spoon apples over and cover with pastry tops. Garnish with pastry stem and leaves and fresh leaves, if using. Serve immediately with ice cream or yogurt, if desired.

MAKES: 2 servings.

CHIC CANDLELIGHT CHICKEN

*N*o matter what the age, taste preferences, or diet restrictions of your guests, chicken is a sure bet. My challenge was to present this ubiquitous bird in an exciting new way. It took marinating, stuffing pockets in the breasts, dipping them in crumbs, and cloaking them with sauce to make a dish majestic enough for a grand dinner. Even so, the breasts take less than an hour to prepare, require no stovetop cooking, and go straight from refrigerator to oven. They even freeze well.

To begin the evening, offer two completely different vegetable-based dips. The bean puree is smooth, white, and creamy; the salsa is coarse, colorful, and spicy. Both go well with Tuscany Toasts, so you can do without vegetable dippers, if you choose.

My choice as an opener for the meal itself is a dressy salad merger of hot shrimp and cold greens with cool crunchy vegetables. If the last-minute searing of the shrimp poses a problem, Spinach-Grapefruit Salad with Blue Cheese and Pine Nuts (see page 250) can be made ahead.

You'll want to keep the starch simple here. Pasta lightly coated with a nutty roasted garlic sauce fits the fare perfectly. Two alternate choices for oven-baked side dishes with the same baking time as the chicken are Roasted Red-Skin Potatoes with Rosemary (see page 119) or Potato–Mushroom–Blue Cheese Galette (see page 222). As a vegetable, snow peas, sugar snaps, *haricots verts,* and green beans are interchangeable, according to your preference or the season.

The Black and White Chocolate–Banana Tart will be the pièce de résistance, from its glamorous profile to its layered indulgences. ''Seconds'' will be the cry heard here. This menu serves eight.

GAME PLAN

1 Month Ahead	**Make and freeze Tuscany Toasts**
	Make and freeze Puree of White Beans
	Make and freeze crust for Black and White Chocolate–Banana Tart
	Make and refrigerate or freeze Marbled Chocolate Shavings
2 Weeks Ahead	**Marinate, stuff, and freeze chicken breasts**
	Make and freeze sauce for chicken
1 Day Ahead	**Prepare greens and vinaigrette for salad**
	Make and refrigerate Italian Salsa
	Defrost chicken breasts and sauce
	Defrost Tuscany Toasts
	Defrost Puree of White Beans
	Defrost crust for tart
	Make sauce for pasta
	Cook Sugar Snap Peas

DAY OF PARTY

6 Hours Ahead	**Complete dessert**
1 Hour Ahead	**Marinate shrimp**
15 Minutes Before Serving	**Bake chicken breasts and reheat sauce**
Shortly Before Serving	**Toss salad**
	Stir-fry shrimp for salad
	Cook pasta and reheat sauce
	Reheat Sugar Snap Peas

EXTRA ◆ POINTS

◆

THE TABLE

Place a runner down the table or drape swatches of fabric or scarves in a free-form style down the center. Instead of the typical symmetrical floral arrangement, tie a long bouquet of flowers with multiple color ribbons. Lay the flowers down on the fabric with the ribbons streaming down the runner. Tie tiny bouquets of flowers with matching ribbons and place one on each guest's napkin. For name cards, insert a name into each bouquet.

THE MOOD

Don't forget the music: romantic, classical, jazz, or whatever fits your guests' taste.

For a spectacular salad, perch hot, moist, juicy shrimp atop crisp greens and mushrooms and dress it all with a lively mint vinaigrette. Since mint varies so much in intensity, you may want to supplement it with some dried if yours is an insipid bunch.

PREP TIME: 30 minutes

MARINADE TIME: 1 hour

ADVANCE PREP: Greens and vinaigrette may be refrigerated overnight. Cook shrimp just before serving.

SEARED SHRIMP SALAD WITH RASPBERRY-MINT VINAIGRETTE

Salad
1 large head curly endive or friseé (about 1½ pounds)
1 large head green leaf lettuce (about 1 pound)
3 medium heads Belgian endive (about ¾ pound)

Raspberry-Mint Vinaigrette
¼ cup raspberry vinegar
2 tablespoons red wine vinegar
1 tablespoon sugar
2 tablespoons fresh lemon juice
½ cup chopped fresh mint or 2 tablespoons dried mint
⅓ cup olive oil
¼ teaspoon salt, or to taste
Freshly ground black pepper

1½ pounds extra-large shrimp, peeled and deveined (22 to 25 per pound)
¾ pound mushrooms, cleaned, trimmed, and sliced
1 to 2 tablespoons vegetable oil

To Prepare Salad: Clean lettuces and tear into bite-size pieces. Cut core off Belgian endive, cut large leaves in half, and slice remainder into ½-inch slices. Wrap in paper towels, place in plastic bag, and refrigerate. (Greens may be refrigerated overnight.)

To Make Vinaigrette: Whisk vinegars, sugar, lemon juice, mint, oil, salt, and pepper to taste in a small bowl until blended. If fresh mint is not fragrant, add some dried. (Vinaigrette may be refrigerated overnight.)

To Marinate Shrimp: About 1 hour before serving, rinse shrimp, blot dry, place in a plastic zipper bag or bowl, and pour ¼ cup vinaigrette over. Toss to coat. Refrigerate for 1 hour.

To Cook Shrimp and Assemble Salad: Just before serving, drain shrimp and blot lightly. Place greens in bowl, add sliced mushrooms and remaining vinaigrette, and toss to coat. Divide among salad plates. Heat 1 tablespoon oil in a wok or large skillet until very hot and smoking. Over high heat, stir-fry shrimp in batches without crowding, stirring, until cooked through, about 2 minutes per side, adding more oil if needed. Divide shrimp among salads and serve immediately.

MAKES: 8 to 10 servings.

Leaner: Arrange marinated shrimp on skewers and grill or broil them. Remove from skewers and place atop salad.

PASTA WITH ROASTED GARLIC SAUCE

2 large heads garlic, cloves as
  large as possible
No-stick cooking spray
1½ cups chicken or vegetable
  broth
½ cup regular or light sour
  cream

¼ cup heavy cream
1 package (16 ounces) fusilli
Salt
Freshly ground rainbow
  peppercorns or seasoned
  pepper blend

To Roast Garlic: Preheat oven to 450°F.

Peel outer skin from garlic bulb. Keeping the bulb intact, cut a small slice off the top. Separate unpeeled cloves and place them in a pie dish. Spray with cooking spray. Bake, uncovered, for 15 to 20 minutes or until soft when squeezed. When cool enough to handle, remove peel and chop coarsely. In a 4-cup microwavesafe measure, combine garlic, broth, sour cream, heavy cream, and salt and pepper to taste. (Sauce may be refrigerated overnight.)

Shortly Before Serving: Bring a large pot of salted water to a boil. Cook pasta according to package directions, until tender to the bite. Microwave sauce, covered with plastic wrap, on high (100%) for 2 to 4 minutes, or until hot. Drain pasta, return to saucepan and toss well with sauce. If too dry, add more broth or cream. Season with salt and pepper to taste. Serve immediately. Pasta will absorb sauce as it sits.

MAKES: 8 servings.

Leaner: Substitute ¾ cup low-fat (2%) milk for ¼ cup heavy cream and ½ cup of the chicken broth.

When cooking teacher Bonnie Rapoport Marshall was testing recipes for me, she developed this dish as a companion for the chicken breasts. Roasted garlic, so different from raw or sautéed, lends an unobtrusive but compelling flavor.

PREP TIME: 10 minutes

COOK TIME: Garlic, 15 to 20 minutes; pasta, about 10 minutes

ADVANCE PREP: Sauce may be refrigerated overnight.

NUTRITIONAL ANALYSIS

Per serving (with light sour cream)
264 calories
6 g fat
65 mg cholesterol
301 mg sodium

Im this no-fail, surefire, prepare-ahead recipe the chicken breasts are filled with a smoky-fruity stuffing, wrapped in a delicate nut crust, and napped with an orange-tinged sauce. This impressive entree works best with six-ounce boned breasts, which are not always available prepackaged, so you may want to order them ahead. It can be multiplied for any size crowd.

PREP TIME: 45 minutes

MARINADE TIME: 4 to 12 hours

BAKE TIME: 12 to 15 minutes

ADVANCE PREP: Stuffed chicken breasts may be refrigerated overnight or frozen. Sauce may be refrigerated overnight or frozen.

NUTRITIONAL ANALYSIS

Per serving
497 calories
17 g fat
81 mg cholesterol
847 mg sodium

DRIED APRICOT, HAM, AND LEEK– STUFFED CHICKEN BREASTS

8 large boneless, skinless chicken breast halves (about 6 ounces each)

Marinade
1½ cups orange juice
1 cup chicken broth
½ cup imported dry vermouth or dry white wine
¼ cup soy sauce
2 tablespoons Dijon mustard
1 tablespoon honey

Stuffing
⅓ cup dried apricots (about 10)
2 tablespoons golden raisins
3 medium leeks, cleaned and thickly sliced (see page 11)
4 ounces lean smoked ham or Canadian bacon, cut into 1-inch pieces (about 1 cup)
2 tablespoons olive oil
⅓ cup egg or Italian bread crumbs, toasted (see page 10)

Crust
¾ cup chopped shelled pistachios, hazelnuts, or almonds, toasted (3 ounces) (see page 11)
1¼ cups egg or Italian bread crumbs, toasted (see page 10)
Salt and pepper to taste

Sauce
¼ cup heavy cream
4 teaspoons cornstarch
No-stick cooking spray

Garnish (optional)
Apricot Roses (recipe follows)
Garden leaves (see page 10), or parsley or watercress

To Prepare Chicken: Cut off all fat from chicken. Cut a pocket horizontally into each breast by holding the knife parallel to the counter and cutting back as far as possible without cutting in half. Leave a small edge uncut on 3 sides. Place in shallow glass casserole or large plastic zipper bag.

To Marinate: Whisk all marinade ingredients in a medium bowl. Pour 1¼ cups over chicken, turning to coat all surfaces. Refrigerate for 4 to 12 hours, turning occasionally. Refrigerate remaining marinade.

To Make Stuffing: In a food processor with the metal blade, pulse apricots until coarsely chopped. Add raisins, leeks, and ham and pulse until diced into ¼-inch pieces. In a large skillet, preferably nonstick, heat olive oil over moderate heat. Add apricot mixture and bread crumbs and sauté until leeks are soft and mixture is lightly browned, 5 to 7 minutes. Stir in 2 tablespoons reserved marinade. Cool. (Stuffing may be refrigerated overnight.)

Remove chicken from marinade; do not dry. Discard marinade. Fill each pocket with about 2 tablespoons stuffing. Press edges to close.

To Make Crust: In a pie plate or other shallow dish, stir together nuts and bread crumbs. Sprinkle chicken with salt and pepper. Dip both sides into crumbs, pressing to adhere. Place at least 1 inch apart on greased or foil-lined and greased baking sheet. Refrigerate until ready to bake. (Chicken may be refrigerated overnight or frozen up to 2 weeks. Freeze on baking sheet until firm and then transfer to a plastic freezer bag or wrap in heavy-duty foil. Return to baking sheet and defrost overnight in the refrigerator. Refrigerate or freeze reserved crumbs.)

To Make Sauce: Pour reserved marinade into a small saucepan. Simmer for 2 to 3 minutes. Remove from heat. In a small bowl, stir cream and cornstarch together. Whisk into sauce. Return to heat and bring to a boil, whisking constantly. (Sauce may be refrigerated overnight or frozen. Reheat before serving. If too thick, thin with orange juice, broth, or wine.)

To Bake: Place oven rack in upper third of oven and preheat to 450°F. Sprinkle tops of breasts with remaining crumbs and spray with no-stick cooking spray. Bake chilled breasts for 12 to 15 minutes, or until cooked through. Remove to plates, drizzle with sauce, and pass remaining sauce. If desired, garnish with apricot roses and leaves or greens.

MAKES: 8 servings.

Leaner: In stuffing, substitute smoked chicken or turkey for the ham. In crust, substitute ¾ cup toasted bread crumbs for the nuts.

APRICOT ROSES

For each rose, flatten 5 to 6 dried apricot halves with fingers. For large roses, use more apricots. Roll one up tightly for the center. Wrap remainder around for petals, fanning them out as you go, and squeezing the base to hold them together.

A cross between common garden peas and snow peas, the delightfully sweet, plump, crisp sugar snap is entirely edible—pod and all. Because all peas come out greener, crisper and more flavorful when cooked on top of the stove, I am not including a microwave alternative.

PREP TIME: 15 minutes

COOK TIME: 3 to 4 minutes

ADVANCE PREP: May be cooked 1 day ahead.

NUTRITIONAL ANALYSIS

Per serving
53 calories
1 g fat
0 cholesterol
71 mg sodium

SUGAR SNAP PEAS

2 pounds sugar snap peas   **Salt**
1 teaspoon oriental sesame oil
  or olive oil (optional)

Rinse peas, cut off stem end and string, if necessary. Pour about ¾ inch water into a large skillet and bring to a boil over moderate heat. Add peas, cover, and boil gently for 3 to 4 minutes, or until tender, tossing with a spatula once or twice. If water evaporates before peas are tender, reduce heat and add more water. Drain any remaining water. Add oil, if using, and salt to taste and toss to coat. (Peas may be refrigerated overnight. Reheat, covered, in a microwave for 2 to 4 minutes or until hot, stirring once.)

MAKES: 8 servings.

Faster: Substitute 2 pounds frozen sugar snap peas for the fresh. Defrost on several layers of paper towels until at room temperature. Cook for 1 minute, tossing once or twice, until heated through.

Change of Pace: To cook snow peas, cut off stem end and string, if necessary. Cook covered in ¾ inch of water for 3 to 5 minutes, tossing every minute.

To cook green beans, cut stem ends off beans. Cook, covered, in 1 inch of water for 5 to 7 minutes, tossing once or twice.

To cook haricots verts (thin baby beans), for 8 servings, cut stem ends off 1½ pounds of beans. Cook, covered, in ¾ inch water for 5 to 7 minutes, stirring once or twice.

BLACK AND WHITE CHOCOLATE–BANANA TART

Cookie Pastry
¼ pound (1 stick) butter or margarine, cold and cut into 8 pieces
2 tablespoons sugar
1 large egg
1½ cups all-purpose flour
¼ teaspoon salt

Dark Chocolate Truffle
4 ounces semisweet chocolate, cut into small pieces
1 tablespoon heavy cream
1 tablespoon white crème de cacao

White Chocolate Mousse
2 bars (3½ ounces each) white chocolate, cut into small pieces, or 6 ounces white chocolate chips
2 tablespoons plus ¾ cup heavy cream, divided
3 tablespoons white crème de cacao
½ cup light sour cream

3 ripe but firm bananas
Marbled Chocolate Shavings, for garnish (see page 101) (optional)

To Make Pastry: Place butter and sugar in food processor with metal blade or bowl with electric mixer and pulse or mix until mixture holds together. Add egg and pulse 5 or 6 times or mix to blend. Add flour and salt all at once and pulse several more times or mix until moistened. Scrape down sides and pulse or mix until a cookielike dough is formed. If using food processor, remove metal blade, place a large plastic bag over top of workbowl, invert bowl, and turn dough into bag. Shape pastry in bag into a ball and flatten into a disk. If using mixer, remove dough and shape into a disk. If dough is too sticky to work with, refrigerate until it firms up. With your hands, press into the bottom and up the sides of an 11-inch tart pan with a removable bottom. Trim edges even with top of pan. Prick bottom and sides of dough with a fork. Refrigerate for at least 30 minutes to keep pastry from shrinking when baked.

Place oven rack in bottom third of oven and preheat to 375°F.

Place tart on baking sheet and bake for 15 to 18 minutes, or until shell is lightly golden and pulls away from the sides. After 5 minutes, it may be necessary to reprick with a fork any areas that have puffed up. Remove to a rack and cool completely. (Baked crust may be covered with foil and held at room temperature overnight or frozen up to 1 month.)

(continued)

The affinity of chocolate for bananas led to the creation of this monument of decadence. Designed to show textural variety, from the crisp cookie crust, soft sliced bananas, fudgy truffle filling, and creamy white mousse to the brittle chocolate curls, this one is a winner.

PREP TIME: 35 minutes

CHILL TIME: Crust, 30 minutes

BAKE TIME: Crust, 15 to 18 minutes

ADVANCE PREP: Crust may be baked and stored at room temperature overnight or frozen. Chocolate shavings may be frozen. Assembled tart may be refrigerated up to 6 hours.

NUTRITIONAL ANALYSIS

Per serving (with light sour cream)
481 calories
30 g fat
86 mg cholesterol
185 mg sodium

To Make Truffle Filling: Up to 6 hours before serving, place chocolate, cream, and crème de cacao in a small microwavesafe bowl. Microwave, uncovered, at 60% power for 60 to 90 seconds, or until chocolate is melted. Stir until smooth. Or melt on stove in top of double boiler. Spread into bottom of baked pastry shell.

To Make Mousse: Place white chocolate, 2 tablespoons heavy cream, and crème de cacao in medium microwavesafe bowl. Microwave on 60% power for 70 to 90 seconds, or until chocolate is melted. Stir until smooth. Or melt on stove in top of double boiler. Cool to room temperature. In small mixing bowl with electric mixer, beat ¾ cup heavy cream until soft peaks form. Add sour cream and continue beating on high speed until stiff peaks form. Fold in cooled chocolate-cream mixture.

To Assemble: Slice bananas on a diagonal and arrange over dark chocolate in pastry shell, covering it completely. Spoon mousse over bananas, spreading top smoothly. Sprinkle with chocolate shavings, if using. Cover with plastic wrap and refrigerate until serving or up to 6 hours.

MAKES: 8 to 10 servings.

Faster: Substitute 1 refrigerated already prepared pie crust for a 9-inch pie. Roll into a 12-inch circle and fit into 11-inch tart pan. Prick with a fork. Refrigerate at least 30 minutes before baking and bake according to package directions. It will shrink slightly.

Change of Pace: To make Black and White Chocolate–Raspberry Tart, substitute ½ pint (8 ounces) fresh raspberries for the bananas.

MARBLED CHOCOLATE SHAVINGS

2 ounces semisweet chocolate, chopped, or chocolate chips

2 ounces white chocolate, chopped, or white chocolate chips

Place each type of chocolate in a small microwavesafe bowl and microwave at 60% power until melted, about 40 to 80 seconds. Stir until smooth. Spoon chocolates into a 5-ounce paper cup, alternating colors. Marble gently with a knife. Refrigerate until firm.

Tear off paper cup. You now have a marbled block of chocolate. Leave it in a warm spot or microwave at 20% power for 1 to 3 minutes, or until soft enough to peel with vegetable peeler. Working over a sheet of heavy foil, peel to get a mixture of shavings and curls. If the block is too cold, they will break off in shattered pieces; if too warm, they will stick to the peeler. Refrigerate or freeze the shavings on the foil until firm. When chilled, transfer to a covered container and store in the refrigerator or freezer. The shavings and curls are very fragile, so you may wish to use a toothpick to move the curls onto the tart.

PARTY WRAPPED FISH in PHYLLO

Entrees baked in phyllo are the ultimate in elegance. And now that we've discovered that phyllo pastry works every bit as well with no-stick cooking spray instead of being smeared with butter or oil, such entrees make a splendid low-fat choice for dinner parties. And they are practical—assembled ahead, refrigerated on a baking sheet, and popped right into the oven. Talk about being a relaxed host! The only concern in baking fish in phyllo is the same as with all fish recipes: Don't overcook. Remember, food goes on cooking after you take it out of the oven. It's also important not to crowd the packets on the baking sheet. If too close together, they will steam and not get brown and crisp. Phyllo roses add a touch of whimsy and refinement.

With an entree wrapped in pastry, you want to keep the rest of the dinner fairly light, so I suggest a vegetable hors d'oeuvre like Artichokes with Romesco Sauce. You could also offer the sauce as a dip with a variety of vegetables. Other good choices are Eggplant Rolls with Garlic-Herb Cheese (see page 148) or Confetti-capped Mushrooms (see page 150). The Tomato Relish in Plum Tomato Shells is more than a side dish—it emphasizes the sun-dried tomatoes in the fish filling and embellishes it.

Gorgonzola Puffovers will become your rolls of choice whenever you want to impress. It's hard to eat just one—they are full of flavor, breezy as a popover, airy as a cream puff.

Lemon is so well suited to fish that I like to take it the extra step and feature it in the dessert. Present Lemon-Pineapple Trifle in all its glory at the table and spoon it into stemmed goblets or onto small plates. Being self-contained and easy to serve, it's a sensible choice for a buffet as well. Light and Lush Lemon Cake (see page 233) offers another alternative. This menu serves six, but each of the recipes can be doubled.

GAME PLAN

1 Month Ahead	**Make and freeze soup**
	Make and freeze tomato relish
	Make and freeze ladyfingers
3 Days Ahead	**Prepare filling for fish in phyllo**
1 Day Ahead	**Defrost soup**
	Scoop out tomatoes and defrost tomato relish
	Prepare fish in phyllo
	Prepare orzo
	Defrost ladyfingers and complete trifle
	Prepare artichokes and Romesco sauce

DAY OF PARTY

8 Hours Ahead	**Prepare garnish for soup**
2 Hours Ahead	**Prepare Gorgonzola Puffovers**
	Microwave broccoli and stir into orzo
	Garnish trifle
30 Minutes Before Serving	**Bake puffovers**
	Bake fish
	Fill tomato shells with relish
Shortly Before Serving	**Heat soup and microwave garnish**
	Reheat orzo

EXTRA POINTS

THE TABLE

Instead of one centerpiece, arrange flowers in various size vases and place them and votive candles around the table. Tie bows around the vases with lace, ribbons, tapestry, tassels, cord, or fringe. Tie matching bows around the napkins.

GOLDEN VEGETABLE SOUP WITH CORN AND RED PEPPER GARNISH

I n this creamy soup without the cream, the silkiness comes from pureeing potatoes, corn, and squash. A cluster of barely cooked vegetables adds a crunchy mosaic of color.

PREP TIME: 20 minutes

COOK TIME: 30 minutes

ADVANCE PREP: Soup may be refrigerated up to 2 days or frozen. Garnish may be refrigerated up to 8 hours.

2 tablespoons olive oil
3 garlic cloves, minced
3 medium leeks, white part only, cleaned and chopped (see page 11) (about 3 cups)
4½ cups chicken broth
1 medium (6 ounce) potato, chopped (1 cup)
1 medium (8 ounce) yellow crookneck squash, chopped (1¾ cups)
1½ teaspoons dried tarragon
1 package (16 ounces) frozen corn kernels

1 teaspoon ground cumin
½ teaspoon salt, or to taste

Vegetable Garnish
1 cup reserved corn from soup, defrosted
1 large red bell pepper, chopped by hand into ¼-inch dice
8 large green onions, chopped (about 1 cup)
1 large yellow crookneck squash, cut into matchstick strips by hand or with julienne blade of a food processor

To Make Soup: In a 4-quart soup pot over medium heat, heat olive oil. Add garlic and leeks and sauté, stirring, for 1 minute. Cover pot with wax paper and lid, reduce heat to low and cook, covered, for 10 minutes, or until very soft, stirring occasionally. Add broth, potato, squash, and tarragon. Reserve 1 cup of the corn for garnish, and add the rest. Bring to a boil, reduce heat, and simmer, uncovered, until potatoes are soft, about 20 minutes. Cool slightly and puree in batches in the blender. Stir in cumin and salt. (Soup may be refrigerated up to 2 days or frozen up to 1 month.)

To Prepare Garnish: Place all ingredients in a microwavesafe pie dish or shallow casserole. Cover with vented plastic wrap. (May be refrigerated up to 8 hours.)

Before Serving: Heat soup in saucepan until hot. Adjust seasonings, if needed. Microwave garnish for 3 to 5 minutes, stirring once, or until vegetables are hot and cooked through but still crunchy. Divide soup among bowls and add a spoonful of vegetables in the center.

MAKES: 6 to 8 servings.

NUTRITIONAL ANALYSIS

Per serving (including garnish)
162 calories
5 g fat
1 mg cholesterol
592 mg sodium

GORGONZOLA PUFFOVERS

6 tablespoons regular, low-fat, or nonfat milk
6 ounces gorgonzola or other blue cheese, crumbled (1½ cups)

¼ pound (1 stick) butter or margarine, cut into small pieces
1¼ cups all-purpose flour
5 large eggs
Butter, for serving (optional)

To Make Batter: Grease twelve 3-inch muffin cups. In a medium saucepan over medium-high heat, bring milk, cheese, butter or margarine, and 6 tablespoons water to a rolling boil, whisking until cheese melts. Remove from heat and stir in the flour all at once. Return to heat and cook, stirring constantly until mixture pulls always from the sides of the pan, about 3 minutes. Remove from heat and with electric hand beater or in mixing bowl with electric beater, mix in eggs, one at a time, incorporating each egg thoroughly before adding the next one. Fill each muffin cup almost to the top. (Batter may be covered with foil and held at room temperature up to 2 hours.)

To Bake: As close to serving as possible, preheat oven to 425°F. Bake in center of oven for 15 minutes, reduce oven temperature to 350°F. and continue baking for 10 to 15 minutes more, or until firm and golden brown. Go around edges with a sharp knife and remove from cups. Serve with butter, if desired.

MAKES: 12 puffovers.

When you bake a cheese-laden cream-puff batter in a muffin cup like a popover, you get a crisp and airy hybrid. These gems are adapted from the ones served at Sophie's Restaurant in New York.

PREP TIME: 20 minutes

BAKE TIME: 25 to 30 minutes

ADVANCE PREP: Batter may be held in muffin cups up to 2 hours before baking.

NUTRITIONAL ANALYSIS

Per puffover (with nonfat milk)
199 calories
14 g fat
120 mg cholesterol
306 mg sodium

FILLETS OF SALMON AND SOLE IN PHYLLO

Sun-dried Tomato Filling
12 sun-dried tomatoes (see page 12)
2 tablespoons regular or light sour cream
4 tablespoons regular, light, or fat-free mayonnaise
1 tablespoon plus 1 teaspoon fresh lemon juice
1 tablespoon plus 1 teaspoon madeira wine
1 teaspoon dry mustard
1 teaspoon Dijon mustard
1 teaspoon dried tarragon

18 ounces sole or flounder fillets, about ½ to ¾ inch thick

Salt
12 ounces salmon fillets, skinned, about ⅜ inch at thickest part
12 tablespoons dry bread crumbs (see page 10)
6 sheets phyllo dough, at room temperature (see page 12) (half a 1-pound package)
No-stick cooking spray

Garnish (optional)
6 sheets phyllo dough, at room temperature, for phyllo roses (recipe follows)
Fresh tarragon or parsley stems and leaves

To Prepare Filling: Rehydrate tomatoes by placing in a 1-cup glass measure. Cover with water and microwave, uncovered, on high (100%) for 2 to 3 minutes, or until very soft. Cool slightly, remove to cutting board, and chop into small pieces. Meanwhile, in a small bowl, stir together sour cream, mayonnaise, lemon juice, madeira, mustards, and tarragon. Stir in tomatoes. (Filling may be refrigerated up to 3 days.)

To Prepare Fish: Rinse fish and pat dry. Place half the sole fillets on a work surface to make 6 equal portions, cutting and patching them if necessary. Sprinkle with salt and spread each with 2 heaping teaspoons filling. Measure thickness of salmon fillets. If thicker than ⅜ inch, cover with wax paper and pound very lightly. Do not be concerned if some parts are slightly thinner. Arrange salmon fillets over the sole, cutting to fit. Sprinkle with salt and spread with remaining filling. Top with remaining sole.

To Wrap in Phyllo: Place 2 sheets of phyllo on work surface. Keep remainder covered so it doesn't dry out. Spray 1 sheet with cooking spray. Sprinkle with 2 tablespoons bread crumbs. Top with second sheet and spray. Cut in half crosswise. Sprinkle 1 tablespoon bread crumbs over each half, leaving a 1-inch border. Place a fish "sandwich" in the

Your guests will love this surprise package of delicate white and pink fish fillets sandwiching a mellow madeira and creamy sun-dried tomato filling. Just be sure to purchase the fish the same day you prepare it, particularly if you plan to serve the dish the following day. The recipe can be multiplied to serve any number—allow three ounces sole and two ounces salmon per serving. For a spectacular presentation, make ruffled phyllo roses to place on top of each packet.

PREP TIME: Fish, 45 minutes; optional phyllo roses, 15 minutes

BAKE TIME: 15 to 28 minutes

ADVANCE PREP: Fish in phyllo may be refrigerated overnight. Phyllo roses may be stored at room temperature for up to 4 days or frozen.

NUTRITIONAL ANALYSIS

Per serving (with light sour cream, nonfat mayonnaise)
295 calories
4 g fat
52 mg cholesterol
297 mg sodium

center, fold a short end over, fold in sides, and fold up remaining end like a wrapped package. Spray top and sides. Place, seam side down, on greased baking sheet at least 2 inches apart. Do not crowd. Repeat with remaining fish and phyllo. (Fish may be refrigerated overnight covered with plastic wrap.)

To Bake Fish: Preheat oven to 400°F.

Bake chilled fish for 22 to 28 minutes, or until edges of phyllo are golden and a knife inserted in the center of the fish feels hot against your lips. The center of the phyllo may be pale, but the roses will cover it. If fish has not been refrigerated after preparing, bake for 15 to 20 minutes. If using 2 baking sheets, rotate their positions after 12 minutes. Transfer packets with a spatula to plates and top each with a rose, if using, and tarragon or parsley stems and leaves.

MAKES: 6 servings.

PHYLLO ROSES

Preheat oven to 400°F.

Spray 1 sheet of phyllo with cooking spray. Cut crosswise into 3-inch-wide strips. Holding the bottom edge of 1 strip, crinkle and roll from 1 end to form center of rose. Loosely crinkle second strip around the outside to make ruffled petals, squeezing the base to hold them in place. Use as many strips as desired. Place on greased baking sheet. If the rose does not stand upright, cut a portion off the bottom with scissors. Repeat to make as many roses as needed, allowing one per serving. Bake for 3 to 5 minutes, or until golden. (Roses may be stored in an airtight container at room temperature up to 4 days or frozen. Reheat at 400°F. for 2 minutes while baking fish.)

The rice-shaped pasta called orzo (sometimes called *Seme di melone* or melon seeds) takes very well to being coated with a vivid uncooked broccoli pesto, then studded with bright green steamed florets.

PREP TIME: 20 minutes

COOK TIME: About 10 minutes

ADVANCE PREP: Orzo with pesto may be refrigerated overnight. Add cooked broccoli florets up to 4 hours before serving.

NUTRITIONAL ANALYSIS

Per serving
166 calories
4 g fat
32 mg cholesterol
176 mg sodium

ORZO WITH BROCCOLI PESTO

1¼ cups uncooked orzo pasta (10 ounces)
1 tablespoon plus 2 tablespoons olive oil, divided

Broccoli Pesto
½ cup (packed) fresh basil leaves
1 cup broccoli florets
2 garlic cloves, peeled
4 teaspoons dry sherry or madeira

1½ cups small broccoli florets
2 to 4 tablespoons grated parmesan cheese
2 to 4 tablespoons pine nuts, toasted (see page 12)
Salt and freshly ground black pepper

To Cook Orzo: Bring a medium saucepan of salted water to a boil. Cook orzo until tender to the bite, about 10 minutes. Drain, transfer to a medium bowl (microwavesafe if you wish to reheat it), and toss with 1 tablespoon olive oil.

To Make Pesto: While orzo cooks, in a food processor with the metal blade, process basil, broccoli, and garlic until minced. Pulse in sherry or madeira until mixture is pureed. Add pesto to cooked orzo and toss to coat. (Orzo may be refrigerated overnight.)

To Cook Broccoli: Up to 4 hours before serving, place 1½ cups broccoli florets in a microwavesafe pie dish and add ¼ inch of water. Cover with vented plastic wrap and microwave on high (100%) for 2 to 4 minutes, or until tender but still bright green. Drain and stir into orzo. If not serving immediately, cover and leave at room temperature.

To reheat, microwave orzo with broccoli on high (100%) for 2 to 4 minutes, or until heated through, stirring once. Add olive oil and as much parmesan cheese, pine nuts, and salt and pepper as desired and toss well.

MAKES: 6 to 8 servings.

TOMATO RELISH IN PLUM TOMATO SHELLS

Tomato Relish
12 medium plum tomatoes (about 8 ounces), seeded (see page 12)
2 tablespoons olive oil
4 teaspoons minced shallots or onion
2 small garlic cloves, minced
2 teaspoons raspberry vinegar

4 teaspoons finely chopped fresh basil leaves or 1 teaspoon dried basil
1 teaspoon sugar
Salt and freshly ground black pepper

6 medium plum tomatoes
Basil sprigs, for garnish (optional)

To Make Relish: Chop tomatoes in a food processor or by hand into about ⅜-inch pieces. In a medium skillet over moderate heat, heat olive oil until hot. Cook shallots and garlic until softened, 3 to 5 minutes. Add tomatoes and cook, stirring, until they come to a boil and begin to wilt, about 3 to 5 minutes. Remove from heat and stir in vinegar, basil, sugar, and salt and pepper to taste. Cool and refrigerate. (Relish may be refrigerated up to 2 days or frozen up to 1 month.)

To Prepare Tomato Shells: Cut 6 tomatoes in half through stem end and scoop out pulp, leaving ¼-inch shells. Refrigerate, covered.

Before Serving: Bring tomato shells and relish to room temperature. Drain off excess juices from relish and mound into tomato halves. Garnish each with a sprig of fresh basil, if desired.

MAKES: 6 servings; 2 halves each.

Flash-cooked tomatoes brightened with a splash of raspberry vinegar are a fine accompaniment for baked fish in phyllo or for grilled steaks, chops, fish, or chicken.

PREP TIME: 15 minutes

COOK TIME: 7 to 10 minutes

ADVANCE PREP: Relish may be refrigerated up to 2 days or frozen. Tomatoes may be scooped out a day ahead. Fill before serving.

NUTRITIONAL ANALYSIS

Per serving
63 calories
5 g fat
0 cholesterol
185 mg sodium

There is nothing trivial about this trifle. Time and time again I'm amazed by the raves this layered pudding of lemon ladyfingers and lemon-pineapple custard evokes. It's an ethereal pairing of sweet and tart.

PREP TIME: Ladyfingers, 25 minutes; custard, 20 minutes plus assembly time

BAKE TIME: Ladyfingers, 12 to 14 minutes

ADVANCE PREP: Ladyfingers may be frozen. Trifle may be refrigerated overnight.

NUTRITIONAL ANALYSIS

Per serving
340 calories
11 g fat
160 mg cholesterol
52 mg sodium

LEMON-PINEAPPLE TRIFLE

Lemon Ladyfingers
3 large eggs, separated
6 tablespoons plus 3 tablespoons sugar, divided
1 tablespoon finely grated lemon peel (see page 11)
3 tablespoons fresh lemon juice (see page 11)
⅔ cup all-purpose flour

Lemon Custard
2 large eggs
1¼ cups sugar
4 teaspoons cornstarch

⅔ cup fresh lemon juice (see page 11)
1 tablespoon grated lemon peel (see page 11)
½ cup heavy cream
½ cup light sour cream
1 can (8 ounces) crushed pineapple, drained

Garnish (optional)
½ cup heavy cream, whipped
1 small lemon, sliced
Mint leaves

To Make Ladyfingers: Place racks in middle and upper third of oven (or middle of 2 ovens) and preheat to 350°F. Line 2 baking sheets with parchment or wax paper and grease the paper. In a large mixing bowl with electric mixer, beat egg yolks with 6 tablespoons sugar until thick and light in color, about 2 minutes. Mix in lemon peel and juice. In a small mixing bowl with clean beaters, beat egg whites until soft peaks form. Beating continuously, add remaining 3 tablespoons sugar, 1 tablespoon at a time, until stiff peaks form. Sift half the flour over top of egg yolk mixture. Spoon half the whites over and gently fold together. Gently fold in remaining flour and whites until incorporated. Do not overmix.

Spoon the mixture into a large pastry bag fitted with a ½-inch plain round tip. Squeeze fingers of batter onto prepared baking sheets, about 1 inch wide and 3 inches long, about 1 inch apart. Bake for 12 to 14 minutes, or until lightly browned, rotating baking sheets in oven after 6 minutes. Cool 5 minutes, loosen bottoms from paper, and leave on paper to cool. (Ladyfingers may be stored in 1 layer, covered, overnight. Do not pile up or they will stick together. Or freeze on baking sheets until firm and then layer in airtight containers, separating layers with plastic wrap. Defrost in single layers, lightly covered with foil.)

To Make Custard: In a heavy medium saucepan off the heat, whisk eggs, sugar, cornstarch, lemon juice and peel until blended. Cook over medium heat whisking constantly, making sure to get into the edges of the pan, until the custard comes to a boil and thickens. Remove from heat and immediately pour into a bowl. Cover with plastic wrap placed directly on the surface and refrigerate until chilled. Or place the bowl in a large bowl of ice water and stir until chilled.

Spoon half the custard into another bowl and set aside. In a small mixing bowl, beat heavy cream until stiff peaks form. Add sour cream and beat until soft peaks form. Fold the pineapple and cream into half the chilled custard.

To Assemble: Line the bottom and sides of a 2-quart glass bowl, preferably one with straight sides, with ladyfingers. Spread half the plain lemon custard over the ladyfingers in an even layer. Spread with half the pineapple-lemon cream. Cover with remaining ladyfingers. Spread with remaining lemon custard and top with pineapple cream, smoothing the top. (Trifle may be covered with plastic wrap and refrigerated overnight.)

To Garnish: Pipe rosettes of whipped cream around the top and decorate with lemon slices and mint leaves, if desired.

MAKES: 8 servings.

Faster: Substitute 24 storebought ladyfingers for the homemade. (They are usually sold 12 to a package.) About 15 minutes before assembling, separate them into halves and brush the insides lightly with a mixture of ¼ cup lemon juice and 3 tablespoons sugar.

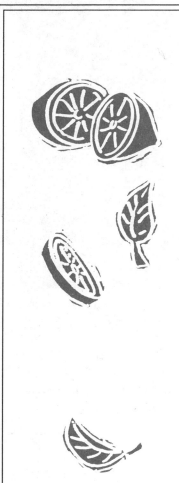

Menu

SAVORY SCOTCH BISCOTTI
WITH CANADIAN BACON AND
MUSTARD SEED SPREAD

◆

SALAD GREENS WITH PASTA
PINWHEELS AND WARM
TOMATO VINAIGRETTE

◆

BEEF TENDERLOIN CRUSTED
WITH BLUE CHEESE AND
TOMATO CHUTNEY

◆

ROASTED RED-SKIN POTATOES
WITH ROSEMARY OR
QUINOA AND WILD
MUSHROOM PILAF IN ACORN
SQUASH RINGS

◆

CRISP GARLIC GREEN BEANS

◆

EBONY, IVORY, AND MILK
CHOCOLATE TORTE

FANCIED-UP FILLET *of* BEEF

A whole beef tenderloin always deserves star billing. This one, made by simply spreading a roast with chutney and cheese, is one of the most outstanding I know. A fabulous choice for an extravagant sit-down dinner, it's also terrific for a large party because you can make as many as your oven will hold. Just be sure to leave space between the roasts or they will steam instead of getting brown and crusty.

A versatile hors d'oeuvre, Savory Scotch Biscotti can be dressy or casual, hot or at room temperature; they are sturdy and hasslefree. The first course is a glamorous salad of mixed greens topped with a chunky tomato vinaigrette and colorful pinwheels of rolled up lasagna noodles. It makes an outstanding entree for an important luncheon as well. Any of my first-course soups can stand in for the salad if you prefer.

For a side dish, roasted potatoes bake at the same temperature as the beef. Or serve a refined Quinoa and Wild Mushroom Pilaf. Guests often ask why Crisp Garlic Green Beans taste so much better than others. It's the combination of sautéing and steaming in a little oil and water that helps them retain their bright flavor, vivid color, and snappy texture without being crackly underdone.

A European-style torte comprised of three nutty layers in different shades of chocolate, which are repeated in the garnish of tricolor triangles, is a fitting end to an elegant meal. This dinner serves six to eight.

GAME PLAN

1 Month Ahead	**Make and freeze biscotti**
	Make and freeze torte layers
	Make and refrigerate tomato chutney
	Make and freeze chocolate triangles for torte, if using
	Make Canadian Bacon and Mustard Seed Spread, if using

| 2 Days Ahead | **Make quinoa and bake squash rings, if serving** |
| | **Make pasta pinwheels for salad** |

1 Day Ahead	**Defrost biscotti**
	Defrost bacon spread
	Prepare greens and vinaigrette for salad
	Defrost torte layers and complete torte
	Prepare green beans

DAY OF PARTY

| 2 Hours Before Serving | **Prepare tenderloin** |

| 40 to 50 Minutes Before Serving | **Roast tenderloin** |

30 Minutes Before Serving	**Slice pasta pinwheels**
	Roast potatoes, if serving
	Assemble quinoa on squash rings, if serving

Shortly Before Serving	**Warm tomato vinaigrette and assemble salad**
	Reheat green beans
	Reheat quinoa, if serving

EXTRA POINTS

THE TABLE

For a natural look, make or purchase a centerpiece that is light and airy, using dried flowers, leaves, twigs, and vines. Keep the bulk of the centerpiece under twelve inches so it doesn't hamper conversation. Sprinkle potpourri over the arrangement and around the table. Intersperse votive candles. Use an array of pastel or earth-tone napkins. For favors and/or name cards, place small packets of potpourri at each place.

When these peppery wafers bake, the aroma wafting from the Scotch in the batter is intoxicating. When you taste them, though, you'll wonder where all the liquor went. The biscotti are terrific plain, extra terrific when topped with a smoky Canadian Bacon and Mustard Seed Spread. (See color photo, page 6.)

PREP TIME: 15 minutes

BAKE TIME: 45 to 50 minutes plus 5 minutes standing time

ADVANCE PREP: May be stored at room temperature up to 1 week or frozen.

NUTRITIONAL ANALYSIS

Per biscotti
62 calories
3 g fat
0 cholesterol
41 mg sodium

SAVORY SCOTCH BISCOTTI

2½ cups all-purpose flour
3 tablespoons sugar
¾ teaspoon salt, or to taste
1½ teaspoons coarsely ground rainbow peppercorns or black pepper
½ cup Scotch whisky
½ cup olive oil
1 teaspoon Worcestershire sauce
Fresh flowers and garden leaves, for garnish (see page 10) (optional)
Canadian Bacon and Mustard Seed Spread, for serving (recipe follows) (optional)

To Make Dough: Preheat oven to 325°F.

Place flour, sugar, salt, and pepper in a food processor with the metal blade and pulse to combine. Add Scotch, oil, and Worcestershire sauce and pulse until the mixture holds together and is the consistency of wet sand. With your hands, shape the dough into a ball and divide in half. Place on a greased baking sheet and shape into 2 logs, each 10 inches long, 1 inch high, and 1½ inches wide, spacing them at least 2 inches apart.

To Bake: Bake for 20 minutes, or until tops are set and color is pale. With a spatula, remove to a cutting board and let cool 5 minutes. Leave oven at 325°F. With a serrated knife, slice diagonally about ⅜ inch thick. Return the slices, cut side down, to the baking sheet and bake until dry and firm, about 25 to 30 minutes. Cool on baking sheet. (Biscotti may be stored airtight at room temperature up to 1 week or frozen.)

Serve biscotti at room temperature garnished with flowers and leaves, if desired. Serve with spread, if you like.

MAKES: 40 biscotti.

Change of Pace: To make Scotch Thumbprints, which require only a single baking, divide dough into 40 pieces. Roll with hands into ¾-inch balls. Place ½ inch apart on lightly greased baking sheets. Press the handle of a wooden spoon into the center of each ball to form an indentation. Bake for 25 to 30 minutes, or until bottoms are pale golden and the tops are firm. Serve with spread, if desired.

CANADIAN BACON AND MUSTARD SEED SPREAD

2 teaspoons whole mustard
  seeds
1 tablespoon Scotch
2 teaspoons water
¼ teaspoon salt
1 teaspoon balsamic vinegar
3 ounces lean Canadian bacon or
  smoked ham, coarsely
  chopped (⅔ cup)

3 ounces regular or low-fat
  cream cheese, softened
2 teaspoons honey
1 tablespoon Dijon mustard
Savory Scotch Biscotti or
  crackers, for serving

In a 1-cup microwavesafe measure, combine mustard seeds, Scotch, water, salt, and vinegar. Cover with plastic wrap and microwave on high (100%) for 75 to 95 seconds, or until boiling. Set aside for 15 minutes or until lukewarm.

Meanwhile, in a food processor with the metal blade, process bacon and cream cheese until well blended. Add honey and mustard and pulse until incorporated. Add mustard seed mixture and pulse until blended. Remove to a bowl and refrigerate until serving. (Spread may be refrigerated for up to 3 days or frozen up to 1 month.)

Serve with biscotti or crackers.

MAKES: 1 cup.

The flavor really pops when Scotch-plumped mustard seeds unite with Dijon mustard and smoky ham. (See color photo, page 6.)

PREP TIME: 20 minutes

ADVANCE PREP: May be refrigerated up to 3 days or frozen.

NUTRITIONAL ANALYSIS

Per tablespoon (with lean
ham, low-fat cream cheese)
27 calories
1 g fat
4 mg cholesterol
157 mg sodium

When my cooking friend wine connoisseur Nick Brown and I donated a dinner for a fund raiser auction, the price tag climbed into the thousands. As an opener, I chose this salad of chilled greens with a warm fresh tomato dressing crowned with lasagna noodles rolled up with pink smoked salmon, emerald spinach, and creamy white cheese. (See color photo, page 3.)

PREP TIME: Pasta pinwheels, 30 minutes; salad, 25 minutes

CHILL TIME: Pasta, at least 1 hour

ADVANCE PREP: Pasta may be refrigerated up to 2 days. Greens and dressing may be refrigerated overnight.

NUTRITIONAL ANALYSIS

Per serving
279 calories
13 g fat
25 mg cholesterol
293 mg sodium

SALAD GREENS WITH PASTA PINWHEELS AND WARM TOMATO VINAIGRETTE

Pasta Pinwheels
6 lasagna noodles
9 ounces mild goat cheese or garlic-herb cheese, at room temperature
6 to 10 large fresh spinach leaves
½ pound thinly sliced smoked salmon

Salad
1 small head romaine lettuce, preferably center leaves, torn into bite-size pieces (about 6 cups loosely packed)
3 ounces stemmed and trimmed spinach, torn into bite-size pieces (about 4 cups)

2 medium heads Belgian endive, thickly sliced (about 8 ounces)
1 medium head radicchio, torn into bite-size pieces (about 8 ounces)

Warm Tomato Vinaigrette
6 tablespoons olive oil
4 green onions with tops, chopped (about ½ cup)
3 garlic cloves, minced
2 pounds plum tomatoes, chopped into ¼-inch pieces (16 medium)
6 tablespoons raspberry or red wine vinegar
2 tablespoons chopped fresh basil leaves
Salt and freshly ground black pepper

To Make Pasta Pinwheels: Fill a wide shallow pan half full of salted water. Bring to a boil and cook noodles until tender. Drain, rinse under cold water, and pat dry. Meanwhile, rinse spinach leaves and while still damp, place in a microwavesafe pie plate. Microwave, covered, on high (100%) for 1 to 2 minutes, or until wilted. Blot very dry. Cut out large stems.

Arrange a layer of spinach over each noodle. Slice salmon diagonally into 1-inch-wide strips. Place diagonally across noodles at ½-inch intervals. The strips should touch the short end of the noodles. Spread with a heaping tablespoon of cheese, spreading to the edges. (If cheese is difficult to spread, warm it in a microwave until soft and stir in ½ to 1 teaspoon milk.) Roll up tightly. Place on a plate, seam side down. Wrap in plastic wrap and refrigerate for at least 1 hour. (Pinwheels may be refrigerated up to 2 days.)

To Prepare Salad: Prepare lettuce, spinach, endive, and radicchio, wrap in paper towels, place in a plastic bag, and refrigerate. (May be refrigerated overnight.)

To Make Vinaigrette: In a large skillet over high heat, heat olive oil. Add green onions, garlic, and tomatoes and cook, stirring, just until the tomatoes begin to soften, 1 to 2 minutes. Remove from heat and stir in vinegar, basil, and salt and pepper to taste. (Dressing may be refrigerated overnight.)

To Assemble: About 10 to 30 minutes before serving, slice pasta rolls ⅜ to ½ inch thick and let stand at room temperature. Reheat vinaigrette in the microwave or on top of the stove until warm. Divide greens among salad plates, spoon warm dressing over, and top each with 2 to 3 slices of pasta.

MAKES: 8 servings.

Faster: Substitute 8 to 10 ounces (about 12 cups) mesclun (a mixture of baby greens available at some supermarkets) for the romaine, spinach, endive, and radicchio.

After dabbling with slews of sauces to embellish the classic beef tenderloin, as good as they were, I wanted something more exciting. Taking a new tack, I packed tangy-sweet tomato chutney and pungent blue cheese over the beef. With this approach, you save time, dirty dishes, and the worry of coordinating an extra sauce. To ensure the roast is done to your liking, use a meat thermometer.

PREP TIME: Chutney, 10 minutes; beef, 10 minutes

COOK TIME: Chutney, 45 to 55 minutes in microwave; beef 25 to 35 minutes plus 10 to 20 minutes standing time

ADVANCE PREP: Chutney may be refrigerated up to 1 month. Assemble roast 2 hours before baking.

BEEF TENDERLOIN CRUSTED WITH BLUE CHEESE AND TOMATO CHUTNEY

Tomato Chutney
10 garlic cloves, peeled
1 piece peeled fresh ginger (about 1 × 4 inches)
½ cup balsamic vinegar
¼ cup red wine vinegar
6 tablespoons sugar
1¼ teaspoons salt

¾ teaspoon cayenne, or to taste
12 large plum tomatoes (1¼ pounds), seeded and quartered (see page 12)

1 fillet of beef (3 to 4 pounds)
1½ to 2 cups blue or mild Roquefort cheese, crumbled (about 6 to 8 ounces)

To Make Chutney: In a food processor with the metal blade, mince garlic and ginger. Add vinegars, sugar, salt, and cayenne. Add tomatoes and pulse into small pieces. Remove to an 8-cup microwavesafe bowl and microwave, uncovered, on high (100%) for 45 to 55 minutes, stirring every 10 minutes, until the mixture is very thick and the small amount of liquid on the top is absorbed when stirred. Cool thoroughly. (Chutney may be refrigerated up to 1 month.)

To Prepare Tenderloin: Up to 1 hour before roasting, remove meat from refrigerator. Trim off fat. Sprinkle with salt. Place on a rack in a shallow pan. Sprinkle ½ to 1 cup cheese over the top, pressing it into meat. Spoon enough chutney over the top to press into a ¼-inch-thick layer; you will not use it all.

To Cook: Preheat oven to 450°F. Roast meat for 15 minutes. (Don't be concerned if some of the chutney falls off.) Sprinkle top with remaining cheese. Continue baking for a total of 25 to 30 minutes for rare (120°F.), 35 to 40 minutes for medium rare or medium (130°–135°F.). The temperature will go up 10 degrees as it stands. Let rest 10 to 20 minutes. Carve into ½-inch slices. Pass remaining chutney.

MAKES: 6 to 8 servings.

ROASTED RED-SKIN POTATOES WITH ROSEMARY

2 pounds small (1½ to 2 inches) red-skin or White Rose potatoes

2 tablespoons olive oil

1 teaspoon salt, preferably coarse

1 tablespoon chopped fresh rosemary leaves

Preheat the oven to 450°F.

Scrub potatoes, dry well, and cut in half lengthwise. Choose a rimmed baking sheet into which the potatoes fit comfortably. (Do not use the cushioned type because the potatoes won't brown.) Pour olive oil in pan and heat in oven until oil is hot, about 3 minutes. Swirl to coat pan and place potatoes, cut side down, in hot oil. Sprinkle with salt. Bake for 25 to 35 minutes, or until cut side is golden brown. Remove from oven, turn with a spatula, sprinkle with rosemary, and toss to coat. Serve immediately.

MAKES: 6 to 8 servings.

Potatoes can be sort of "oven-fried" by heating oil in a baking pan and placing the potatoes, cut side down, in it. The cut side becomes golden and crusty. They don't need tossing and are as easy to make as to eat.

PREP TIME: 10 minutes

BAKE TIME: 25 to 35 minutes

ADVANCE PREP: Bake potatoes as close to serving as possible.

NUTRITIONAL ANALYSIS

Per serving
136 calories
4 g fat
0 cholesterol
272 mg sodium

The "mother grain" of the Andes for over five hundred years, quinoa (pronounced KEEN-wah), Peruvian lore has it, was named back in 1520 when Francisco Pizarro took his first taste and exclaimed, "Quiera!" Although he was saying "Fantastic!" it was misheard and has been aptly misquoted ever since. Look for quinoa in your supermarket or health food store and store it in the refrigerator. Spooning it over sweet golden squash enhances its robust flavor and brownish hue.

PREP TIME: Quinoa, 15 minutes; squash, 10 minutes

COOK TIME: Quinoa, 12 to 15 minutes; squash, microwave 10 to 15 minutes, conventional oven, 30 minutes

ADVANCE PREP: Quinoa and squash rings may be refrigerated separately up to 2 days.

NUTRITIONAL ANALYSIS

Per serving
84 calories
2 g fat
0 cholesterol
200 mg sodium

QUINOA AND WILD MUSHROOM PILAF IN ACORN SQUASH RINGS

2 medium acorn squash (1 to 1¼ pounds each—not larger or they will be difficult to slice)

Quinoa Pilaf
2 teaspoons olive oil
¾ cup quinoa, rinsed with cold water
2 large shallots or ¼ onion, chopped (¼ cup)

¼ pound fresh wild or cultivated mushrooms, such as shiitakes, chanterelles, or porcini, chopped into ½-inch pieces
⅔ cup chicken or vegetable broth
1 tablespoon soy sauce
¼ cup chopped pimiento or roasted red pepper
⅓ cup chopped green onions

Salt and freshly ground black pepper

To Prepare Squash: Preheat oven to 400°F. Using a large butcher knife, cut ends off squash. Carefully slice each squash into 4 rings, about ½ to ¾ inch thick.

Place slices in a rimmed baking sheet, add ¼ inch water and bake, covered, for 30 minutes, or until tender when pierced with a knife.

When cool, cut off peel and cut out seeds and stringy fibers. (Squash may be refrigerated covered up to 2 days.)

To Make Pilaf: In a medium saucepan over medium-high heat, heat oil until hot. Sauté quinoa, stirring, for 1 minute. Add shallots and mushrooms and sauté until lightly golden, about 3 to 5 minutes. Add broth, ½ cup water, and soy sauce. Bring to a boil, cover, reduce heat to low, and simmer for 12 to 15 minutes, or until liquid is absorbed and quinoa is tender. Remove from heat and stir in pimiento and green onions. (Quinoa may be refrigerated up to 2 days.)

To Serve: Place squash rings on a microwavesafe platter and sprinkle with salt and pepper. Mound quinoa in the center of each ring. Cover with plastic wrap and microwave on high (100%) for 2 to 4 minutes or until hot. With a wide spatula, transfer to serving plate.

MAKES: 8 servings.

Change of Pace: For a more substantial vegetarian entree, serve half a squash filled with quinoa per person. Cut squash in half, scoop out seeds, and microwave or bake until soft. Spoon quinoa into squash cavities.

CRISP GARLIC GREEN BEANS

2 tablespoons olive oil, divided
2 pounds green beans, stem end trimmed, divided. (the youngest, smallest available)

4 garlic cloves, minced, divided
Salt

In a large nonstick skillet over moderate heat, heat 1 tablespoon oil until hot. Add 1 pound beans and stir to coat. Stir in 2 tablespoons water, cover, and cook over moderate heat until almost tender, stirring occasionally, about 4 to 5 minutes. The beans will smoke and sputter. Stir in half the garlic, cover, and cook for 2 minutes more, stirring once, until crisp-tender. Toss with salt to taste. Remove to serving platter. Repeat with the remaining beans. Serve warm or at room temperature. (Beans may be refrigerated overnight and reheated in the microwave, if desired.)

MAKES: 8 servings.

Change of Pace: To cook haricots verts using this method, first blanch them in boiling water for 2 to 3 minutes and run under cold water with ice to stop the cooking, then proceed with recipe.

In celebration of one of Alice Waters' new books, I hosted a party with an array of fresh dishes. To simplify the buffet, I took my favorite green beans and served them at room temperature fanned out on a huge platter. They were the main topic of conversation until Alice took the floor. With this cooking technique, it's important not to overcrowd the pan; that's why the beans are cooked in two batches.

PREP TIME: 10 minutes

COOK TIME: 12 to 16 minutes for 2 batches

ADVANCE PREP: May be refrigerated overnight.

NUTRITIONAL ANALYSIS

Per serving
72 calories
4 g fat
0 cholesterol
137 mg sodium

Felicia Driscoll, pastry chef at the Old Lyme Inn in Connecticut, has won several prizes for her three-layer Chocolate Trinity Cake, and when I asked for the recipe, she happily obliged. Unfortunately, her cake contains dried chestnuts, difficult for the home cook to obtain, and lots of time-consuming steps. I shortened the technique, substituted almonds for chestnuts, and although the result is not quite the same, I think you'll agree it's a show-stopper.

PREP TIME: Cake, 45 minutes; frosting, 15 minutes

BAKE TIME: 25 to 30 minutes

ADVANCE PREP: Cake layers may be stored at room temperature overnight or frozen. Frosted cake may be stored at room temperature overnight. Chocolate Triangles may be frozen.

NUTRITIONAL ANALYSIS

Per serving
631 calories
46 g fat
228 mg cholesterol
114 mg sodium

EBONY, IVORY, AND MILK CHOCOLATE TORTE

Batter
9 large eggs, separated
½ cup plus ¼ cup sugar, divided
4 ounces white chocolate, preferably Lindt Blancor or Tobler Narcisse
4 ounces semisweet chocolate
4 ounces milk chocolate, preferably Lindt
3 tablespoons B & B or brandy
½ pound (2 sticks) unsalted butter, softened
1 cup slivered blanched almonds, very finely ground (see page 11)

6 tablespoons all-purpose flour
¾ teaspoon baking powder
2 tablespoons unsweetened cocoa powder
Salt

Chocolate Frosting
8 ounces semisweet chocolate
2 tablespoons butter
⅔ cup heavy cream
5 teaspoons sugar
3 tablespoons B & B or brandy

Tricolor Chocolate Triangles, for garnish (recipe follows) (optional)

Place rack in center of oven and preheat to 375°F. Line the bottom of three 8- or 9-inch cake pans with wax paper or parchment. Grease pans and paper.

To Make Batter: In a large mixing bowl with electric mixer, beat egg yolks with ½ cup sugar until very light and thick, about 5 minutes. Meanwhile, place each kind of chocolate in a large microwavesafe bowl. Microwave each separately, uncovered, on 60% power for 2 to 4 minutes, stirring every 60 seconds, until smooth. Watch white chocolate carefully; it scorches easily. Beat B & B or brandy and butter into egg yolks. Add almonds, flour, and baking powder and mix on low speed until incorporated.

Stir 1¼ cups batter into white chocolate. Add 2 tablespoons cocoa powder to remaining batter, mixing until incorporated. Stir half the remaining batter (1 cup) into the semisweet chocolate and the other half into the milk chocolate, stirring until smooth. In a small mixing bowl with clean beaters, beat egg whites with a dash of salt until soft peaks form. Beat in remaining ¼ cup sugar, 2 tablespoons at a time, until stiff but not dry peaks form. Fold a third of the whites (about 2¼ cups) into each chocolate mixture. Pour each batter into a prepared pan and smooth the top.

To Bake: If space permits, stagger the 3 pans on 1 oven shelf. Bake for 25 to 30 minutes, or until a toothpick inserted in the center comes out clean. If necessary, rotate pans after 15 minutes. Cool 10 minutes and invert onto racks. Cool completely. (The cooled cake layers may be wrapped and held at room temperature overnight or frozen up to 1 month.)

To Make Frosting: In a large microwavesafe bowl, combine chocolate, butter, cream, and sugar and microwave, uncovered, on high (100%) until chocolate is melted, about 1½ to 3 minutes, stirring every 60 seconds, until smooth. Stir in B & B or brandy. Place bowl in larger bowl half full of ice water and stir often until thick enough to spread, about 15 to 25 minutes. Watch carefully or it will turn to fudge and need to be remelted. Or leave at room temperature, stirring occasionally until thick, about 1 to 2 hours.

To Frost: Line a cake plate with strips of wax paper to catch the drippings. Place semisweet cake layer on plate and spread with scant ⅓ cup frosting. Top with white chocolate layer. Spread with scant ⅓ cup frosting. Top with milk chocolate layer. Spread remaining frosting over top and sides. If using chocolate triangles, arrange as many as desired in a free-form pattern over top and sides of cake, standing some up and laying others flat, varying the colors. Carefully remove wax paper strips. (Torte may be stored at room temperature overnight.) Serve at room temperature.

MAKES: 12 servings.

TRICOLOR CHOCOLATE TRIANGLES

2 to 3 ounces white chocolate, chopped or chips

2 to 3 ounces semisweet chocolate, chopped or chips

2 to 3 ounces milk chocolate, chopped or chips

Place each chocolate in a small microwavesafe bowl or measuring cup. Microwave, uncovered, at 60% power for 1½ to 4 minutes, stirring after each minute, until smooth. Melting times vary with types of chocolate.

Pour each chocolate onto a separate sheet of heavy foil and spread into an even, smooth layer about ¼ inch thick. Cool at room temperature until firm but not brittle. With a sharp knife, working right on the foil, cut each into various size triangles, from 1 to 3 inches long. Remove from foil and refrigerate until firm. (Triangles may be frozen.)

DRESS-DOWN DINING

ere are two dinners for those occasions that require something fast and fancy-free. When time is shorter than usual but expectations remain high, turn to the "don't panic" party. Whether it's for last-minute guests, a family get-together, a graduation celebration, or an evening with friends, it proves that tiny efforts can produce gigantic results. Open your kitchen for a family reunion, neighborhood block party, or an office potluck and let your guests help themselves to broths, brews, and breads. Whether you give each guest a recipe to prepare or make them all yourself, keep the stove fires burning, the soup pot(s) bubbling and beverages flowing. The gang's all here—let's celebrate.

IMPROMPTU
"Don't Panic"
PARTY

have yet to meet the person who doesn't break into a sweat when hearing that out-of-town guests or business associates will be arriving for dinner in two to three hours. Here's a menu designed to keep palpitations to a mere murmur. I think you'll find that the dishes are so good you'll make them no matter how much advance notice you have.

The two speediest dishes, the soup and pasta, also happen to be the most colorful. To make the most of the velvety Red Bell Pepper Soup, keep jars of the peppers on hand; the other ingredients are basic pantry staples. The croutons take extra time, so if you are really rushed, sprinkle the soup with packaged ones instead. When you're racing against the clock, you'll especially appreciate the shortcuts for making the Salad Bar Pasta. Precut florets of broccoli and cauliflower cook right in the water with the pasta, and the spinach wilts in the colander when the hot pasta is poured over it.

There is a choice of main dishes here because I couldn't decide between them. Cornish hens cut in half, richly glazed, and baked at a high temperature become toasty umber and crackly crisp. They also reheat beautifully. When you remove the rib bones (very easy to do after they're cooked) and spruce up the birds with cherry sauce, they are formal fare. The fish, more humble, is so tasty and simple to prepare, you'll find yourself making it often for your family.

Your last hurdle, dessert, is cleared in record time with Chambord Grapes under Snow. This menu serves four, but each of the recipes can be multiplied as desired.

Menu

◆

ROASTED RED PEPPER SOUP
WITH RED PEPPER–GARLIC
CROUTONS

◆

DILL YOGURT–TOPPED
FISH FILLETS
OR
SWEET AND STICKY
CORNISH HENS WITH
TART CHERRY SAUCE

◆

SALAD BAR PASTA WITH
PARMESAN SHAVINGS

◆

CHAMBORD GRAPES
UNDER SNOW

GAME PLAN

| 1 Month Ahead | **Make and freeze soup**
Make and freeze toast for croutons |
| 1 Day Ahead | **Make red-pepper butter for croutons**
Defrost soup and croutons
Roast hens and make sauce, if serving |

DAY OF PARTY

8 Hours Ahead	**Prepare Chambord grapes** **Prepare ingredients for pasta**
4 Hours Ahead	**Prepare fish, if serving** **Spread red-pepper butter on croutons**
20 Minutes Before Serving	**Bake fish, if serving** **Reheat hens and sauce, if serving** **Put on water for pasta**
Shortly Before Serving	**Reheat soup** **Broil croutons** **Make pasta**

· 127 ·

EXTRA ◆ POINTS ◆

THE TABLE

Make an impromptu center-piece using things you have around the house or purchase from the market. Tie ribbons around plants and place them in groupings on the table or in a basket. Arrange paper, fabric, or plastic mâché fruits and flowers in a tray, bowl, or basket. Display a grouping of fresh fruit or vegetables, such as lemons, apples, or tomatoes with some greenery in a basket or bowl. Or arrange them in groupings right on the table, inserting fresh flowers and leaves here and there. Place a leafy cabbage on a tray and garnish with sprigs of baby's breath.

When I learned a group of food editors were coming to my home for dinner in less than two hours, I chose to serve this soup. Its bright taste, velvety texture, and cheery orange hue wowed them. Toasty red pepper–garlic croutons top off each bowl with style.

PREP TIME: Soup and croutons, 15 minutes

COOK TIME: Soup, 30 minutes; croutons, 10 minutes

ADVANCE PREP: Soup may be refrigerated up to 2 days or frozen. Croutons may be refrigerated up to 4 hours.

NUTRITIONAL ANALYSIS

Per serving
193 calories
13 g fat
22 mg cholesterol
699 mg sodium

ROASTED RED PEPPER SOUP WITH RED PEPPER–GARLIC CROUTONS

1 tablespoon vegetable oil
1 medium onion, chopped
1½ jars (7½ ounces each) roasted red bell peppers, well drained and chopped, remaining ½ jar reserved for croutons
1 tablespoon all-purpose flour

1 teaspoon sugar
3½ cups chicken or vegetable broth
2 tablespoons dry sherry
¼ cup heavy cream
Salt and freshly ground black pepper
Red Pepper–Garlic Croutons (recipe follows)

To Make Soup: Heat oil in a medium saucepan over medium-high heat. Add onion and sauté, stirring, for 1 minute. Cover pan with a sheet of wax paper and a lid and cook over low heat, stirring occasionally, until wilted, about 10 minutes. Add peppers and sauté, stirring occasionally, until onions are very soft, but not brown, about 10 minutes.

Stir in flour until incorporated. Stir in sugar, broth, and sherry. Bring to a boil and simmer, uncovered, for 10 minutes, stirring occasionally. Cool slightly and puree in a blender until smooth. (Soup may be refrigerated up to 2 days or frozen.)

Before Serving: Stir in cream and cook, stirring occasionally, until heated through. Season to taste with salt and pepper. Ladle into soup bowls and top with croutons.

MAKES: 4 servings.

Leaner: Omit the cream. The soup tastes terrific without it, too.

RED PEPPER–GARLIC CROUTONS

**8 slices firm white, whole wheat,
or egg bread
1 small garlic clove, peeled
½ (7½ ounce) jar roasted red
peppers, drained and patted
very dry (scant ½ cup)**

**4 tablespoons (½ stick) butter or
margarine, at room
temperature**

Preheat oven to 325°F.

Remove crusts from bread. Cut diagonally into triangles or desired shapes with a 1½ to 2-inch cookie cutter. Place on a baking sheet and bake for 10 minutes or until very dry and crisp. (Toasts may be stored airtight up to 1 week or frozen.)

In a food processor with the metal blade, process garlic until minced. Add red peppers and process until pureed. Add butter and process until blended; the mixture will not be smooth. (Butter may be refrigerated for up to 2 days.)

Up to 4 hours before serving, spread butter generously on croutons. Refrigerate until serving. Preheat broiler. Place croutons on baking sheet and broil until bubbling and edges are brown, 2 to 4 minutes, watching carefully so they don't burn.

MAKES: about 16 toasts.

NUTRITIONAL ANALYSIS

**Per 2-inch toast
61 calories
4 g fat
8 mg cholesterol
88 mg sodium**

When my daughter Cheryl gave birth to my first grand-daughter, another doting grand-mother, Bonnie Wall, donated this dish for dinner. We thought it was a winner, and Cheryl confirmed it by serving it at her next three dinner parties.

PREP TIME: 10 minutes

BAKE TIME: 12 to 16 minutes

ADVANCE PREP: May be refrigerated up to 4 hours before baking.

NUTRITIONAL ANALYSIS

Per serving (with halibut, nonfat yogurt)
311 calories
9 g fat
64 mg cholesterol
760 mg sodium

DILL YOGURT–TOPPED FISH FILLETS

4 whitefish fillets, such as mahimahi, halibut, red snapper, or grouper, skin removed and cut ¾-inch thick (6 to 8 ounces each)
½ lemon
Salt and freshly ground black pepper
1 cup regular, low-fat, or nonfat plain yogurt

4 tablespoons plus 1 tablespoon dry bread crumbs, divided
⅔ cup plus 1 tablespoon grated parmesan cheese, divided
2 tablespoons fresh chopped dill or 1 tablespoon dried dillweed
No-stick cooking spray

Place oven rack on top rung. Preheat oven to 425°F.

If fish is more than ¾ inch thick, cover with wax paper and pound lightly. Rinse and pat dry. Place fillets in a baking dish about 1 inch apart and sprinkle lightly with lemon juice. Sprinkle with salt and pepper.

In a medium bowl, stir together yogurt, 4 tablespoons bread crumbs, ⅔ cup cheese, and 2 tablespoons dill. Divide mixture over top of fish and spread to form an even layer. (Fish may be refrigerated, covered, up to 4 hours.) Sprinkle tops with 1 tablespoon crumbs and 1 tablespoon parmesan cheese. Spray tops with cooking spray. Bake for 12 to 16 minutes, or until opaque when cut into. Turn on broiler and broil until tops are golden.

MAKES: 4 servings.

SWEET AND STICKY CORNISH HENS WITH TART CHERRY SAUCE

4 Cornish hens, at room temperature (about 1¼ pounds each)
2 teaspoons prepared mustard
1 tablespoon dry mustard
½ cup sweet orange marmalade
1 cup catsup
1 can (16 ounces) tart red cherries, drained, juice reserved

1½ teaspoons cornstarch

Garnish (optional)
Orange slices, twisted into butterflies
Watercress or parsley

Preheat oven to 425°F.

Using poultry or kitchen shears, cut hens in half through the breast and down the back. Cut out the row of bones from each side of the back bone. Line a shallow roasting pan with a double thickness of heavy-duty foil and place hens on it, skin side up.

To Make Glaze: In a small bowl, stir together mustards, marmalade, catsup, and 1 tablespoon of the reserved cherry juice. Set aside ½ cup glaze for sauce. With a brush, dab half the glaze over hens.

To Bake: Roast for 40 to 45 minutes, basting with remaining glaze after 15 minutes. Hens are done when juices run clear when a sharp knife is inserted between the drumstick and breast. The glaze will look runny but will set up. If browner tops are desired, place under broiler. If desired, cut out small rib and back bones with scissors. (Hens and reserved ½ cup glaze may be refrigerated separately overnight. Bring to room temperature and reheat at 425° for 10 to 15 minutes.)

To Make Sauce: While hens bake, drain cherry juice into a medium saucepan. Stir in reserved ½ cup glaze and cornstarch, whisking until cornstarch is dissolved. Cook over medium heat, stirring, until sauce comes to a boil and thickens. Stir in 1 cup of the cherries; reserve remainder for another use. (Sauce may be refrigerated overnight. Reheat before serving in microwave or on top of stove. If too thick, thin with a little orange juice.) If desired, garnish hens with orange slices and greens. Spoon a small amount of sauce over hens and pass remainder.

MAKES: 4 servings.

Leaner: Before baking, remove skin from hens by pulling it off with your fingers and a knife. Brush glaze directly over meat.

Practical but elegant still, these hens are cut in half and thickly coated with a cherry glaze. They are easier to eat if you cut out the small rib and back bones after roasting.

PREP TIME: 15 minutes

BAKE TIME: 40 to 45 minutes

ADVANCE PREP: Hens may be cooked 1 day ahead and reheated. Sauce may be refrigerated overnight.

NUTRITIONAL ANALYSIS

Per serving without sauce
983 calories
56 g fat
203 mg cholesterol
390 mg sodium

Per 2 tablespoons sauce
44 calories
1% calories percent from fat
less than 2 g fat
0 cholesterol
136 mg sodium

SALAD BAR PASTA WITH PARMESAN SHAVINGS

ash to your supermarket salad bar for the vegetables you need already washed and cut up. Organize the ingredients before you begin—this gets done in a wink.

PREP TIME: 10 minutes

COOK TIME: 2 to 4 minutes

ADVANCE PREP: Assemble ingredients ahead and cook at last minute.

1 chunk (1½ to 2 ounces) parmesan cheese
1 cup (packed) fresh spinach leaves, cut into ½-inch strips
2 medium tomatoes, cut into ½-inch pieces (1½ cups)
½ cup canned garbanzo beans (chick peas), rinsed and drained
2 tablespoons chopped fresh basil or 2 teaspoons dried basil
1 cup broccoli florets, cut into ½-inch pieces
1 cup cauliflower florets, cut into ½-inch pieces
¼ pound dried capellini (angel hair) pasta, broken in thirds
2 to 3 tablespoons olive oil
2 to 3 tablespoons fresh lemon juice
Salt and freshly ground black pepper

Fill a 4-quart saucepan with salted water and bring to a boil. Meanwhile, with a vegetable peeler, shave parmesan cheese into long thick strips. Place spinach in a colander in the sink and place tomatoes, garbanzo beans, and basil in a large bowl.

When water comes to a boil, add broccoli, cauliflower, and pasta. Boil until pasta is tender to the bite, 2 to 4 minutes. Drain in colander over spinach and transfer to the bowl with the tomatoes. Add olive oil, lemon juice, salt and pepper to taste. Add cheese and toss well. Serve immediately.

Faster: Substitute ¼ cup grated or shredded parmesan cheese for the shavings.

MAKES: 4 servings.

NUTRITIONAL ANALYSIS

Per serving
265 calories
12 g fat
33 mg cholesterol
342 mg sodium

CHAMBORD GRAPES UNDER SNOW

¾ **pound seedless grapes, mixed green, red, and black, if available (2 cups)**
2 tablespoons Chambord liqueur
⅓ **cup heavy cream, chilled**
⅓ **cup light sour cream, chilled**

⅓ **cup regular or low-fat plain yogurt, chilled**
½ **cup chopped chocolate-coated toffee bars, such as Heath or Skor Bars (about 4 ounces)**

Cut grapes in half and divide among 4 goblets or dessert dishes. Stir ½ tablespoon Chambord into each. In a small mixing bowl with electric mixer, beat heavy cream until soft peaks form. Add sour cream and yogurt and mix until soft peaks form. Spread over grapes, covering completely. (May be refrigerated, covered, until ready to serve or up to 8 hours.) Before serving, sprinkle with toffee.

MAKES: 4 servings.

Change of Pace: Stir 1 orange, peeled, quartered, and sliced, in with the grapes.

When grapes are doused with raspberry-flavored Chambord, blanketed with thickly whipped yogurt cream, and sprinkled with toffee, they are an exception to my rule that fruit is not dessert. I would happily conclude any meal with this combination. Regular or low-fat yogurt is preferred to nonfat because it is thicker.

PREP TIME: 15 minutes

ADVANCE PREP: May be refrigerated up to 8 hours.

NUTRITIONAL ANALYSIS

Per serving
309 calories
20 g fat
53 mg cholesterol
95 mg sodium

SOUPS *and* SUDS PARTY

If your entertaining has slipped into a recession, here's an idea that won't increase inflation or cause a deficit in your budget. To nourish the spirit as well as the body, invite friends over for a sampler of soups, suds, and breads. Depending on the number of guests at your gathering, serve one, two, or all three of these stalwart main-dish soups. They are ideal party selections since each can be made and simmered in about an hour, can be refrigerated or frozen ahead, and can sit on the stove over low heat virtually unattended throughout the party. And you needn't fret over a shortage of soup bowls. Just dig out your new, old, and seldom used mugs or borrow some from friends; ask guests to rinse them out between courses.

For starters, you might wish to put out a big bowl of Guacamole and Corn Salsa (page 170), Chunky Italian Salsa (page 285), or Roasted Provençale Vegetable Salsa (see page 180) with appropriate dippers.

Some people make bread because they find it therapeutic, so they are happy to knead, whack, pull, pummel, and caress the dough. Not me. I make bread because I want to warm my friends with love by serving a homemade loaf. To meet my time constraints, I am happy to make the dough in the food processor, rise it in the microwave, and bake it without forming any human bonding. Because my breads are intended to be eaten without butter, you'll find them bursting with exciting ingredients—dried fruits, nuts, seeds, herbs, cheese, and such savory condiments as sun-dried tomatoes and olives.

For the suds, fill big coolers or washtubs with a bevy of imported and domestic brews or purchase a keg. Offer some light and nonalcoholic varieties as well.

Close with a fruit crisp, warmed and peaked with a dollop of whipped cream, ice cream, or frozen yogurt. If you serve all the soups and breads in this menu, you will have enough for sixteen to eighteen people. You will either need to make two crisps or supplement one with Amaretti Streusel Apple Squares (see page 27).

GAME PLAN

1 Month Ahead	**Make and freeze smoked turkey soup**
	Make and freeze Tortilla Crab Soup
	Prepare and freeze tortilla strips for crab soup
	Make and freeze sausage soup and rouille
	Make and freeze Currant-Walnut Baguettes
	Make and freeze Wheatberry Multigrain Bread
2 Weeks Ahead	**Make and freeze crisp**
1 Day Ahead	**Make Italian braid**
	Defrost soups
	Defrost tortilla strips
	Defrost rouille
	Defrost breads
DAY OF PARTY	
Morning of Party	**Defrost crisp at room temperature**
1 Hour Before Serving	**Prepare condiments for Tortilla Crab Soup**
	Bring Italian braid to room temperature
20 Minutes Before Serving	**Reheat breads**
	Reheat soups
	Reheat crisp

EXTRA POINTS

For a cozy, homespun look, throw a quilt or lap blanket over your table and wrap soup spoons in bandanas, which do double duty as napkins.

When I lived in southern California, I often would go to George's Restaurant at the Cove in La Jolla to devour a bowl of this fabulous smoky soup. Now that I live in Baltimore, I keep a batch in the freezer to satisfy my homesick pangs. To save time, chop the vegetables in a food processor.

PREP TIME: 30 minutes

COOK TIME: About 45 minutes

ADVANCE PREP: May be refrigerated up to 2 days or frozen.

SMOKED TURKEY, BROCCOLI, AND BLACK BEAN SOUP

Stock Base
2 tablespoons olive oil
1 cup diced peeled broccoli stems (1 medium head)
½ cup chopped carrots (2 medium)
½ cup chopped onion (½ onion)
½ cup chopped celery (2 medium stalks)
2 teaspoons dried thyme, crumbled
2 teaspoons dried oregano, crumbled
1 teaspoon dried basil, crumbled
½ cup dry white wine or imported dry vermouth

5 cups chicken broth

2 cups broccoli florets
1 can (16 ounces) black beans, drained
½ pound smoked turkey or chicken, chopped into ½-inch pieces
1 tablespoon Worcestershire sauce
½ teaspoon hot-pepper sauce, such as Tabasco
2 tablespoons cornstarch
1 cup heavy cream
Salt and freshly ground black pepper

To Make Stock Base: Heat oil in a 4-quart Dutch oven or soup pot over medium-high heat. Add broccoli stems, carrots, onion, celery, thyme, oregano, and basil and sauté, stirring occasionally, until vegetables are soft, about 10 minutes. Add wine and broth and bring to a boil. Boil gently, stirring occasionally, until liquid is reduced by about half, about 20 minutes.

To Finish Soup: Add broccoli florets, beans, turkey, Worcestershire, and hot-pepper sauce and simmer 5 minutes, stirring occasionally. Remove pan from heat. Stir cornstarch into cream to dissolve and stir into soup. Return to heat and bring to a boil, stirring, until soup thickens. Season to taste with salt and pepper. (Soup may be refrigerated up to 2 days or frozen. It will appear separated, but will smooth out when reheated.)

MAKES: 6 servings.

Leaner: Reduce cream to ½ cup. Do not substitute milk for the cream; it will turn the soup gray.

TORTILLA CRAB SOUP

3 garlic cloves, peeled
½ pickled or fresh seeded
   jalapeño (½ to 1 inch), halved
   (see page 10) (optional)
1 large onion, peeled and cut
   into eighths
1 tablespoon vegetable oil
½ cup plus 3½ cups chicken
   broth, divided
1 can (28 ounces) Italian plum
   tomatoes
1 can (10¾ ounces) tomato
   puree
2 teaspoons chile powder
2 teaspoons ground cumin
3 tablespoons fresh lime juice

Salt
1½ cups fresh or frozen corn
   kernels
½ pound crab meat, picked over

Condiments
1 package corn tortillas, 6 to 7
   inches in diameter
1 cup chopped cilantro leaves
1 large avocado, cut into small
   cubes
1 cup shredded sharp cheddar
   cheese
Minced jalapeños
Lime wedges

In a food processor with the metal blade, process garlic and jalapeño, if using, until finely minced. Add onion and pulse until chopped. In a 4-quart Dutch oven or saucepan over high heat, heat oil. Sauté onion mixture for 1 minute. Stir in ½ cup chicken broth, cover, reduce heat to medium-low and simmer 5 minutes, or until onion is soft. In same processor bowl, pulse tomatoes until coarsely chopped. Add them with their juice, the remaining 3½ cups broth, tomato puree, chile powder, cumin, and lime juice to soup pot. Bring to a boil, reduce heat, and simmer, uncovered, for 15 minutes. Season with salt to taste. Stir in corn and cook 5 minutes. (Soup may be refrigerated up to 2 days or frozen. Reheat before serving.)

To Bake Tortilla Strips: While soup simmers, preheat oven to 350°F. Stack tortillas, cut into ⅜-inch strips, and cut strips in half. Grease or spray a large baking sheet with cooking spray. Place tortillas on baking sheet and bake for 15 to 18 minutes or until dry, crisp, and lightly browned. (Strips may be stored airtight at room temperature for several days or frozen.)

As close to serving as possible, prepare remaining condiments and place in separate serving bowls.

Before Serving: Stir crab into hot soup. Serve with assorted condiments.

MAKES: 6 servings.

Change of Pace: To make Tortilla Chicken Soup, substitute ¾ pound boneless, skinless chicken breasts for the crab. Cut into bite-size strips and add to soup 10 minutes before serving. Simmer until cooked through.

This thick tomato-based soup, dotted with corn and swimming with crab, is served with help-yourself condiments. Guests add their own heat with jalapeños and crunch with baked tortilla strips.

PREP TIME: 20 minutes

COOK TIME: 30 minutes

ADVANCE PREP: Soup may be refrigerated up to 2 days or frozen. Tortilla strips may be stored at room temperature for several days or frozen.

NUTRITIONAL ANALYSIS

Per serving (without condiments)
190 calories
4 g fat
23 mg cholesterol
1070 mg sodium

If you're searching for a robust potage that tastes as if it cooked all day but actually simmered for only thirty minutes, then look no further. The broth is lightly seasoned, so that each guest can add a spoonful of the spicy, garlicky rouille to taste. In French, the word "rouille" means rust, and that aptly describes the hue of this pungent paste.

PREP TIME: 30 minutes

COOK TIME: 45 minutes

ADVANCE PREP: Soup and rouille may be refrigerated up to 2 days or frozen.

NUTRITIONAL ANALYSIS

Per serving (without rouille)
250 calories
6 g fat
19 mg cholesterol
1057 mg sodium

Per tablespoon rouille
15 calories
1 g fat
2 mg cholesterol
89 mg sodium

SAUSAGE AND CABBAGE SOUP WITH SUN-DRIED TOMATO ROUILLE

Soup
2 tablespoons olive oil
¼ pound lean smoked ham, chopped into ¼-inch pieces
½ pound regular or low-fat kielbasa sausage, cut in half lengthwise and sliced ¼-inch thick
2 medium onions, chopped (about 2 cups)
3 large garlic cloves, minced
1 pound turnips, peeled and cut into ½-inch cubes
½ head green cabbage, cut in half, cored and cut into 1-inch pieces (about 1½ pounds)
6 cups chicken broth
¾ cup dry sherry

1 cup water
4 cups (loosely packed) spinach leaves, cut into ½-inch strips (about 6 ounces)
2 cans (16 ounces each) butter beans (large limas), rinsed and drained

Sun-dried Tomato Rouille
¾ cup sun-dried tomatoes (see page 12)
3 medium garlic cloves, peeled
½ can (2 ounces) flat anchovy fillets (optional)
1 plum tomato, seeded and quartered
Scant ½ teaspoon cayenne
1 tablespoon olive oil

To Make Soup: In an 8-quart Dutch oven or soup pot over medium-high heat, heat olive oil. Sauté ham and sausage until browned, about 8 minutes, stirring occasionally. Add onions, garlic, turnips, and cabbage and sauté, stirring occasionally, until soft, about 6 minutes.

Stir in chicken broth, sherry, and 1 cup water. Bring to a boil, reduce heat, and simmer, partly covered, for 15 minutes. Add spinach and beans and simmer 5 minutes, or until heated through. (Soup may be refrigerated up to 2 days or frozen. Reheat before serving.)

To Make Rouille: While soup simmers, place sun-dried tomatoes in a 2-cup glass measure. Cover with water and microwave, covered with plastic wrap, on high (100%) for 3 to 4 minutes, or until soft. In food processor with metal blade, mince garlic. Add anchovies if using, and process until minced. Squeeze water from sun-dried tomatoes and add them, the fresh tomato, and cayenne to processor. Process until minced. Add oil and mix until pureed. (Rouille may be refrigerated for several days or frozen.) Serve at room temperature.

To Serve: Ladle hot soup into bowls and pass rouille, letting each guest stir desired amount into soup.

MAKES: 8 to 10 servings.

CURRANT-WALNUT BAGUETTES

½ cup golden raisins
¾ cup currants
1½ cups bread flour
1½ cups whole wheat flour
1 package quick-rising yeast
1 teaspoon salt

¾ cup walnut halves or pieces
1 tablespoon honey
2 tablespoons walnut oil or
  olive oil
1 egg, lightly beaten, for glaze

To Make Dough: Pour 1¼ cups water into a 4-cup microwavesafe glass measure and stir in raisins and currants. Microwave, covered with wax paper, on high (100%) for 2 to 3 minutes. Let steep until water feels very warm to the touch. Remove raisins and currants from water and set aside, reserving water.

In a food processor with the metal blade, pulse the flours, yeast, and salt until combined, about 30 seconds. Add walnuts and pulse 3 or 4 times to incorporate. Stir honey and oil into water; if not very warm to the touch (about 125° to 130°F.), reheat in microwave. With the machine running, pour liquid through feed tube, reserving about 1 tablespoon. The dough should leave the sides of the bowl and form a ball. If it doesn't, gradually add the remaining liquid until a ball is formed. With the machine running, knead for 60 seconds. Remove dough to a lightly floured surface and knead lightly, adding more flour only if too sticky. Shape into a ball.

To Rise in the Microwave: You need a microwave with 10% power. Make a hole in the center of the dough, like a doughnut, and return it to food processor bowl without the blade. Spray top with cooking spray or brush lightly with oil. Cover loosely with a damp towel or plastic wrap. Place an 8-ounce glass of water in back of oven. Place bowl in center. Microwave at 10% power for 5 minutes and rest 5 minutes. Rotate bowl and microwave 5 more minutes and rest 5 minutes. The dough should be double in bulk and when you poke it with your finger, a hole should remain. If not, repeat process one more time.

To Rise at Room Temperature: Coat a large bowl with oil and place dough in bowl, turning to coat all sides. Cover with a damp towel and let rise in a warm place (see page 9) for about 1 to 1½ hours, or until double in size and a hole remains when poked with your finger.

To Shape: Punch dough down, turn out onto a lightly floured surface and knead in the currants and raisins. Divide into 2 equal parts. Roll

(continued)

When Renée Carisio of the Ma Cuisine Cooking School in Los Angeles shared this recipe with me, she warned me that one taste and I wouldn't be able to stop eating it. Rustic brown baguettes, crammed with currants, raisins, and walnuts, make a perfect partner for hearty soups, entree salads, fruit, and cheese. But I prefer eating mine solo—ever since I devoured an entire loaf in one sitting. Renée is certainly a woman of her word.

PREP TIME: 30 minutes

RISE TIME: First rise: Microwave, 20 to 30 minutes; warm place, 60 to 90 minutes. Second rise: 45 minutes.

BAKE TIME: 30 minutes

ADVANCE PREP: May be stored at room temperature up to 2 days or frozen.

NUTRITIONAL ANALYSIS

Per 1-inch slice
44 calories
1 g fat
3 mg cholesterol
35 mg sodium

each into a 6 × 15-inch sheet. With your hands, roll the sheets into long cylinders, pinching the edges to seal. Transfer to a greased baking sheet, seam side down, or 2 baguette pans. Cover with plastic wrap and a towel and let rise in a warm place until the loaves are almost doubled, about 45 minutes.

To Bake: Preheat oven to 375°F. Brush loaves with beaten egg and slash each with a sharp knife several times on the diagonal. For a crisp crust, see page 9. Bake for 30 to 35 minutes, or until nicely browned. (Loaves may be stored in a plastic bag up to 2 days or frozen. To reheat, see page 9.)

MAKES: 2 loaves.

WHEATBERRY MULTIGRAIN BREAD

½ cup regular or quick rolled
    oats
⅓ cup bulgur wheat
½ cup rye flour
½ cup whole wheat flour
2½ to 3 cups all-purpose flour
1 package quick-rising yeast
3 tablespoons oat bran high-
    fiber hot cereal
1½ teaspoons salt
⅔ cup molasses

2 tablespoons vegetable oil
½ to ⅔ cup very warm water
    (125° to 130°F.)
⅓ cup Grape Nuts cereal
⅓ cup plus 1 tablespoon
    sunflower seeds, divided
2 tablespoons plus 1 tablespoon
    sesame seeds, divided
1 egg white, mixed with 1
    teaspoon water, for wash

In a 2-quart microwavesafe bowl, stir together oats, bulgur, and 1 cup cold water. Microwave, uncovered, on high (100%) for 2 to 4 minutes, or until water is absorbed and mixture is soft. Cool to lukewarm.

To Make in a Food Processor: You need a large food processor (at least 11-cup bowl). Place rye flour, whole wheat flour, and 2½ cups white flour, yeast, oat bran, and salt in bowl fitted with the metal blade. Pulse to combine, about 10 seconds. Add molasses, oil, and oatmeal mixture and pulse until incorporated, about 10 seconds. With the motor running, drizzle the warm water very slowly through the feed tube, reserving 1 to 2 tablespoons. The batter should leave the sides of the bowl and form a ball. If it doesn't, gradually add the remaining liquid until a ball is formed. With the machine running, process 60 seconds to knead, adding additional flour a very small amount at a time if dough seems sticky. The sides of the bowl should be clean. Pulse in Grape Nuts, ⅓ cup sunflower seeds, and 2 tablespoons sesame seeds until incorporated.

I f ever I owned a restaurant, this wholesome, crusty round loaf would be my signature bread. Molasses adds a dark sweetness; seeds make it nutty; and whole grains provide a dense, nubby texture.

PREP TIME: 20 minutes

RISE TIME: First rise: microwave, 30 minutes plus additional time at room temperature; warm place, 1½ to 2 hours. Second rise: 45 minutes

BAKE TIME: 35 to 40 minutes

ADVANCE PREP: May be stored at room temperature up to 2 days or frozen.

NUTRITIONAL ANALYSIS

Per 1-inch slice
208 calories
5 g fat
0 cholesterol
224 mg sodium

Remove dough to a lightly floured surface and knead lightly, adding more flour only if dough is too sticky. Shape into a ball.

To Make with Electric Mixer: Place rye flour, whole wheat flour, 2½ cups white flour, yeast, oat bran, and salt in bowl of electric mixer. Add molasses, oil, and oatmeal mixture and mix on low speed to incorporate, about 30 seconds. Add ½ cup warm water and mix until a dough is formed. Add remaining water only if needed to make a slightly sticky dough. Add remaining flour as needed if dough is too sticky. Mix in the Grape Nuts, ⅓ cup sunflower seeds, and 2 tablespoons sesame seeds. Remove to a floured surface and knead by hand for 5 to 7 minutes, or until soft and elastic.

To Rise in the Microwave: You need a microwave with 10% power. Make a hole in the center of the dough, like a doughnut, and return it to food processor bowl without the blade. Spray top with cooking spray or brush lightly with oil. Cover loosely with plastic wrap and a damp towel. Place an 8-ounce glass of water in back of oven. Place bowl in center. Microwave at 10% power for 5 minutes and rest 5 minutes. Rotate bowl and microwave 5 more minutes and rest 5 more minutes. Repeat one more time for a total of 30 minutes rising time. The dough should be nearly double in bulk and when you poke it with your finger, a hole should remain. If not, cover and let rise in a warm place until almost doubled in bulk. It may take 30 minutes or longer.

To Rise at Room Temperature: Coat a large bowl with oil and place dough in bowl, turning to coat all sides. Cover with a damp towel. Let rise in a warm place (see page 9) for about 1½ to 2 hours, or until nearly double in size and a hole remains when poked with your finger.

To Shape and Rise Again: Punch dough down, turn out onto a lightly floured surface, and knead by hand a few times. Shape into a ball and place in a greased 2- to 3-quart ovenproof bowl or round casserole. Cover with plastic wrap and a towel and set in warm place to rise until doubled, about 45 minutes. Brush top with egg white and sprinkle with 1 tablespoon sunflower and 1 tablespoon sesame seeds, pressing them in lightly to adhere.

To Bake: Preheat oven to 375°F. For a crisp crust, see page 9. Bake for 35 to 40 minutes, or until the bread is deeply browned. Transfer to a rack to cool. (Bread may be stored in a plastic bag at room temperature up to 2 days or frozen. To reheat, see page 9.)

MAKES: 1 loaf

Here's a braided cal-zone packed with pesto, olives, goat cheese, and sun-dried tomatoes.

PREP TIME: 35 minutes

RISE TIME: 15 minutes

BAKE TIME: 15 to 20 minutes plus 15 minutes cooling time

ADVANCE PREP: May be refrigerated overnight.

WHITE, RED, AND GREEN ITALIAN BRAID

Dough
2¾ cups all-purpose flour
1 package quick-rising yeast
1 tablespoon sugar
1 teaspoon salt
2 tablespoons olive oil
1 egg, at room temperature
⅔ cup very warm water (125° to 130°F.)

Filling
¼ cup basil pesto sauce, storebought or homemade (see page 152)
¼ cup sliced pitted Mediterranean olives, such as niçoise (see page 12)

1 cup shredded regular or low-fat mozzarella cheese (about 4 ounces)
¼ cup crumbled goat or blue cheese (about 1½ ounces)
¼ cup chopped roasted red peppers, blotted dry
¼ cup sun-dried tomatoes rehydrated (see page 12) and chopped

1 egg, mixed with 1 tablespoon water, for glaze
1 teaspoon sesame or poppy seeds (optional)

Fill a large shallow pan or roaster half full of water and bring to a boil to use for rising.

To Make Dough: Place flour, yeast, sugar, and salt in food processor fitted with the metal blade and pulse to combine. Add oil and egg and process until incorporated. With the motor running, drizzle the water slowly into the dry ingredients, reserving 1 to 2 tablespoons. The batter should leave the sides of the bowl and form a ball. If it doesn't, grad-ually add the remaining liquid until a ball is formed. Process 60 seconds to knead. Cover with a towel and let rest for at least 10 minutes. Mean-while, prepare filling ingredients.

To Assemble: On a lightly floured surface, roll dough to a 14 × 10-inch rectangle. Place on greased or sprayed baking sheet. Spread pesto lengthwise down center third of dough. Sprinkle with olives, cheeses, red peppers, and tomatoes. Make cuts at 1-inch intervals from filling to edges of dough. Alternating the sides, fold strips at an angle across filling. Cover with a towel.

To Rise: Place rack in upper third of oven. Preheat oven to 400°F. Remove pan of boiling water from heat. Place baking sheet with bread over pan. Let rise 15 minutes. It will begin to swell like a pizza crust. Brush egg over loaf and sprinkle with seeds, if desired.

To Bake: Bake for 15 to 20 minutes, or until golden. Remove to rack and cool 15 minutes before slicing. Serve warm or at room temperature. (Loaf may be refrigerated overnight. Reheat at 350°F. for 10 minutes before serving.)

MAKES: 1 loaf.

If you think a crisp is a pie with an upside-down identity crisis that belongs only with homespun dinners, take another look. This combination of sweet and tart fruit touched with honey and baked under a crunchy oatmeal topping can hold its own against any right-side-up pie or high falutin' torte. It even makes a great breakfast entree. To serve six, divide the recipe in half and bake in a two-quart rectangular baking dish.

PREP TIME: 30 minutes

BAKE TIME: 40 to 50 minutes

ADVANCE PREP: May be refrigerated overnight or frozen.

NUTRITIONAL ANALYSIS

Per serving
316 calories
7 g fat
15 mg cholesterol
154 mg sodium

PEAR, RASPBERRY, AND RHUBARB CRISP

1 package (12 ounces) frozen unsweetened raspberries, partially thawed
1 pound fresh or frozen rhubarb, partially thawed, chopped into ½-inch pieces
6 medium ripe but firm pears, preferably Bosc, peeled, cored, and chopped into 1-inch pieces
¾ cup honey
¼ cup all-purpose flour
2 teaspoons ground cinnamon
Vanilla ice cream, frozen yogurt, or whipped cream, for serving (optional)

Oatmeal Streusel
1 cup regular or quick rolled oats
1½ cups all-purpose flour
½ cup (packed) light brown sugar
1½ teaspoons ground cinnamon
½ teaspoon salt
6 tablespoons butter or margarine
2 tablespoons seedless raspberry preserves or jelly

Preheat oven to 375°F.

In a large bowl, gently stir together raspberries, rhubarb, pears, honey, flour, and cinnamon. Pour into a greased 9 × 13-inch baking dish or 12-cup gratin dish.

To Make Streusel: In a medium bowl stir together oats, flour, brown sugar, cinnamon, and salt. Combine butter or margarine and preserves and heat or microwave until melted. Stir into flour mixture until crumbly. Sprinkle evenly over fruit. Bake for 40 to 50 minutes, or until pears are tender and topping is golden. Cool slightly and serve with ice cream, frozen yogurt, or whipped cream, if desired. (Crisp may be held at room temperature for several hours or refrigerated overnight or frozen up to 2 weeks. Defrost covered at room temperature. Before serving, reheat uncovered at 375°F. for 20 to 30 minutes.)

MAKES: 10 to 12 servings.

Team Cuisine

ommunal cooking can dish up good times and elaborate meals in short order. For the easiest and speediest get-togethers, gather some friends and select one of the following game plans: a traditional potluck, where everyone brings a dish; a pizza party, where guests bring the toppings and cook together; or a progressive journey, with each course at another person's home. All you need is a team manager, a group of good sports, and a desire to play the game.

TOP YOUR OWN PIZZA PARTY

Menu

ANTIPASTO PLATTER:

EGGPLANT ROLLS WITH
GARLIC-HERB CHEESE

ASPARAGUS SPEARS WITH
SMOKED SALMON

CONFETTI-CAPPED
MUSHROOMS

CARAMELIZED ONION,
WALNUT, AND BLUE CHEESE
PIZZA

PESTO, SHRIMP, AND BRIE
PIZZA

SICILIAN PIZZA

PEACH TORTONI

Here's a way to compose a menu for dinner or a teen-age birthday or graduation party and allow your guests to be entertained while they make their own meal. When inviting your friends, request they bring an apron as well as a food item they would put on pizza. Each one should bring enough for all the guests. You could suggest a specific ingredient to fit in with the recipes you are planning or ask them to bring one that begins with the first letter of their name.

When the guests arrive, collect the toppings and assemble them in bowls. Usher the guests into the kitchen, form them into teams of two or three, and have each group top its pizza as directed in recipes you provide or as their imagination dictates. To ensure optimum participation, keep glasses filled with the chefs' favorite beverages and offer assorted vegetable antipasti to ward off pangs of hunger. You might ask someone to bring a salad, or else toss together a Mediterranean Caesar Salad (see page 186), or Garden Salad with Tortilla Strings and Grainy Mustard Vinaigrette (without the tortilla strings) (see page 172), or Green, Gold, and Orange Slaw with Lima Grands (see page 51).

This menu begs for a cool, creamy dessert. Remove individual Peach Tortoni from the freezer and take a well-deserved bow for orchestrating such a fun event. This menu serves eight to ten.

GAME PLAN

1 Month Ahead	**Make pesto for pizza** **Make and freeze Sicilian sauce for pizza**
2 Weeks Ahead	**Make and freeze tortoni**
2 Days Ahead	**Marinate eggplant rolls** **Make caramelized onions for pizza**
1 Day Ahead	**Cook asparagus** **Make couscous filling for mushrooms** **Defrost pizza sauces** **Remove eggplant rolls from marinade and refrigerate** **Prepare mushrooms and toppings for Sicilian Pizza**

DAY OF PARTY

6 Hours Ahead	**Assemble asparagus** **Sauté mushrooms for Sicilian Pizza** **Assemble pizza toppings** **Marinate and stuff mushrooms**
20 Minutes Before Serving	**Slice eggplant** **Assemble and bake pizzas**

EXTRA POINTS

◆ ◆

THE INVITATIONS

Write a message on the top of a personal-size pizza carton and send it in a padded envelope.

THE TABLE

Accent a white tablecloth with strips of red and green felt, broadcloth, or crepe paper in a diagonal or criss-cross pattern. Or use gingham or red-and-white checked cloth and/or napkins. Arrange terra-cotta pots with daisies and candles around the table.

THE KICKER

Take Polaroid pictures of the cooks in action, along with their finished creations, and give them as mementos.

When I cook eggplant, I usually skip the step of salting and draining to remove excess moisture and bitter juices. But in these marinated pinwheels, the eggplant should be as mellow as possible, so it is important to do it.

PREP TIME: 45 minutes including salting and draining eggplant

BAKE TIME: 12 to 14 minutes

MARINADE TIME: 2 to 24 hours

ADVANCE PREP: Marinated rolls may be refrigerated for 2 days.

EGGPLANT ROLLS WITH GARLIC-HERB CHEESE

2 medium eggplants (about 1 pound each)
1 teaspoon salt
½ pound regular or light garlic-herb cheese, softened

Marinade
¼ cup raspberry vinegar
½ cup olive oil

1 garlic clove, minced
1 tablespoon herbes de Provence, fines herbes, or desired blend of dried herbs
Salt and freshly ground black pepper
Fresh herbs or garden leaves, for garnish (see page 10) (optional)

To Prepare Eggplant: Peel eggplant and slice lengthwise into ⅜-inch slices. Place on paper towels, sprinkle with salt and let stand for at least 30 minutes. Pat dry. Preheat oven to 375°F. Line 2 baking sheets with parchment paper or heavy foil; grease or spray with cooking spray. Place eggplant slices on baking sheets and bake for 10 to 14 minutes, turning after 6 minutes, until slices are soft enough to roll. Loosen bottoms with a spatula and leave on sheets to cool to room temperature.

To Assemble: Spread each slice of eggplant with about 2 teaspoons cheese. Roll up jelly-roll fashion. Place, seam side down, in a shallow glass dish.

To Marinate: In a small bowl, whisk together vinegar, oil, garlic, herbs, and salt and pepper to taste. Pour over eggplant rolls, cover with plastic wrap, and refrigerate for at least 2 hours or overnight.

Remove from marinade. (Rolls may be refrigerated covered up to 2 days.)

Before Serving: Cut each roll into 3 pieces. Arrange on a platter and garnish with sprigs of fresh herbs or leaves, if desired.

MAKES: 36 to 40 slices.

ASPARAGUS SPEARS WITH SMOKED SALMON

32 thin asparagus spears

Honey Mustard
1 tablespoon Dijon mustard
1½ teaspoons regular, low-fat,
  or nonfat mayonnaise
1½ teaspoons honey

⅓ **pound smoked salmon, thinly
  sliced**

Freshly ground rainbow
  peppercorns, seasoned pepper
  blend, or black pepper
Smoked salmon roses, for
  garnish (see page 33)
  (optional)

To Cook Asparagus: Cut off bottom of asparagus, leaving spears about 4 inches long. Separate into bundles of 6 to 8 spears each, with tips pointing in the same direction. Tie with string. In a large skillet, bring about 1 inch of water to a boil. Add asparagus and cook, uncovered until just tender, about 4 minutes. Remove bundles, cut string, and run under cold water to stop the cooking. Blot well with paper towels. (Asparagus may be refrigerated wrapped in a double thickness of paper towels overnight.)

To Make Honey Mustard: In a small bowl, stir together mustard, mayonnaise, and honey.

To Assemble: Up to 6 hours before serving, using a very sharp knife, cut slices of salmon in half lengthwise. Spread each with a thin coating of honey mustard. Blot asparagus with paper towels and wrap salmon around middle of 2 spears, spiraling it towards the thick ends. Sprinkle generously with pepper. Refrigerate covered until serving.

Arrange on a platter and garnish with smoked salmon roses, if desired.

MAKES: 16 spears.

Faster: Substitute 4 teaspoons thick storebought honey mustard dressing for the honey mustard.

When you spy pencil-thin asparagus in your market, snatch them up and wind them up with sunset-tinged smoked salmon. (See color photo, page 6.)

PREP TIME: 25 minutes

COOK TIME: About 4 minutes

ADVANCE PREP: Asparagus may be cooked 1 day ahead. Spears may be assembled up to 6 hours before serving.

NUTRITIONAL ANALYSIS

Per appetizer (with nonfat mayonnaise)
22 calories
1 g fat
2 mg cholesterol
111 mg sodium

My now-grown-up daughter Caryn was so fond of vegetables that at the age of eight she gave up eating meat and fish. Although it took her a while to discover couscous, she now makes an entire meal of these marinated stuffed mushrooms—a salad in a bite. The couscous can also be used as a filling for cherry tomatoes or zucchini boats. It makes a great side-dish salad too.

PREP TIME: 30 minutes

MARINADE TIME: 1 to 4 hours

ADVANCE PREP: Filling may be refrigerated overnight. Stuffed mushrooms may be refrigerated up to 6 hours.

NUTRITIONAL ANALYSIS

Per mushroom (with nonfat yogurt)
19 calories
1 g fat
0 cholesterol
37 mg sodium

CONFETTI-CAPPED MUSHROOMS

25 to 30 medium mushrooms (1 pound)

Marinade
¼ cup balsamic vinegar
⅓ cup olive oil
2 garlic cloves, minced
¼ teaspoon salt, or to taste

Couscous Filling
3 tablespoons couscous
½ pickled or fresh seeded jalapeño (½ to ¾ inch) (see page 10)
½ small zucchini, quartered (½ cup chopped)

3 tablespoons fresh cilantro sprigs
⅓ cup finely chopped red bell pepper, chopped by hand
⅓ cup fresh or frozen corn kernels, thawed
⅓ cup cooked or canned black beans, rinsed and patted dry
1 teaspoon ground cumin
2 tablespoons regular, low-fat, or nonfat sour cream or yogurt
Salt
Fresh cilantro sprigs, for garnish (optional)

To Marinate: Wipe mushrooms clean and with a small knife or spoon, cut out stems to make deep cups. Reserve stems for another use. To make marinade, in a plastic zipper bag or glass bowl, combine vinegar, oil, garlic, and salt. Add mushrooms, shake or toss well to coat, and marinate in the refrigerator from 1 to 4 hours, tossing once or twice.

To Make Filling: Place couscous and ⅓ cup water in a medium microwavesafe bowl. Microwave, covered, on high (100%) 3 to 4 minutes, or until water is absorbed. Remove from oven and stir. Meanwhile, in a food processor with the metal blade, process jalapeño until minced, scraping sides. Add zucchini and cilantro and pulse until very finely chopped but not pureed. (Do not process red pepper or it will bleed into the other vegetables.) Remove to a medium bowl and stir in red pepper, corn, beans, cumin, 1 teaspoon marinade from mushrooms, sour cream or yogurt, and salt to taste. (Filling may be refrigerated overnight.)

To Assemble: Up to 6 hours before serving, blot mushrooms with paper towels. Salt the insides and fill with rounded teaspoonfuls of filling. If not serving immediately, cover with plastic wrap and refrigerate up to 6 hours. Before serving, garnish each with a small sprig of cilantro, if desired.

MAKES: 25 to 30 mushrooms.

CARAMELIZED ONION, WALNUT, AND BLUE CHEESE PIZZA

5 medium red onions, peeled
2 tablespoons butter or margarine
Salt and freshly ground black pepper

1 (16-ounce) baked Italian bread shell, such as Boboli
½ cup crumbled blue cheese
½ cup walnut pieces

To Cook Onions: Thinly slice onions by hand or in a food processor with the thin (2 mm) slicing blade; you should have about 5 cups. Melt butter in large skillet. Add onions and cook slowly over low heat, stirring occasionally, until soft and golden. This should take about 30 minutes. It may be necessary to adjust the heat. Season generously with salt and pepper. Cool. (Onions may be refrigerated up to 2 days.)

To Bake: Preheat oven to 450°F.

Place pizza shell on baking sheet. Spread the onion mixture evenly over the top. Sprinkle with blue cheese and walnuts. Bake for 10 minutes. Let cool 2 minutes before slicing.

MAKES: 8 servings.

This pizza with pure California pizzazz owes its roots to talented chef Joyce Goldstein of Square One Restaurant in San Francisco. Cut it into small pieces for a deluxe appetizer.

PREP TIME: 15 minutes

COOK TIME: Onions, 30 minutes

BAKE TIME: 10 minutes

ADVANCE PREP: Cooked onions may be refrigerated up to 2 days.

NUTRITIONAL ANALYSIS

Per serving
313 calories
15 g fat
21 mg cholesterol
677 mg sodium

Although traditional pesto with basil works well on this pizza, one made with cilantro and spicy chiles is far more interesting. For ease in chopping the brie, place it in the freezer for 30 minutes, or until firm, and remove the rind.

PREP TIME: 15 minutes

BAKE TIME: 10 minutes

ADVANCE PREP: Pesto may be refrigerated up to 2 days or frozen.

PESTO, SHRIMP, AND BRIE PIZZA

Cilantro-Jalapeño Pesto
4 garlic cloves, peeled
1 pickled or fresh seeded
    jalapeño (about ¾ to 1 inch)
    (see page 10)
¼ cup grated parmesan cheese
    (1 ounce)
2 tablespoons pine nuts or
    walnuts
¾ cup (loosley packed) cilantro
    leaves

2 tablespoons olive oil
¼ teaspoon salt, or to taste

1 (16-ounce) baked Italian bread
    shell
½ pound uncooked medium
    shrimp, peeled
½ cup finely chopped brie, rind
    removed (2 ounces)
¼ cup shredded regular or low-
    fat mozzarella cheese
    (1 ounce)

Preheat oven to 450°F.

To Make Pesto: In a food processor with the metal blade, process garlic and jalapeño until finely minced. Add parmesan and nuts and process until ground. Add cilantro and pulse 3 or 4 times until coarsely chopped. Add oil and salt and pulse until distributed. (Pesto may be refrigerated up to 2 days or frozen.)

To Bake: Place pizza crust on baking sheet and spread the pesto evenly over the top. Arrange shrimp in circles over pesto. Distribute brie over shrimp and sprinkle with mozzarella. Bake for 10 minutes, or until shrimp are cooked through. Cool 2 minutes before slicing and serving.

MAKES: 8 servings.

NUTRITIONAL ANALYSIS

Per serving (with low-fat
mozzarella)
263 calories
11 g fat
57 mg cholesterol
556 mg sodium

SICILIAN PIZZA

Sicilian Sauce
2 tablespoons olive oil
1 medium onion, chopped
1 tablespoon dried basil
2 teaspoons dried oregano
4 large garlic cloves, minced
2 tablespoons tomato paste
1 can (28 ounces) crushed
    tomatoes with puree or whole
    tomatoes including juice,
    chopped
¼ to ½ teaspoon dried red
    pepper flakes
¾ teaspoon salt, or to taste

1 tablespoon vegetable oil
6 ounces fresh mushrooms,
    thickly sliced

1 (16-ounce) baked Italian bread
    shell
1 cup shredded regular or low-
    fat mozzarella cheese (about
    4 ounces)
1 cup shredded regular or low-
    fat fontina cheese (about
    4 ounces)
1 can (4 ounces) sliced black
    olives, drained
1 can (4¾ ounces) caponata
    eggplant appetizer (optional)
Peperoni, cooked sausage, and/
    or anchovies (optional)

To Make Sauce: Heat oil in a heavy medium saucepan over medium heat. Add onion, basil, and oregano and cook, stirring occasionally, until onion is soft. Stir in garlic and tomato paste and cook, stirring, for 2 minutes. Add tomatoes and bring to a simmer. Break up tomatoes with back of a spoon. Simmer uncovered until sauce is very thick, about 45 minutes. Season with pepper flakes and salt. (Sauce may be refrigerated up to 1 week or frozen). Makes 3 cups sauce, enough for 2 or 3 pizzas.

To Cook Mushrooms: Heat 1 tablespoon oil in a medium skillet over high heat. Add mushrooms and sauté 1 minute. Add 1 tablespoon water and cook over high heat, stirring constantly, until all the juices evaporate and mushrooms begin to brown. (Mushrooms may be refrigerated overnight.)

To Bake: Preheat oven to 450°F.

Place pizza shell on baking sheet and spread with 1½ cups of the sauce. Sprinkle with ½ cup mozzarella and ½ cup fontina. Distribute olives, mushrooms, and caponata, peperoni, sausage, and anchovies, if using, evenly over cheese. Top with remaining cheese. Bake for 10 minutes. Cool several minutes before slicing.

MAKES: 8 servings.

Trendy pizzas come and go, but Americans have remained faithful to the sun-drenched flavors of southern Italy. This thick, robust tomato sauce makes enough for two or three pizzas; you may even wish to double the recipe and keep an extra supply in the freezer.

PREP TIME: 30 minutes

COOK TIME: Sauce, 45 minutes

BAKE TIME: 10 minutes

ADVANCE PREP: Sauce may be refrigerated up to 1 week or frozen. Toppings may be prepared 1 day ahead.

NUTRITIONAL ANALYSIS

Per serving (with low-fat
mozzarella and fontina)
289 calories
12 g fat
11 mg cholesterol
640 mg sodium

Some of the simplest things make your taste buds smile, like these chilled fruity creams with a fruity crunch.

PREP TIME: 20 minutes

FREEZE TIME: At least 6 hours.

ADVANCE PREP: May be frozen up to 2 weeks.

PEACH TORTONI

12 foil muffin papers
½ cup slivered almonds, toasted (see page 11)
½ cup granola without raisins
½ cup graham cracker or gingersnap cookie crumbs

⅓ cup plus ½ cup peach jam or preserves, divided
1½ pints frozen vanilla yogurt or ice cream, softened slightly
3 tablespoons peach schnapps

Place muffin papers in muffin cups.

In a medium bowl, stir together almonds, granola, crumbs, and ⅓ cup peach jam. Spoon 1 teaspoon into bottom of each muffin cup, pressing in lightly.

Spoon yogurt or ice cream into a medium bowl and stir in ½ cup jam and peach schnapps. Spoon a heaping tablespoon into each cup. Top with 1 teaspoon crumbs and another heaping tablespoon peach mixture. Sprinkle remaining crumbs over the top. Cover with foil and freeze until firm. (Tortoni may be frozen up to 2 weeks.) If desired, pull off paper before serving.

MAKES: 12 tortoni.

Change of Pace: To make Peach Tortoni Pie increase recipe by half: For crumb mixture, combine ¾ cup almonds, ¾ cup granola, ¾ cup crumbs and ½ cup jam and press a third into bottom of 9-inch pie plate. Stir ¾ cup jam and 4½ tablespoons peach schnapps into 2½ pints frozen yogurt or ice cream. Spoon half over crumbs, sprinkle with half the remaining crumbs, add the remaining peach mixture, and top with remaining crumbs.

NUTRITIONAL ANALYSIS

Per serving (with graham cracker crumbs, low-fat frozen yogurt)
196 calories
4 g fat
7 mg cholesterol
32 mg sodium

Menu

◆

HORS D'OEUVRES FROM SOUTHEAST ASIA:

MINI THAI CRAB CAKES

·

RANGOON SPRING ROLLS IN PHYLLO

◆

SOUP FROM INDIA:

BENGAL CURRY APPLE SOUP WITH SAMBALS

·

SPICED POPADAMS

◆

SALAD AND ENTREE FROM ITALY:

TUSCAN BREAD SALAD WITH ROMAINE RIBBONS

·

GRATIN OF POLENTA, TOMATOES, AND WILD MUSHROOMS

◆

DESSERT FROM NEW ORLEANS:

CHOCOLATE–CARAMEL PRALINE ROLL

◆

AROUND THE WORLD COFFEE BAR

PROGRESSIVE DINNER AROUND *The* WORLD

When hankering for an adventurous soiree with little time to spare, enlist a group of fellow enthusiasts for a culinary journey spanning the globe. As coordinator, ask the participants to choose a course they would like to serve at their house, and either give them a recipe or let them use their own. Each of the dishes in this menu requires a minimum of reheating, so the food will be ready soon after the voyagers arrive, you among them. Here are some tips for serving, as well as theme suggestions for those who want to do more than just prepare food. This menu serves ten to twelve people, allowing for extra appetizers.

GAME PLAN

There is none. This menu is designed to be eaten in progress—not in one home.

◆ EXTRA POINTS ◆

THE INVITATIONS

Use a copied page of a passport listing the times, ports of call, and hosts for each course. For example: 5:30 Appetizers—Port of Hong Kong, The Smiths; 6:45 Soup—Bay of Bengal, The Johnsons.

FIRST STOP:
Southeast Asia for appetizers

Both the Mini Thai Crab Cakes and Rangoon Spring Rolls in Phyllo bake in the same oven at the same temperature for a short time. To keep the spring rolls crisp, do not crowd them on the baking sheet. Both appetizers use the same dipping sauce so you might want to provide each guest with an individual bowl. (Chinese teacups work well.) A chilled, quickly assembled alternative would be Crudités with Peanut Dipping Sauce (see page 212). You won't need a centerpiece for the cocktail hour, but to enhance the Asian theme, you could serve the appetizers on straw or brass platters garnished with orchids and paper parasols.

SECOND PORT:
India for soup

Sambals, or condiments, enhance the exotic but simple to prepare Bengal Curry Apple Soup. For a dramatic presentation, line a large copper or brass vessel or bucket with fabric and tuck the bowl or tureen of soup in it. Accompany the soup with crisp, crackly popadams. Set the table with brightly colored cloth or paper table runners accented with swirls of chiffon, netting, or tissue lamé. Use a profusion of colored napkins, embroidered fabrics, and any brass or copper pieces and accessories you have, like bells, vases, and candlesticks.

THIRD STOP:
Italy for the entree

Rustic terra-cotta pots filled with basil, rosemary, and bouquets of loose blossoms; red white and green tablecloths or place mats; posters with gondoliers; and strains of ''That's Amore'' set the scene. Make, reheat, and serve the Gratin of Polenta, Tomatoes, and Wild Mushrooms in a brass or pottery casserole and toss the salad in an earthenware bowl. For a centerpiece, scoop out an Italian bread, fill it with floral foam, and stick flowers and groupings of pasta into it. Stuff napkins into dried manicotti pasta for napkin rings.

FOURTH PORT:
New Orleans for dessert

With the first bite of the Chocolate–Caramel Praline Roll, guests will think themselves on Bourbon Street. You may wish to serve coffee or tea with the cake. Decorate the table and platter with glittery beads, glitzy masks and dazzling feathers. The more the better.

FINAL DESTINATION:
Rio de Janeiro for a coffee extravaganza

Complete your journey at a coffee buffet with recipe cards for make-your-own coffees. Rent or borrow coffee urns, servers, or thermos pots as well as Irish coffee mugs or tempered footed glasses. Cover the table with world maps and decorate with globes (inflatable ones are fine), toothpick flags, and various replicas of modes of transportation—ships, cars, trains, planes, and even hot air balloons. Bon voyage!

My friend Barbara Tropp, chef/owner of China Moon in San Francisco, inspired me to infuse good old American crab cakes with the flavors of Asia. It may take a trip to a specialty market to find unsweetened coconut milk and Chinese chile sauce, but these hors d'oeuvres are well worth the detour.

PREP TIME: 25 minutes

CHILL TIME: At least 30 minutes

BAKE TIME: 12 to 15 minutes

ADVANCE PREP: May be refrigerated overnight or frozen. Sauce may be refrigerated indefinitely.

NUTRITIONAL ANALYSIS

Per crab cake
24 calories
1 g fat
6 mg cholesterol
132 mg sodium

Per teaspoon dipping sauce
2 calories
less than 1 g fat
0 cholesterol
229 mg sodium

MINI THAI CRAB CAKES

2 slices French or Italian bread, crusts removed (¾ cup fresh bread crumbs)
1 cup (lightly packed) cilantro leaves
1 piece peeled fresh ginger, (about 1 × 1½ inches)
2 medium green onions with tops, cut into 1-inch pieces
2 teaspoons Chinese chile sauce (see page 10)
½ cup unsweetened coconut milk (see page 10)

1 tablespoon fresh lime juice
2 tablespoons fruit-based chutney, such as Major Grey mango chutney
1 egg or 2 egg whites, lightly beaten
1 pound fresh crabmeat, picked over and blotted dry with paper towels

Asian Dipping Sauce
½ cup soy sauce
3 tablespoons rice wine vinegar

To Make Crab Cakes: In a food processor with the metal blade, process bread into crumbs. Measure ¾ cup and remove to a medium bowl; discard the rest. In same processor bowl, process cilantro, ginger, and green onions until minced. Add chile sauce and coconut milk and pulse until incorporated. Add lime juice, chutney, and egg and pulse 3 or 4 times to incorporate. Stir crabmeat into bread crumbs. Add contents of food processor and stir gently to combine. Cover and refrigerate for at least 30 minutes or overnight to firm up.

To Make Sauce: In a small bowl, stir together soy sauce, vinegar, and 1 tablespoon water. (Sauce may be refrigerated indefinitely.)

To Bake: Place rack in upper third of oven and preheat to 400°F. Grease or spray a baking sheet. Using about 1 tablespoon crab mixture per cake, gently shape into small mounds and place about 1 inch apart on baking sheet. Bake for 12 to 15 minutes, or until golden. (Crab cakes may be refrigerated overnight or frozen. Reheat uncovered at 400°F. for 10 minutes or until hot.) Serve hot or at room temperature with dipping sauce.

MAKES: about 40 crab cakes.

RANGOON SPRING ROLLS IN PHYLLO

Filling
About 2 ounces bean threads or cellophane noodles (half a 3¾-ounce package)
1 ounce dried shiitake mushrooms (1 cup)
⅓ cup chunky or smooth peanut butter
2 tablespoons plus 2 teaspoons soy sauce
2 tablespoons raspberry vinegar
1 to 2 teaspoons Chinese chile sauce (see page 10)

½ small head green cabbage
1 large carrot, peeled
1 piece peeled fresh ginger (about 1 × 1 inch)
4 garlic cloves, peeled
4 green onions, cut into chunks
2 tablespoons sesame oil

1 pound phyllo dough (see page 12), at room temperature
3 egg whites
⅓ cup olive oil
Asian Dipping Sauce (see page 158)

To Make Filling: Place 3 cups water in a large microwavesafe bowl, cover, and microwave on high (100%) for 5 to 6 minutes, or until boiling. Add bean threads and mushrooms (they will separate when heated), cover with plastic wrap or lid, and microwave on high (100%) for 4 to 5 minutes, or until soft. Let steep 10 minutes. Drain, cut off stems from mushrooms, and squeeze dry. With scissors, cut noodles into about thirds.

Meanwhile, in a medium bowl, stir together peanut butter, soy sauce, vinegar, ¼ cup water, and chile sauce to taste. Set aside. With a knife or slicing blade (4 mm) of food processor, slice cabbage into ¼ × 1-inch long shreds. Remove to a bowl. In food processor with the shredding disc or with a hand grater, shred carrot. Add to cabbage. With the metal blade, pulse ginger and garlic until minced. Add green onions and mushrooms and pulse into small pieces. In a medium skillet over medium high heat, heat sesame oil until hot. Sauté mushroom mixture, carrots, and cabbage, stirring, for 3 to 5 minutes, or until softened slightly but still crisp. Stir in peanut butter mixture and bean threads.

To Assemble: Grease or spray baking sheets. In a small bowl, whisk together egg whites and olive oil until frothy. Remove 2 sheets phyllo from package. Cover remaining sheets so they don't dry out. Brush 1 sheet lightly with egg white mixture. Top with second sheet and brush again. Cut into 6 rectangles by first cutting in half crosswise, and then cutting each half into 3 strips. Place 1 tablespoon filling on one end of each rectangle, leaving ½-inch border on sides. Roll up egg-roll style by rolling once lengthwise, tucking in sides and continuing to roll.

(continued)

These little phyllo-wrapped packets are ample appetizers of fresh vegetables and cellophane noodles, bound with peanut sauce. Brushing the phyllo with a mixture of egg white and olive oil gives the rolls an extra-crisp, substantial glaze, making them especially durable for freezing.

PREP TIME: 60 to 90 minutes

BAKE TIME: 14 to 18 minutes

ADVANCE PREP: Baked rolls may be refrigerated overnight or frozen.

NUTRITIONAL ANALYSIS

Per spring roll (not including dipping sauce)
83 calories
4 g fat
0 cholesterol
87 mg sodium

Brush top and sides with egg white mixture and place on baking sheet, seam side down, at least 1 inch apart. Repeat with remaining phyllo and filling.

To Bake: Preheat oven to 400°F. Bake for 14 to 18 minutes, or until edges and bottoms are golden brown and tops are tan and crispy. If baking 2 sheets in 1 oven, rotate halfway through the baking time. (Baked rolls may be refrigerated overnight or frozen up to 1 month. Reheat frozen or defrost uncovered in single layers at room temperature for 1 hour. Reheat at 400°F. for 8 minutes if defrosted, 12 minutes if frozen, or until heated through.) Serve with dipping sauce.

MAKES: about 40.

BENGAL CURRY APPLE SOUP WITH SAMBALS

1½ ounces dried shiitake mushrooms (1½ cups)

3 cups plus 4½ cups chicken broth, divided

1 cup sherry, sweet or dry

2 tablespoons olive oil

3 pounds fresh mushrooms, cleaned and sliced ¼ inch thick

5 tablespoons all-purpose flour

1½ teaspoons turmeric

2¼ teaspoons ground ginger

2¼ teaspoons ground cumin

2¼ teaspoons curry powder

¾ teaspoon ground coriander

3 medium tart green apples, peeled and chopped into ½-inch pieces (about 3¾ cups)

¾ cup heavy cream

Sambals or Condiments, for Serving

5 tablespoons minced jalapeños

1 cup chopped green onions

1½ cups toasted coconut (see page 12)

1½ cups chopped dry-roasted peanuts or cashews

To Prepare Mushrooms: Place shiitakes, 3 cups chicken broth, and sherry in an 8-cup microwavesafe bowl. Cover with plastic wrap and microwave on high (100%) for 6 to 8 minutes or until boiling. Remove and let steep 10 minutes. Remove mushrooms from liquid, cut off stems, and slice caps into ¼-inch strips about ¾ inch long. Set aside liquid.

To Make Soup: In a large soup pot, heat olive oil over medium-high heat until hot. Add sliced fresh mushrooms and sauté, stirring, until soft, about 5 minutes. Stir in flour. Stir in reserved broth-sherry mixture, remaining 4½ cups chicken broth, shiitakes, spices, apples, and cream. Bring to a boil, stirring occasionally. Reduce heat and simmer 15 minutes, stirring occasionally. (The soup may be refrigerated up to 2 days. Reheat before serving. The condiments, except for the green onions, may be prepared 2 days ahead.) Serve soup in individual bowls accompanied by small bowls of the sambals.

MAKES: 12 servings.

Leaner: Reduce cream to ⅓ cup or eliminate it.

My son Kenny is an avid enthusiast of fine food, so when he returned from India raving about a special curried broth brimming with sweet apples and dark, woodsy mushrooms, I was determined to duplicate it. Although my kitchen is near the Chesapeake Bay, not the Bay of Bengal, my version transports him to those distant shores. The taste of this soup is tempered so guests can spike their own with sambals or condiments.

PREP TIME: 40 minutes

COOK TIME: 30 minutes

ADVANCE PREP: May be refrigerated up to 2 days.

NUTRITIONAL ANALYSIS

Per serving (not including condiments)

191 calories

9 g fat

21 mg cholesterol

341 mg sodium

SPICED POPADAMS

For a crisp bread replacement, look for packages of wafer-thin East Indian lentil bread called popadams (also spelled popadums) at your local supermarket or Indian specialty store. They are fun to cook, because when they hit hot oil, they puff up to almost double their volume. They come with or without spices (I prefer the spiced variety) and in various sizes, usually around four inches. Plan on two popadams per person. A four-ounce package usually contains twelve. Since the package directions are so sketchy, here are more detailed ones.

COOK TIME: About 40 minutes for 20 popadams

ADVANCE PREP: May be stored at room temperature up to 2 weeks or frozen.

NUTRITIONAL ANALYSIS

Per 2 popadams
78 calories
2 g fat
0 cholesterol
275 mg sodium

Line a baking sheet with paper towels. In a wok or deep skillet over medium heat, heat 2 to 3 inches of oil to 400°F. on a deep-fry thermometer, or until a small cube of bread browns in 40 seconds. Fry 1 to 2 popadams at a time by dropping each gently but quickly into hot oil. Be careful. They will grow and curl within 2 seconds. Quickly turn with tongs and fry on other side, about 2 seconds more. They should be pale brown, a shade lighter than camel, but not golden. Remove to baking sheet to drain, propping them on their sides to drain off as much oil as possible. (Popadams may be stored in an airtight container up to 2 weeks or frozen. Defrost and serve at room temperature.)

TUSCAN BREAD SALAD WITH ROMAINE RIBBONS

9 cups Italian bread with crusts, cut into 1-inch cubes (10-ounce loaf)

Italian Vinaigrette
⅓ cup chicken or vegetable broth
¼ cup balsamic vinegar
¼ cup plus 2 teaspoons fresh lemon juice (see page 11)
2 medium garlic cloves, minced
½ cup olive oil
½ cup regular, low-fat, or nonfat plain yogurt
¼ teaspoon salt, or to taste
Freshly ground black pepper

Salad
1 medium red onion, halved and thinly sliced
1 seedless or 2 regular cucumbers, cut into ½-inch cubes (about 4 cups)
⅔ cup sliced kalamata olives (see page 12)
3 tablespoons capers, rinsed and drained
2 heads romaine lettuce, cut into 1-inch strips, with ribs (about 12 cups)

To Toast Bread Cubes: Preheat oven to 350°F.

Place bread cubes on baking sheet and bake for 20 to 25 minutes, tossing occasionally, until crisp and dry. If necessary, leave in turned-off oven until thoroughly dry in the center. Cool to room temperature. (Bread cubes may be stored airtight for several days or frozen.)

To Make Vinaigrette: In a medium bowl, whisk together broth, vinegar, lemon juice, and garlic. Whisk in oil and yogurt until thoroughly blended. Season with salt and pepper to taste. Do not use food processor or it will break down yogurt. (Dressing may be refrigerated up to 3 days. It will thicken as it sits. Shake or stir well before using.)

To Assemble Salad: About 5 minutes before serving, place onion, cucumbers, olives, capers, and bread cubes in salad bowl. Add half the vinaigrette and toss to coat. Let stand at room temperature 5 minutes. Add lettuce and remaining vinaigrette, toss, and serve immediately.

MAKES: 10 to 12 servings.

This is an adaptation of the classic Tuscan bread salad, which was created as a way of using up stale bread but included no greens. The bread cubes are toasted until crisp and then tossed in the dressing about five minutes before serving, so the outside softens, but the inside remains crunchy.

PREP TIME: 30 minutes

TOAST BREAD: 20 to 25 minutes

ADVANCE PREP: Bread cubes may be stored at room temperature for several days or frozen. Dressing may be refrigerated up to 3 days. Lettuce may be refrigerated overnight.

NUTRITIONAL ANALYSIS

Per serving (with nonfat yogurt)
219 calories
3 g fat
less than 1 mg cholesterol
566 mg sodium

Substitute creamy layers of polenta for traditional lasagna noodles and alternate them in a rustic earthenware or copper casserole with a chunky tomato-meat sauce and sprinkles of parmesan cheese for a dish worthy of any occasion. To multiply the recipe, do not double the polenta; you need to make it twice. The sauce, however, may be doubled or even tripled.

PREP TIME: 30 minutes

COOK TIME: Sauce, 75 minutes; polenta, 25 to 35 minutes

BAKE TIME: 20 minutes plus 20 minutes standing time

ADVANCE PREP: Unbaked casserole may be refrigerated up to 2 days or frozen.

NUTRITIONAL ANALYSIS

Per serving (with milk)
274 calories
12 g fat
38 mg cholesterol
827 mg sodium

GRATIN OF POLENTA, TOMATOES, AND WILD MUSHROOMS

Polenta
2 cups yellow cornmeal
6½ cups water
2 teaspoons salt

Tomato Sauce
1 ounce dried wild mushrooms, such as shiitake or porcini (about 1 cup)
3 medium garlic cloves, peeled
1 medium onion, peeled and quartered
2 medium carrots, peeled and cut into 1-inch pieces
1 medium celery stalk, cut into 1-inch pieces

2 tablespoons olive oil
1 pound lean ground beef
1 teaspoon salt, or to taste
1 cup dry white wine or imported dry vermouth
1 can (28 ounces) Italian plum tomatoes, coarsely chopped, with juice
3 tablespoons tomato paste
¼ cup heavy cream or whole milk
Salt and freshly ground black pepper
⅔ cup grated parmesan cheese

To Make Polenta: Place cornmeal, water, and salt in a 3 to 4-quart microwavesafe bowl or casserole. Microwave, covered, on high (100%), stirring every 6 minutes, for 25 to 35 minutes, or until the mixture is thick enough to form soft mounds, but still jiggles when the bowl is shaken. Grease or spray a large, flat baking sheet and spread polenta into a ¼-inch-thick 12 × 18-inch rectangle. To spread evenly, cover with a sheet of wax paper and roll with rolling pin. Let stand, covered, until cool and firm. (Polenta can be refrigerated up to 2 days or frozen. If desired, divide in quarters and wrap in foil.)

To Make Sauce: Place mushrooms in a small microwavesafe bowl, add 1 cup water, and microwave, covered, on high (100%) for 2 to 3 minutes, or until very hot. Soak for 15 minutes, or until soft. Reserve liquid. Squeeze mushrooms dry, remove tough stems, and chop caps into ½-inch pieces.

Meanwhile, in a food processor with the metal blade, chop garlic. Add onion, carrots, and celery and pulse until finely chopped. Heat olive oil in a large skillet over medium-high heat and sauté vegetables for 2 minutes. Add ¼ cup water, cover, and simmer over medium-low heat until soft, about 10 minutes, stirring every 3 minutes. Increase heat to medium-high, add ground beef and salt, and sauté, breaking the meat up with a fork, until lightly browned, about 5 minutes. If necessary, drain off fat. Stir in mushroom liquid and wine. Bring to a boil, lower heat, and simmer until most of the liquid has evaporated, about 10 minutes. Add tomatoes with their juice, tomato paste, and cream or milk. Cook over low heat, stirring occasionally, until thickened, about 40 minutes. Stir in mushrooms and simmer 10 minutes more. Season to taste with salt and pepper. (Sauce may be refrigerated up to 2 days or frozen.)

To Assemble: Arrange half the polenta in bottom of a greased 9 × 13-inch casserole, cutting and patching to fit. Spoon half the sauce over and sprinkle with half the cheese. Repeat with another layer of each. (Casserole may be refrigerated up to 2 days or frozen up to 1 month. Bring to room temperature before baking.)

To Bake: Preheat oven to 450°F. Bake, uncovered, in middle of oven for 20 minutes, or until heated through and sides are bubbling. Let stand 20 minutes before serving.

MAKES: 10 to 12 servings.

Leaner: Substitute 1 pound freshly ground chicken or turkey breast for the beef.

CHOCOLATE–CARAMEL PRALINE ROLL

Chocolate Cake Roll
⅓ cup plus 1 tablespoon cocoa,
   preferably Droste Dutch
   process
2 tablespoons butter or
   margarine, at room
   temperature
4 tablespoons boiling water
1 teaspoon vanilla extract
6 large eggs, separated
½ cup plus ¼ cup sugar, divided
2 tablespoons all-purpose flour

Caramel Praline Filling
¾ cup chopped pecans
1 cup sugar

2 tablespoons light corn syrup
4 tablespoons (½ stick) butter or
   margarine, at room
   temperature
½ cup plus ¾ cup heavy cream

Chocolate Glaze and Garnish
4 ounces semisweet chocolate,
   chopped
½ cup heavy cream
1 tablespoon light corn syrup
1 teaspoon vanilla extract
8 to 16 pecan halves, for garnish

To Make Cake: Preheat the oven to 350°F. Line a 15½ × 10½ × 1-inch rimmed baking sheet (jelly-roll pan) with parchment or foil, allowing several inches to extend over short ends. Grease or spray the paper (if using foil, flour it also).

Place cocoa and butter in a small bowl. Stir in boiling water and vanilla. In a large mixing bowl with electric mixer, beat egg yolks with ½ cup sugar until very light, about 5 minutes. On low speed, mix in chocolate. Mix in flour. In small mixing bowl with clean beaters, beat egg whites until soft peaks form. Slowly mix in remaining ¼ cup sugar, beating until stiff peaks form. Fold whites into chocolate mixture. Pour batter into prepared pan, spreading evenly. Bake for 20 to 24 minutes, or until cake springs back when lightly pressed and sides begin to pull away from pan. Remove from oven and immediately place a damp dish towel directly over the top. Cool to room temperature.

To Make Filling: Toast pecans at 350°F. for 10 to 15 minutes, or until golden. Meanwhile, in a heavy medium saucepan, stir together sugar, ¼ cup water, and corn syrup. Bring to a boil over medium heat and boil, without stirring, until mixture turns amber in color, about 4 to 6 minutes. When the sugar begins to color around the sides of the pan, it is all right to stir. Remove from heat and immediately stir in hot pecans. Carefully stir in butter and ½ cup cream. The mixture will bubble. Cool to room temperature. (Caramel may be held, covered, at room temperature up to 2 hours, if desired.)

This melt-in-your-mouth chocolate cake roll may be the most popular dessert I've ever taught. The trick to candying the nuts is to make sure they are hot when you drop them into the caramel. If you toast them ahead of time, wrap them in foil and reheat them in the oven or toaster oven.

PREP TIME: Cake, 20 minutes; Filling, 20 minutes; Frosting, 10 minutes

BAKE TIME: 20 to 24 minutes

CHILL TIME: 4 hours

ADVANCE PREP: Unfrosted cake may be refrigerated up to 2 days or frozen. Frosted cake may be refrigerated overnight.

NUTRITIONAL ANALYSIS

Per serving
534 calories
37 g fat
203 mg cholesterol
131 mg sodium

Whip remaining ¾ cup cream until stiff peaks form. Add caramel and mix on high speed only until incorporated, about 30 seconds. Do not overmix or cream will separate.

To Assemble: Lift cake with paper or foil out of the pan and place on a work surface. Spread filling over cake. Beginning with a short end, roll the cake up, using the paper to help roll. Wrap tightly in foil and refrigerate for several hours before frosting. (Cake may be refrigerated up to 2 days or frozen up to 1 month.)

To Frost and Garnish: Cut a piece of cardboard smaller than the cake roll and place cake on it. Set on a rack over a baking sheet. Place chocolate, cream, and corn syrup in a medium microwavesafe bowl. Microwave, uncovered, on high for 1 to 2 minutes, or until chocolate is melted and smooth. Stir in vanilla. Dip half of each pecan half in the chocolate and place on a baking sheet lined with wax paper. Freeze until firm.

Pour remaining chocolate glaze over the cake, tilting to cover, and spreading with a knife only if necessary. (If glaze is too thick, rewarm in microwave.) Arrange pecans in a line of Vs across top of cake. Refrigerate until serving. (Cake may be refrigerated overnight.)

MAKES: 8 to 10 servings.

AROUND THE WORLD COFFEE BAR

Kaffee Vienna
1 cup hot coffee
Unwhipped heavy cream
1 cinnamon stick
Grated chocolate
Ground nutmeg

Mexican Fiesta
1 cup hot coffee
1 ounce Grand Marnier
1 ounce Kahlúa
1 teaspoon sugar
Twist of orange peel
Cinnamon stick

Café del Rio
1 cup coffee
1 ounce amaretto liqueur
1 ounce cognac or brandy
Whipped cream

Café de Bruxelles
1 cup hot coffee
1 ounce chocolate mint liqueur
Whipped cream
Chocolate mint stick
Grated chocolate

For an international closing to a grand event, offer rich strong coffee like Viennese or French roast (both regular and decaf). Set your buffet with bowls of whipped and unwhipped cream, grated dark and white chocolate, cinnamon sticks, colored party sugar, chocolate mint sticks, and twists of orange peel. Put out an array of liqueurs such as brandy or cognac, Kahlúa, amaretto, chocolate mint, Grand Marnier, and appropriate spices. Write out cards with instructions for making the various coffees.

POTLUCK PARTY

Back in 1956, at the height of the can-opener era, the Culinary Arts Institute's *Casserole Cookbook* declared, "Every homemaker dreams of creating memorable main dishes. These dreams come true when she's cooking a casserole. Often, with minutes and hours so precious, she can fill her convenient casserole the day or night before—or even a month before if she has a freezer." These dishes, often a merger of cans (usually condensed soups) and refrigerator remnants, became the basis for a whole genre of parties—the potluck or covered-dish supper. Each guest would bring a different casserole, from chafing dish hors d'oeuvres to cobblers or custards, and, according to Barbara I. Gillard's book *Potluck* (1952), "the only rule is everything has to be made ahead of time and reheated at the party."

Today we are witnessing a revival of co-op cooking. When you consider the money, time, and energy saved, this is good luck for everyone. In the past too many cooks might have spoiled the broth; these days there are often too few cooks, and sometimes no broth at all.

Potluck parties take some coordinating and there are several ways to synchronize them:

- The host chooses the entree and each guest selects a course to complement it.
- The participants all get together and decide what they want to prepare.
- The host plans the entire menu and gives each guest a recipe.

Remember, the method you choose to put the food on the table is secondary to being together with friends and having fun. My only rule is that whoever makes the dish brings everything needed to serve it—garnishes, platters, serving utensils, and so on.

Each of the dishes in this menu is self-contained, sturdy, and vehicle tested. Use a bath towel as a brace to keep them from slipping, to insulate the heat, and catch any mishaps. Mexican Chicken Lasagna fits all the fifties criteria for a communal casserole—and it's probably the easiest lasagna you'll ever throw together. It's a great selection for teen parties as well as grown-up get-togethers. Pork Picadillo (see page 78) and Veal and Orzo with a Garlic Crumb Crust (see page 252) also tote well. For lighter meals consider any of the sandwiches. Tuscan Bread Salad with Romaine Ribbons (see page 163) or Green, Gold, and Orange Slaw with Lima Grands (see page 51) make good alternatives for the Garden Salad with Tortilla Strings.

And, "if they finish everything on their plate," bring out another throwback to the fifties, a bundt cake. You'll find my apricot-almond one a far cry from the cake-mix versions of the past (and a tube pan will work just as well). You might also want to offer the Pear, Raspberry, and Rhubarb Crisp (see page 144). This menu serves eight.

GAME PLAN
For the host who prefers cooking solo

1 Month Ahead	**Make and freeze cake** **Make and freeze tortilla strings**
2 Weeks Ahead	**Make and freeze lasagna**
3 Days Ahead	**Make vinaigrette for salad**
1 Day Ahead	**Make salsa and prepare vegetables for dipping** **Defrost lasagna** **Prepare salad ingredients** **Defrost tortilla strings** **Defrost cake at room temperature**

DAY OF PARTY

2 Hours Ahead	**Bring lasagna to room temperature**
30 Minutes Ahead	**Reheat lasagna**
Shortly Before Serving	**Toss salad**

EXTRA POINTS

There are none—the whole point here is friendly simplicity with a minimum of effort.

Sometimes the best recipes are made by combining two old favorites—in this case spicy salsa with creamy guacamole.

PREP TIME: 10 minutes

CHILL TIME: 1 hour

ADVANCE PREP: May be refrigerated overnight.

GUACAMOLE AND CORN SALSA

½ pickled or fresh seeded jalapeño (½ to ¾ inch) (see page 10)
2 garlic cloves, peeled
3 green onions with tops, cut into 2-inch pieces
½ cup (loosely packed) cilantro leaves
1 celery stalk, cut into 2-inch pieces
⅔ cup chicken or vegetable broth

2 tablespoons fresh lime juice
1 avocado, peeled, pitted, and cut into chunks
⅔ cup fresh or frozen corn, thawed
Salt
Chips and/or vegetables, such as carrots, celery, cucumber, jícama, and radishes, for dipping

In a food processor with the metal blade, pulse jalapeño and garlic until minced. Add green onions, cilantro, and celery and pulse until chopped. Add broth, lime juice, and avocado and pulse until coarsely chopped. Add corn and pulse 2 or 3 times to incorporate; the mixture should be chunky.

Remove to a bowl and refrigerate for at least 1 hour. (Salsa may be refrigerated overnight. Pour off excess liquid before serving.) Serve with chips and/or vegetables.

MAKES: 2 cups.

Per 2 tablespoons
25 calories
2 g fat
0 cholesterol
41 mg sodium

MEXICAN CHICKEN LASAGNA

Tomato-Salsa Sauce
½ medium onion, cut into
 quarters
1 can (28 ounces) whole
 tomatoes with juice
½ cup jarred salsa picante or
 chunky salsa, medium or mild
1 package (1¼ ounces) taco
 seasoning mix
1 can (16 ounces) black beans,
 rinsed and drained

Ricotta Cheese Layer
1 large egg

1 cup whole or skim milk ricotta
 cheese
2 garlic cloves, minced

10 uncooked dried lasagna
 noodles
4 boneless, skinless chicken
 breast halves, cut into 1-inch
 cubes (about 1 pound)
1 can (4 ounces) whole green
 chiles, cut into thin strips
1½ cups shredded regular or
 low-fat sharp cheddar, jack, or
 mozzarella cheese or a
 combination (about 6 ounces)

Preheat oven to 350°F. Grease a 9 × 13-inch casserole.

To Make Sauce: In a food processor with the metal blade, chop onion. Add tomatoes with juice, salsa, and taco seasoning and pulse until tomatoes are in small pieces, 3 or 4 times. Remove to a medium bowl and stir in beans.

To Make Ricotta Layer: In a small bowl with a fork, break up egg. Stir in ricotta and garlic.

To Assemble: Spread 1 cup sauce over the bottom; it will barely cover. Top with 5 noodles, overlapping slightly. Sprinkle with half the chicken, half the chiles, and 2 cups sauce. Spoon ricotta cheese mixture over and spread lightly. Top with half the shredded cheese, remaining noodles, chicken, chiles, sauce, and cheese.

To Bake: Bake, uncovered, for 40 minutes, or until noodles are tender when pierced with a sharp knife. Cool at least 20 minutes before serving. The casserole will stay warm for up to 1 hour and can be reheated, if desired. (Lasagna may be refrigerated overnight or frozen up to 2 weeks. Bring to room temperature and reheat, covered, at 375°F. for 20 minutes or in a microwave until heated through.)

MAKES: 12 servings.

Leaner: Omit ricotta cheese layer—lasagna will still taste great. Reduce amount of shredded cheese as desired.

A taste of this dish be-
lies its ease of prepa-
ration—it requires no
precooking of
chicken, sauce, or
noodles. If you make the
sauce with medium-hot
salsa, the casserole will have
a hint of heat. Extremely
temperate tastes might prefer mild salsa; fiery ones, a
hotter variety.

PREP TIME: 20 minutes

BAKE TIME: 40 minutes
plus 20 minutes standing
time

ADVANCE PREP: May be
refrigerated up to 2 days or
frozen.

NUTRITIONAL ANALYSIS

Per serving (with low-fat
cheddar and ricotta cheeses)
253 calories
6 g fat
84 mg cholesterol
614 mg sodium

I can never get enough of this pretty salad. The yogurt in the dressing does a wonderful job of coating the fruit and greens and adds its own tang as well.

PREP TIME: Salad and dressing, 15 minutes; tortilla strings, 5 minutes

BAKE TIME: Tortilla strings, 15 minutes

ADVANCE PREP: Tortilla strings may be frozen. Dressing may be refrigerated up to 3 days. Salad ingredients may be prepared a day ahead.

GARDEN SALAD WITH TORTILLA STRINGS AND GRAINY MUSTARD VINAIGRETTE

Tortilla Strings
4 corn tortillas, halved and cut crosswise into thin strips

Grainy Mustard Vinaigrette
2 tablespoons balsamic vinegar
2 tablespoons grainy mustard, such as Moutarde de Meaux
¼ cup olive oil
⅓ cup orange juice
1 medium garlic clove, minced
½ cup regular, low-fat, or nonfat plain yogurt
Salt and freshly ground black pepper

Salad
8 cups loosely packed spinach leaves, washed, stemmed, and cut into ½-inch strips (about ½ pound stemmed)
8 cups Boston or butter lettuce, washed and torn into 1-inch pieces (about ¾ pound)
1 cup sliced radishes
2 papayas or mangos, peeled, pitted, and cut into ½-inch cubes

To Make Tortilla Strings: Preheat oven to 350°F. Place tortilla strips on large baking sheet. Bake for 15 minutes, or until pale golden and crisp. Cool to room temperature. (Strings may be stored airtight for several weeks or frozen.)

To Make Vinaigrette: In a medium bowl, whisk all ingredients until blended. Refrigerate until ready to serve. (May be refrigerated up to 3 days.)

Before Serving: Place salad greens in large bowl. Add radishes and fruit and toss with as much dressing as desired. Season to taste with salt and pepper. Top with tortilla strips.

MAKES: 8 servings

Change of Pace: Two cups chopped fresh pineapple, cantaloupe, or oranges may be substituted for the papaya or mango.

APRICOT-ALMOND MARBLE POUND CAKE

Cake

1½ cups dried apricots (about ½ pound)

½ cup apricot brandy

7 to 8 ounces almond paste, preferably Odense brand

6 ounces (1½ sticks) unsalted butter or margarine, softened

1½ cups sugar

6 large eggs

2 teaspoons vanilla extract

½ teaspoon almond extract

2¼ cups all-purpose flour

2 teaspoons baking powder

½ teaspoon salt

¾ cup regular or light sour cream

Apricot Brandy Glaze

2 cups confectioners' sugar

4 tablespoons apricot brandy

1 to 3 tablespoons milk or heavy cream

Apricot halves, for garnish (optional)

Sliced almonds, for garnish (optional)

To Make Cake: Preheat oven to 350°F. Place apricots in a medium microwavesafe bowl. Pour brandy over, cover, and microwave on high (100%) for 2 to 4 minutes, or until apricots are soft. Uncover and cool slightly.

In a large mixing bowl with electric mixer, beat almond paste and butter until smooth, about 3 minutes. Gradually add sugar and beat on high until creamy, about 2 minutes. Add eggs and beat 3 to 4 minutes until the mixture is very well blended. (It may look slightly curdled.) Beat in vanilla and almond extracts. On low speed, mix in flour, baking powder, salt, and sour cream. Increase speed to high and mix 1 minute until incorporated.

In a food processor with the metal blade, puree apricots with brandy. Add 1¾ cups of the batter and process until blended, about 30 seconds. Spoon apricot mixture over almond batter. Using a rubber spatula, gently fold it into the batter just enough to marble; do not overmix or you will lose the pattern.

To Bake: Grease or spray a 12-cup tube or bundt pan. Spoon the batter into the prepared pan and bake for 1 hour and 10 to 20 minutes, or until a toothpick inserted in the center comes out clean. Remove to a rack and cool 10 minutes. Go around inside edge of pan with tip of a sharp knife and invert onto the rack to cool completely.

(continued)

When you want to leave a lasting impression, serve this rich, buttery almond cake swirled throughout with brandied ribbons of apricot puree.

PREP TIME: 30 minutes

BAKE TIME: 70 to 80 minutes

ADVANCE PREP: May be stored at room temperature up to 2 days or frozen.

NUTRITIONAL ANALYSIS

Per serving (with light sour cream)

481 calories

18 g fat

123 mg cholesterol

161 mg sodium

To Make Glaze: In a medium bowl, stir together confectioners' sugar, brandy, and 1 tablespoon milk. Slowly stir in enough milk to make a thick glaze. Spoon over top of cool cake, letting it drip down the sides. If desired, cut apricot halves into petals and arrange like daisies around the top. Place a sliced almond in the center of each flower. (Cake may be stored covered at room temperature up to 2 days or frozen up to 1 month.)

MAKES: 12 to 14 servings.

GRAND GRILLING

Once upon a time in America, barbecuing was hot. But then we discovered that glowing charcoal and wood chips enhance more than hot dogs, hamburgers, and chicken—and changed the name to grilling. Smoky, seared foods are still the mainstay of backyard picnics and summertime outings, but no longer are they confined to the outdoors, or, for that matter, warm weather. Many kitchens have indoor grills, and restaurants are aglow with flames of every description. Thick tomato-based barbecue sauces are making way for lighter marinades, which pack a powerful punch of flavor without much added fat. This chapter runs the grilling gamut with menus that know no cultural bounds. From the balmy shores of the Mediterranean come a colorful Spanish paella and a Middle Eastern feast. Japan offers a traveling table to set wherever your heart takes you. The tortilla journeys across the globe to enwrap Peking chicken. And a sizzling American menu takes you back home.

GRILLED PAELLA PARTY

If you think paella is a winter party dish especially well suited to small groups, then you probably haven't heard about the Spanish chef Juan Carlos Galbis. As a result of losing a bet he made after consuming too many bottles of wine, he challenged paella history by making paella for twenty-five hundred people in a thirteen-foot pan, cooked over half a ton of firewood, and using two hundred and twenty pounds of rice. This may be a little more than you want to handle, but it's a reminder that when throwing a paella party, you are limited only by the size of your pan and your spirit of adventure.

Exactly when or why Americans began cooking paella in the kitchen instead of outside as the originators did two hundred years ago has never been determined. Even in Spain today, paella is grilled outdoors—always by men—and served right from the pan it is cooked in. Paella takes its name from this round, shallow pan, which is customarily made of iron so it can go directly on the fire. But when the main ingredients are cooked separately, or the dish is baked in the oven, an earthenware pan will work as well.

Most purist cooks believe the secret to a great paella lies in the rice, and the only type to use is a short-grained variety, like Italian Arborio. If you are well organized and can have all the ingredients ready at the same time the rice is al dente, then Arborio is a fine choice. If, however, you prefer some flexibility in serving, I recommend using long-grain white rice, which doesn't get sticky on standing and can be held for at least thirty minutes.

Paella includes lots of ingredients—after all, it's an entire meal in one dish—so the recipe appears lengthy, but it is not at all difficult to prepare. I cook each of the components separately, the rice and fish in a paella pan or Dutch oven, the chicken and shrimp on the grill, the mussels and clams in a skillet, and then assemble them before serving.

For this menu, you will find it particularly helpful to follow the Game Plan and cook in stages.

When your guests arrive, greet them with Sangria Blanco (see page 76) or margaritas and a variety of tapas, Spanish for little bites. Begin the meal with the Mediterranean Caesar Salad or serve it along with the paella, buffet style. The bread staffs are a great addition to any part of the meal, even hors d'oeuvres. Lime Mousse in a Seafoam Shell offers an elegant yet refreshing finale. Other options are Margarita Ice Cream Torte (see page 80), Lemon-Pineapple Trifle (see page 110), or fresh fruit with Jack Daniel's Caramel-Mint Sauce (see page 216). This menu serves eight.

GAME PLAN

1 Month Ahead	**Prepare and freeze pita chips** **Make and freeze croutons for salad** **Make and freeze bread staffs**
2 Days Ahead	**Make roasted salsa** **Cook bacon and prepare dressing for salad**
1 Day Ahead	**Cook artichokes** **Make Romesco Sauce** **Prepare Potato Nachos** **Prepare ingredients for salad** **Make marinade and stock base for paella** **Make Lime Mousse in a Seafoam Shell** **Defrost pita chips, croutons, and bread staffs**
DAY OF PARTY 4 Hours Ahead	**Marinate chicken** **Garnish lime mousse with berries or fruit** **Separate leaves on cooked artichokes**
45 to 60 Minutes Ahead	**Marinate shrimp** **Cook rice mixture** **Prepare coals and soak wood chips**
30 Minutes Ahead	**Reheat and garnish Potato Nachos**
10 Minutes Ahead	**Grill chicken and shrimp** **Cook clams and mussels** **Toss salad**

EXTRA POINTS

THE INVITATIONS

Mail your invitations with castanets or sea shells in a padded envelope or small box (you might even include some beach pebbles or sand).

THE TABLE

Set the table in bright Spanish colors and accent with fish net (or any type of netting that resembles it), an assortment of seashells, and driftwood.

THE KICKER

Stir up the party with strains of flamenco.

This spicy sauce thick-ened with nuts and bread is named after the romesco pepper, a red pepper introduced to Catalonia in the sixteenth century. Though romesco sauce is classically served with fried fish, its reddish hue and gutsy flavors make it a perfect dip for artichoke leaves, raw or cooked vege-tables, and crisp crackers.

PREP TIME: Sauce, 15 minutes; artichokes, 5 minutes

MICROWAVE TIME: Arti-chokes, about 16 minutes

ADVANCE PREP: Sauce and artichokes may be re-frigerated overnight.

NUTRITIONAL ANALYSIS

Per serving artichokes
16 calories
less than 1 g fat
0 cholesterol
29 mg sodium

Per tablespoon sauce
39 calories
3 g fat
0 cholesterol
54 mg sodium

ARTICHOKES WITH ROMESCO SAUCE

Romesco Sauce
1 garlic clove, peeled
½ pickled or fresh seeded jalapeño (about ½ to ¾ inch) (see page 10)
2 slices day-old white, Italian, or sourdough bread, crusts removed (1 cup crumbs)
3 large plum tomatoes, seeded and coarsely chopped (see page 12)

2 teaspoons red wine vinegar
2 tablespoons dry sherry
½ cup hazelnuts, chopped and toasted (see page 11)
¼ cup olive oil
½ teaspoon salt, or to taste

2 large or 3 medium artichokes
½ lemon

To Make Sauce: In a food processor with the metal blade, process garlic and jalapeño until minced. Add bread, tomatoes, vinegar, sherry, and nuts and process until ground. With motor running, slowly pour oil through feed tube. Remove sauce to bowl. (Sauce may be refrigerated overnight. Serve at room temperature or chilled. Stir well before serv-ing.) This makes 1⅔ cups sauce.

To Cook Artichokes: Rinse well and cut stems even with bottom so they stand up straight. Place stem side up in a deep microwavesafe casserole. Add enough water to cover a third of the artichokes. Squeeze lemon over. Cover and microwave on high (100%) for 12 to 16 minutes, or until stem is tender when pierced with the tip of a sharp knife. Turn artichokes in liquid to moisten all leaves. Let stand, covered, for 5 minutes and remove from water. If cooking more than 2 artichokes, increase microwave time 3 to 5 minutes for each additional artichoke. (Artichokes may be refrigerated, covered, overnight.)

To Assemble: Several hours before serving, remove leaves from arti-chokes, discarding small bottom leaves. Snip off tops of sharp leaves with scissors. Scrape fuzzy choke from artichoke bottoms and fill each with a spoonful of sauce. Place bowl with sauce on platter and arrange leaves and filled bottoms around it.

MAKES: 8 appetizer servings.

Change of Pace: Two large heads (4 to 5 ounces each) Belgian endive may be substituted for the artichokes. Separate leaves and arrange fanned out on platter around the bowl of sauce.

POTATO NACHOS WITH ROASTED GARLIC

1 large garlic head, with the largest cloves available
No-stick olive or vegetable oil cooking spray
6 to 7 small red-skin potatoes, peeled (about 1½ pounds)
Salt

Topping
½ pickled or fresh seeded jalapeño (about ½ to ¾ inch) (see page 10)

¼ cup chopped red onion (about ¼ onion)
¼ cup canned green chiles, chopped and drained
⅓ cup pimiento-stuffed green olives
½ cup shredded regular or low-fat jack or mozzarella cheese
½ teaspoon ground cumin
Sour cream, for serving
Cilantro leaves, for garnish

To Roast Garlic: Preheat oven to 450°F.

Peel outer skin from garlic. Cut a small slice off the top. Separate unpeeled cloves and place them in a pie dish. Spray with cooking spray. Bake, uncovered, for 15 to 20 minutes, or until soft when squeezed. Set aside until cool enough to handle.

To Bake Potato Slices: Slice potatoes by hand into ⅜- to ½-inch rounds; you should have about 26 slices. (Do not use a food processor or they will be too thin.) Place on a large greased baking sheet. Spray tops with cooking spray and sprinkle with salt. Bake in the same oven with the garlic for 8 minutes, or until crisp-tender. Remove from oven.

To Make Topping: In a food processor with the metal blade, mince jalapeño. Add onion, chiles, olives, cheese, cumin, and salt to taste. Peel garlic, add to processor and pulse until mixture is chopped into small pieces.

To Assemble: Top each potato slice with a heaping teaspoon of roasted garlic topping and place on baking sheet or broiler pan. Preheat broiler and broil 1 to 2 inches from unit (it may be necessary to raise the pan closer to the element by placing it on an inverted rimmed baking sheet) 3 to 5 minutes, or until flecked with brown and bubbling. (Nachos may be refrigerated overnight. Reheat at 425°F. for 8 to 10 minutes or until hot.) Before serving, top with a tiny dollop of sour cream and a cilantro leaf. Serve hot or at room temperature.

MAKES: about 26 nachos.

Mound baked potato slices with a puree of roasted garlic, cheese, and chiles for a lighter nuance on nachos.

PREP TIME: 15 minutes

BAKE TIME: 12 to 15 minutes

ADVANCE PREP: May be refrigerated overnight.

NUTRITIONAL ANALYSIS

Per nacho (with low-fat mozzarella)
32 calories
less than 1 g fat
less than 1 mg cholesterol
57 mg sodium

Celebrate the heady flavors of northern Spain with this rustic but refined mix of marinated grilled or oven-roasted vegetables. Serve it with pita chips, crackers, tortilla chips, or Tuscany Toasts (see page 285).

PREP TIME: Salsa, 20 minutes; pita chips, 10 minutes

MARINADE TIME: 1 to 4 hours

COOK TIME: Grill, 6 to 12 minutes; oven, 20 minutes; pita chips, 10 to 15 minutes

CHILL TIME: 6 hours

ADVANCE PREP: Salsa may be refrigerated up to 2 days. Pita chips may be stored at room temperature for several days or frozen.

NUTRITIONAL ANALYSIS

Per 2 tablespoons salsa
27 calories
2 g fat
0 cholesterol
122 mg sodium

Per 4 pita chips
26 calories
5% calories from fat
less than 1 g fat
0 cholesterol
54 mg sodium

ROASTED PROVENÇALE VEGETABLE SALSA

Marinade
2 teaspoons oriental sesame oil
2 tablespoons olive oil
⅓ cup red wine vinegar
2 garlic cloves, minced
1 teaspoon dried oregano
Salt and freshly ground black pepper

Vegetables
1 small eggplant (about ¾ pound)
1 small zucchini (about ¼ pound)

1 small yellow or red bell pepper
3 green onions, sliced
1 can (16 ounces) garbanzo beans (chick peas) rinsed and drained
⅔ cup pimiento-stuffed green olives, drained
Toasted Pita Chips (recipe follows), crackers, or bread rounds, for serving

To Marinate: In a plastic zipper bag combine sesame and olive oils, vinegar, garlic, oregano, and salt and pepper to taste. Cut ends off unpeeled eggplant and zucchini and slice lengthwise into ½-inch slices. Remove core from pepper, cut into quarters and remove seeds. Add vegetables to marinade, toss to coat, and marinate at room temperature for 1 hour or in the refrigerator up to 4 hours.

To Grill or Oven-Roast Vegetables: Prepare coals. Oil grill rack and place it 3 to 4 inches from coals. Remove vegetables from marinade and reserve marinade. Grill vegetables over hot coals until lightly charred and soft. Bell pepper wedges will take about 12 minutes, turned once; eggplant and zucchini slices, about 6 minutes, turned once. Cool to room temperature.

To Bake in Oven: Preheat oven to 425°F. Place vegetables on greased baking sheets. Bake for 10 minutes, turn, and bake for 10 minutes more, or until soft.

To Assemble: Pulse garbanzo beans and olives in food processor with metal blade until coarsely chopped. Remove to bowl. Chop cooked vegetables in food processor or by hand into ½-inch pieces. Stir into olive mixture. Stir in reserved marinade and toss well. Refrigerate for at least 6 hours. (Salsa may be refrigerated up to 2 days.) Serve with pita chips, crackers, or bread rounds.

MAKES: about 4½ cups salsa.

TOASTED PITA CHIPS

6 pita breads, 6 to 8 inches in diameter

No-stick olive or vegetable oil cooking spray

Preheat oven to 325°F.

With scissors, cut pitas in half horizontally, making 2 rounds. Cut each round in half and then into thirds or quarters, making 6 to 8 triangles per round. Place close together on baking sheets and spray the tops with cooking spray. Bake for 10 to 15 minutes, or until lightly browned and crisp, rotating baking sheets halfway through the baking time. (Chips may be stored in an airtight container for several days or frozen.)

MAKES: 72 to 96 triangles.

These whimsical chile-flecked breadsticks, created by Wayne Brackman of the Mesa Grill in New York City, will be the conversation piece of your party—especially if you stand them in a tall glass or pitcher to show off their artistry.

PREP TIME: 1 hour

RISE TIME: Microwave, 20 minutes; warm place, 45 minutes

BAKE TIME: 25 minutes

ADVANCE PREP: May be stored airtight for several weeks or frozen.

CHILE BREAD STAFFS

2 large, dried chiles with seeds, such as New Mexican or ancho (about 5 inches each)
3 cups all-purpose flour
1 package quick-rising yeast
1 teaspoon salt
¼ to ½ teaspoon hot chile powder, or to taste
1 tablespoon olive oil

Coating
1 egg white, mixed with ½ teaspoon water
½ cup yellow cornmeal
2 tablespoons coarse kosher or sea salt
1 teaspoon hot chile powder

To Prepare Chiles: With scissors, cut chiles into ½-inch pieces. Place in a 4-cup microwavesafe measure and cover with ¾ cup water. Microwave, covered, on high (100%) for 4 to 5 minutes, or until very soft.

To Prepare Batter: Remove chiles from liquid and place in food processor with the metal blade. Reserve liquid.

Process chiles until finely chopped. Add 1 cup flour and process until crumbly. Add remaining 2 cups flour, yeast, salt, and chile powder and pulse to combine. Check temperature of chile soaking liquid; it should be very warm to the touch (120° to 130°F.). If too cold, reheat in microwave. With motor running, pour liquid and olive oil through the feed tube, processing until dough pulls away from sides and forms a ball. If too dry, add more water 1 teaspoon at a time. Knead by processing 1 minute. Remove dough to work surface and knead several times by hand.

To Rise in Microwave: You need a microwave with 10% power. Make a hole through the middle of the dough like a doughnut and return to food processor bowl without the blade. Cover with a damp towel or plastic wrap. Place an 8-ounce glass of water in back of the microwave. Place bowl with dough in front. Microwave at 10% power for 8 minutes; let rest 5 minutes. Microwave for 5 minutes, let rest 5 minutes. If it is not doubled in bulk and dough does not leave an imprint when poked with your finger, microwave for 3 to 5 minutes more.

To Rise in Warm Place: Place dough in an oiled bowl, cover, and let rise in a warm place (see page 9) for 45 minutes, or until doubled in bulk and a finger poked in dough leaves an imprint.

To Shape: Punch dough down and let rest for 5 minutes. On a lightly floured board, roll dough into a rectangle about ⅛ inch thick and about 12 to 15 inches long. If dough springs back and is difficult to roll, let rest 5 to 10 minutes longer. Brush top with egg white.

To Coat and Cut: In a small bowl, stir together cornmeal, salt, and chile powder. Sprinkle over egg white, pressing it in gently. Using a pizza cutter or knife and a ruler or a cardboard template, cut dough into long strips about ⅜ inch wide. Place strips close together on ungreased baking sheets. Don't be concerned with crumbs that do not adhere. Twist, tie, cut, and shape ends.

To Bake: Preheat oven to 325°F. Bake for 25 to 30 minutes, or until lightly browned. To test for doneness, break off a piece and taste; it should be dry and crisp. (Staffs may be stored airtight at room temperature for several weeks or frozen up to 2 months.)

To serve, stand staffs in drinking glasses.

MAKES: about 30 staffs.

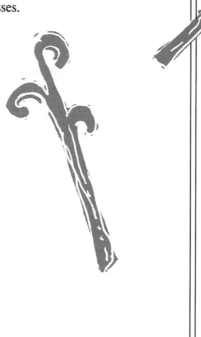

Although this recipe may appear complex, considering it fulfills the entree, starch and vegetable courses, it actually takes less time to prepare than most meals. I would never tackle this dish without my trusty co-chef, Hal, who takes the heat off me in the kitchen by tending the grill. If you have a paella pan that can go directly on the stove, cook the rice in it. If not, transfer everything to an attractive pan or dish for serving.

PREP TIME: About 1 hour

COOK TIME: Stock base, about 15 minutes; rice mixture, about 45 minutes

MARINADE TIME: Chicken, 4 hours; shrimp, 1 hour

GRILL TIME: Chicken, about 10 minutes; shrimp, about 5 minutes

ADVANCE PREP: Marinade and stock base may be refrigerated overnight.

NUTRITIONAL ANALYSIS

Per serving
890 calories
32 g fat
237 mg cholesterol
2070 mg sodium

PAELLA WITH GRILLED CHICKEN AND SHRIMP

Marinade
3 tablespoons fresh chopped oregano leaves or 1 tablespoon dried oregano
1 tablespoon ground coriander
4 garlic cloves, minced
5 tablespoons red wine vinegar
½ to 1 teaspoon cayenne, or to taste
1 tablespoon coarsely ground pepper
3 tablespoons olive oil
¼ cup chicken broth
1 teaspoon salt, or to taste

6 skinless, boneless chicken breast halves
16 jumbo shrimp, peeled and deveined, tails left on

Stock Base
2 bottles (8 ounces each) clam juice
5 cups chicken broth
1 cup dry white wine or imported dry vermouth

2 teaspoons ground coriander
½ teaspoon ground cumin
½ to 1 teaspoon saffron
Salt and freshly ground black pepper

Rice Mixture
1 tablespoon olive oil
1 pound chorizo or spicy Italian sausage, casings removed
2 large onions, chopped
4 garlic cloves, minced
2 cans (15 ounces each) whole tomatoes, drained and broken up
2½ cups uncooked long-grain white rice
¾ pound shark or swordfish, cut into 1-inch pieces
1 cup frozen peas, thawed
¼ cup chopped fresh herbs, preferably oregano and thyme

16 clams, scrubbed
16 mussels, scrubbed

To Make Marinade: Mix all ingredients in glass bowl or jar. Use immediately or refrigerate overnight. Place chicken and shrimp in separate glass dishes or heavy zippered plastic bags. (You may prefer marinating shrimp on skewers to make them easier to grill.) About 4 hours before serving, pour two thirds of the marinade over the chicken. Cover and refrigerate, turning once. About 1 hour before serving, pour remaining marinade over the shrimp. Cover and refrigerate. Remove both from refrigerator 30 minutes before grilling.

To Make Stock Base: In a deep, nonaluminum saucepan, combine all ingredients. Boil slowly over moderate heat until reduced to 5¼ cups. Taste and add additional seasonings and salt and pepper, if needed.

To Make Rice Mixture: In a deep wide saucepan or paella pan, heat olive oil until hot. Add sausage and onions and sauté, breaking up the sausage with a fork, until the onion is tender, about 15 minutes. Pour off any fat. Add garlic and tomatoes and cook several minutes more until liquid is evaporated, stirring occasionally. Stir in stock base. (Mixture may be refrigerated overnight.)

About 45 minutes before serving, bring sausage mixture to a boil. Stir in the rice, reduce heat to a simmer, cover, and cook 10 minutes. Stir in fish and peas, cover, and simmer until the liquid is absorbed and the rice is tender, about 20 to 25 minutes; stirring once or twice. Stir in herbs. The rice will stay warm, covered, for up to 30 minutes.

To Grill: About 45 to 60 minutes before serving, prepare coals and, if desired, soak wood chips in water. When coals are hot, add wood chips, if using. Oil grill rack and place it about 3 to 4 inches from coals.

Remove chicken and shrimp from marinade; do not dry. Grill chicken for 10 minutes, turning once, and shrimp 4 to 6 minutes, turning once, or until cooked through.

To Cook Mollusks: While chicken and shrimp are grilling, bring ¼ inch of water to a boil in a large frying pan. Discard any clams or mussels that are broken or do not clamp shut under water. Add to water, cover, and cook over high heat, shaking the pan occasionally, until they open, about 4 minutes. Remove with slotted spoon to plate and cover with foil. If some are only partially opened, cover, and continue cooking, removing each as it opens fully. Discard any that remain closed.

To Assemble: Spoon rice into paella dish or casserole. Cut breasts in half and arrange them, shrimp, clams, and mussels over the top.

MAKES: 8 servings.

Change of Pace: Grill an assortment of vegetables, such as green onions with tops and chunks of red and yellow peppers, along with the chicken and shrimp.

I'm not sure if it's the olives, the bacon, or the nutty croutons that make this salad so special, but it always elicits kudos. If you can't find small bunches of romaine, use the hearts or inner leaves.

PREP TIME: 40 minutes

BAKE TIME: Croutons, 15 to 20 minutes

ADVANCE PREP: Croutons may be stored at room temperature up to 1 week or frozen. Dressing and bacon may be refrigerated up to 2 days. Salad ingredients may be prepared 1 day ahead.

NUTRITIONAL ANALYSIS

Per serving salad (not including dressing)
131 calories
7 g fat
9 mg cholesterol
443 mg sodium

Per tablespoon dressing
50 calories
5 g fat
0 cholesterol
58 mg sodium

MEDITERRANEAN CAESAR SALAD

6 slices day-old nut or seed-and-grain bread, stale or dried at room temperature for several hours
8 strips bacon
3 to 4 small heads romaine lettuce

Citrus Caesar Dressing
5 tablespoons fresh lemon juice (see page 11)
6 to 8 tablespoons olive oil

3 tablespoons orange juice
2 teaspoons Worcestershire sauce
2 garlic cloves, minced
2 teaspoons dry mustard
2 teaspoons anchovy paste
Freshly ground black pepper

⅓ cup Mediterranean olives, such as niçoise, pitted and quartered (see page 12)
½ cup shredded parmesan cheese

To Make Croutons: Preheat oven to 300°F.

Remove crusts and cut bread into 1- to 1½-inch cubes. Place on a baking sheet and bake for 10 to 20 minutes, tossing occasionally, until toasted and very dry. (If croutons are not thoroughly dry, they will absorb the salad dressing and become soggy.) (Croutons may be stored covered for 1 week or frozen.)

To Prepare Salad: Cut bacon crosswise into 1-inch pieces. Place in microwavesafe casserole, cover with paper towels, and microwave on high (100%) for 5 to 6 minutes, stirring every 2 minutes until crisp. With slotted spoon, remove bacon to paper towels to drain. (Bacon may be refrigerated up to 2 days or frozen.)

Wash lettuce, tear into bite-size pieces, and spin dry. Wrap in paper towels and refrigerate in a plastic bag. (Lettuce may be refrigerated overnight.)

To Make Dressing: In a small bowl or wide-mouth jar, mix lemon juice, 6 tablespoons olive oil, orange juice, Worcestershire sauce, garlic, mustard, and anchovy paste. Taste and if desired, add remaining oil. Add pepper to taste. (Dressing may be refrigerated up to 2 days. Remove from refrigerator at least 1 hour before using and stir well.)

To Assemble: In a large bowl, toss lettuce with bacon, olives, parmesan, croutons and as much dressing as needed. Serve immediately.

MAKES: 10 servings.

Leaner: Substitute low-fat turkey bacon or Canadian bacon for regular bacon. It may take longer than regular bacon to cook until crisp.

LIME MOUSSE IN A SEAFOAM SHELL

Seafoam Shell
8 large egg whites, at room
temperature
½ teaspoon cream of tartar
1½ cups sugar

Lime Mousse
2 large eggs
4 teaspoons cornstarch
1 cup sugar

2 teaspoons grated lime peel
(see page 11)
⅔ cup fresh lime juice (5 to 6
limes) (see page 11)
¾ cup heavy cream
¾ cup light sour cream
Green food coloring (optional)
2 pints medium-size
strawberries, for garnish
Lime slices, for garnish

To Make Seafoam Shell: Preheat the oven to 225°F. Choose an oven-proof 10- to 12-cup (2½- to 3-quart) bowl such as a round glass Pyrex dish. (Don't worry about the little handles.) In a large mixing bowl with electric mixer at medium speed, beat egg whites with cream of tartar for 3 minutes. Increase speed to high and add 1 tablespoon sugar; beat 3 minutes. Add another tablespoon sugar and beat 2 more minutes. Add remaining sugar very slowly, 1 tablespoon at a time, beating continuously at high speed until the mixture is very stiff and glossy, like marshmallow creme. Transfer to ungreased bowl. Using a rubber spatula, make a nest about 1½ inches thick, pushing the meringue up the sides and onto the edge of the bowl, forming a 2-inch-wide border. Place on a baking sheet and bake in center of oven for 1 hour. Check to see if it is very lightly colored. If it is still white, increase oven temperature to 250°F. If it is turning golden, reduce oven temperature to 200°F. Continue baking for 1 hour more. It should be very pale, the color of an egg-shell, and soft and spongy. Remove from oven and cool to room temperature. The shell will fall and crack as it cools.

To Make Lime Mousse: In a medium-size heavy saucepan off the heat, whisk eggs, cornstarch, and sugar until well blended. Whisk in lime peel and juice. Cook over moderate heat, whisking constantly, making sure to get into the edges of the pan, until the custard comes to a boil and thickens, about 4 to 6 minutes. Immediately remove from heat and pour into a bowl. Stir in several drops food coloring to tint pale green, if desired. Cool to room temperature. (To hasten cooling, put bowl in a larger bowl of ice water and stir often.) In a large mixing bowl with electric mixer, beat heavy cream until stiff peaks form. Add sour cream and beat until soft peaks form. Add cooled custard and mix on low speed until incorporated. Pour into the meringue shell. Cover with plas-

(continued)

A huge meringue bowl is filled with a heavenly lime mousse and capped with fresh strawberries—which keep this light-as-air dessert from floating right off the plate. Unlike free-form, crisp, shattering meringue shells, this one is baked in an oven-proof bowl and stays soft and billowy. It is best to make this type of meringue with a free-standing electric mixer, and it is important to follow the directions precisely.

PREP TIME: 1 hour

BAKE TIME: 2 hours

CHILL TIME: At least 12 hours

ADVANCE PREP: May be refrigerated up to 24 hours.

NUTRITIONAL ANALYSIS

Per serving (including strawberry garnish)
249 calories
10 g fat
74 mg cholesterol
72 mg sodium

tic wrap and refrigerate for at least 12 hours or up to 24 hours.

To Garnish and Serve: Up to 4 hours before serving, slice off stem end of strawberries and slice in half or into thick slices through stem end. Arrange overlapping in concentric circles over top of mousse. Twist 2 lime slices in the center. Refrigerate, covered with plastic wrap, until serving. Serve with a large spoon, scooping up some meringue from the bottom and sides with each portion.

MAKES: 8 to 10 servings.

Change of Pace: Substitute or supplement strawberries with sliced kiwi, raspberries, blueberries, or other fruits.

GRILLED MAGIC
Of The
MIDDLE EAST

ven a genie couldn't produce a more exotic and exciting dinner than this one. Fit for sultans when served in the dining room on your most opulent china, it's casual enough for Aladdin when dished up on the patio on a warm summer's eve. When the coals are glowing hot, grill the shrimp mezze (Middle Eastern for appetizers), then toss on more coals to be ready in time for the marinated lamb.

The contrasting flavors of Middle and Near Eastern cuisines—cool and hot, lemony and sweet—are reassuringly recognizable in this menu. Designed to serve eight, the shrimp, lamb, salad, and couscous recipes can be doubled to serve sixteen. For a large party, make as many double recipes as needed. Only the Orange-Pistachio Torte cannot be doubled. You can either make it two or more times, or offer a selection of desserts, such as Lime Mousse in a Seafoam Shell (see page 187), Lemon-Pineapple Trifle (see page 110), or something intriguingly dark, like Chocolate–Caramel Praline Roll (see page 166).

Menu

◆

SHRIMP MEZZE WITH CITRUS AND FETA

◆

TOMATO AND CUCUMBER SALATAT WITH PITA CROUTONS

◆

GRILLED LEG OF LAMB WITH CABERNET FIG SAUCE

◆

COUSCOUS TIMBALES WITH CHICK PEAS AND WALNUTS

◆

VEGETABLES MARRAKESH

◆

SPICED POPADAMS
(See page 162)

◆

ORANGE-PISTACHIO TORTE WITH RICOTTA AND FRESH FRUIT

GAME PLAN

1 Month Ahead	**Bake and freeze croutons for salatat** **Make and freeze sauce for lamb** **Make and freeze Couscous Timbales** **Make and freeze torte layers** **Cook and freeze popadams**
2 Days Ahead	**Make vinaigrette for salatat**
1 Day Ahead	**Make marinade for shrimp** **Marinate lamb** **Defrost sauce for lamb and Couscous Timbales** **Defrost popadams**

DAY OF PARTY

8 Hours Ahead	**Assemble and garnish torte**
6 Hours Ahead	**Prepare vegetables for salad**
4 Hours Ahead	**Cook carrots**
2½ Hours Ahead	**Marinate shrimp**
1½ Hours Ahead	**Prepare coals and soak wood chips**
1 Hour Ahead	**Remove lamb from marinade** **Grill and serve shrimp and put on more coals for lamb**
20 Minutes Ahead	**Grill lamb**
Shortly Before Serving	**Complete vegetables** **Reheat sauce for lamb** **Toss salatat** **Reheat couscous**

EXTRA POINTS

THE THEME

Here's a terrific party idea that might sound farfetched but works like a charm—turn this feast into an Aladdin's Night Party.

THE INVITATIONS

Write an invitation on brown paper—a cut-up grocery bag will do. Burn the edges, roll it up, and insert it into the neck of a small "genie" bottle. (Find small bottles or cruets in your local import store.) Mail in tissue-stuffed boxes.

THE TABLE

Add sparkle to the table with costume jewelry—necklaces, bracelets, pins, belts and copper or brass trays and plates. Drape colorful fabrics down the center of the table and nestle shimmery trinkets in the folds. Fill Aladdin-style or hurricane lamps with lamp oil, candles, or even flowers. For music, play strains of "Persian Market" or "Scheherazade."

THE KICKER

Regale your guests with a belly dancer.

A lime, lemon, and orange juice marinade accented with garlic, tarragon, and Pernod gives these feta-topped shrimp an elusive flavor. Grill and serve them on individual skewers or cook several portions on long skewers and transfer the shrimp to small plates or scallop shells to serve.

PREP TIME: 15 minutes

MARINADE TIME: 1½ to 2 hours

GRILL TIME: 6 to 10 minutes

ADVANCE PREP: Marinade may be prepared 1 day ahead

NUTRITIONAL ANALYSIS

Per serving
112 calories
3 g fat
135 mg cholesterol
179 mg sodium

SHRIMP MEZZE WITH CITRUS AND FETA

Marinade
¼ cup fresh lime juice (see page 11)
3 tablespoons fresh lemon juice
3 tablespoons fresh orange juice
2 tablespoons olive oil
6 garlic cloves, minced
2 tablespoons Pernod
2 teaspoons dried tarragon
Freshly ground black pepper

1½ pounds extra-large or jumbo raw shrimp, peeled and deveined, tails left on (32 extra-large or 16 jumbo)
8 (6-inch) metal skewers, or bamboo skewers soaked in cold water for 30 minutes
About ⅓ cup feta cheese, finely crumbled
Lime wedges, for garnish

To Marinate: In a small bowl whisk together the citrus juices, oil, garlic, Pernod, tarragon, and pepper to taste. (Marinade may be refrigerated overnight.) Thread 4 extra-large or 2 jumbo shrimp on skewers. (If they are wooden, cut to fit.) Place in a shallow glass dish or heavy plastic zipper bag. About 1½ to 2 hours before serving, pour marinade over shrimp, turning to coat both sides. Cover and refrigerate for 1½ hours. Turn and marinate at room temperature for 30 minutes more.

To Grill: While shrimp marinates, soak a handful of mesquite, apple, or other aromatic wood chips for at least 30 minutes before grilling. Prepare coals and when hot, add wood chips. Oil grill rack and place it 3 to 4 inches from coals.

Grill the shrimp, covered with the lid of the barbecue to impart a smokier flavor and keep the flames from flaring up, for 3 to 5 minutes on 1 side, depending on the size of the shrimp. Turn, sprinkle with feta, pressing it in lightly, cover, and cook for 3 to 5 minutes longer, or until cooked through. Do not overcook; shrimp will continue to cook off the heat. Serve on skewers or remove to small plates or scallop shells. Garnish with lime wedges.

MAKES: 8 appetizer servings.

Leaner: Omit feta cheese.

Change of Pace: Shrimp may be baked at 450°F. for 7 to 10 minutes instead of grilled.

TOMATO AND CUCUMBER SALATAT WITH PITA CROUTONS

2 pita breads, about 7 inches in
  diameter

Lemon-Mint Vinaigrette
6 tablespoons olive oil
6 tablespoons orange juice
4 to 5 tablespoons fresh lemon
  juice, or to taste (see page 11)
2 garlic cloves, minced
⅔ cup finely chopped fresh mint
  leaves
Salt and freshly ground black
  pepper

Salad
1 medium hothouse or seedless
  cucumber, peeled and cut into
  ¼-inch dice (about 2½ cups)

¼ teaspoon salt
1 large red bell pepper, cut into
  ¼-inch dice (about 1½ cups)
6 plum or 3 medium tomatoes,
  cut into ¼-inch dice (about
  3 cups)
6 green onions, thinly sliced
  (about ¾ cup)
1 medium head romaine lettuce
Mint sprigs, for garnish
  (optional)

To Make Croutons: Preheat oven to 325°F. Cut the pita into ¾-inch pieces. Place on a rimmed baking sheet and bake, turning occasionally, for 18 to 20 minutes, or until golden brown and crisp. Cool. (Croutons may be stored in an airtight container up to 1 week or frozen.)

To Make Vinaigrette: In a jar or medium bowl, whisk together the oil, orange juice, lemon juice, and garlic. Stir in mint. Season to taste with salt and pepper. (Dressing may be refrigerated up to 2 days. Bring to room temperature and mix well.)

To Prepare Salad: Up to 6 hours before serving, place cucumber in a colander, sprinkle with salt, and let drain in sink or over a plate for 20 minutes or longer. Pat dry. Toss cucumber, bell pepper, tomatoes, and green onions in a large bowl. Refrigerate, covered, until ready to serve. Discard outer leaves from lettuce, cut remainder into ½-inch strips, and refrigerate.

Before Serving: Divide lettuce among salad plates. Pour vinaigrette over vegetables and toss well. Season to taste with salt and pepper and mix in pita croutons. Spoon onto lettuce and serve immediately.

MAKES: 8 servings.

For a delightfully refreshing chopped salatat (Moroccan for *salad*), toss vegetable cubes and pita crisps with a lemony mint-flavored vinaigrette. Be sure to taste the dressing after adding the mint—some strains are very mild and you may wish to add some dried mint. Because the appearance of the salad depends on the way the vegetables are chopped, I recommend cutting them by hand.

PREP TIME: 30 minutes

BAKE TIME: Croutons, 20 minutes

ADVANCE PREP: Croutons may be stored at room temperature up to 1 week or frozen. Dressing may be refrigerated up to 2 days. Vegetables and lettuce may be refrigerated up to 6 hours.

NUTRITIONAL ANALYSIS

Per serving
159 calories
11 g fat
0 cholesterol
131 mg sodium

For lamb that's melt-in-your-mouth tender and very mild, marinate it overnight in yogurt and crème de menthe. When you purchase a boned and butterflied leg, it may remind you of a hilly road in need of repair. But when grilled, that bumpy terrain results in varying degrees of doneness, so your guests can have their choice.

PREP TIME: 40 minutes

MARINADE TIME: 24 hours

GRILL TIME: 16 to 20 minutes

ADVANCE PREP: Sauce may be refrigerated up to 2 days or frozen.

NUTRITIONAL ANALYSIS

Per serving lamb (with nonfat yogurt)
278 calories
10 g fat
115 mg cholesterol
132 mg sodium

Per tablespoon sauce
26 calories
less than 1 g fat
0 cholesterol
50 mg sodium

GRILLED LEG OF LAMB WITH CABERNET FIG SAUCE

1 boned and butterflied leg of lamb (4 to 5 pounds net weight), all fat removed
2 cups regular, low-fat, or nonfat plain yogurt
¾ cup white crème de menthe liqueur
½ teaspoon salt, or to taste
1 teaspoon ground rainbow peppercorns or black pepper

Cabernet Fig Sauce
2 teaspoons olive oil
1 bay leaf

1 medium leek, cleaned and cut into ¼-inch dice (see page 11) (about 1 cup)
1 cup dried figs, preferably baby figlets, stems removed, cut into ½-inch pieces
1¼ cups chicken broth
2 cups Cabernet Sauvignon or other full-bodied red wine
1 tablespoon honey
1 tablespoon cornstarch, mixed with 1 tablespoon water
Salt and freshly ground black pepper

To Marinate: Place lamb in a large plastic zipper bag or shallow glass dish. In a medium bowl, mix yogurt, liqueur, salt, and pepper. Pour over lamb, turning to coat both sides. Close bag or cover dish with plastic wrap and refrigerate overnight, turning once.

To Make Sauce: Heat oil in a medium saucepan over medium-high heat. Add bay leaf, leeks, and figs and sauté, stirring, for 4 minutes. Stir in chicken broth, wine, and honey. Lower heat and boil gently until reduced to about 2¾ cups, about 20 minutes. Remove from heat and stir in dissolved cornstarch. Return to heat and bring to a boil, stirring constantly, until sauce thickens. Season to taste with salt, and pepper. Remove bay leaf. (Sauce may be refrigerated up to 2 days or frozen. Reheat before serving.)

To Grill: One hour before grilling, remove lamb from marinade, blot dry with paper towels, and let stand at room temperature. Prepare coals. Soak a handful of mesquite, apple, or other aromatic wood chips in water for at least 30 minutes. Oil grill rack and place it 3 to 4 inches from coals. When coals are hot, add wood chips. Sprinkle lamb generously with salt and pepper. Grill, covered with the lid of the barbecue to impart a smokier flavor and keep the flames from flaring up, for 7 to 10 minutes. Turn and grill, covered, for 7 to 10 minutes more, or until the thickest parts are rare and the thinner ones medium-well done. Do not overcook; the meat will continue to cook off the heat. Let rest 5 minutes and carve into thin slices. Serve with sauce.

MAKES: 8 servings.

COUSCOUS TIMBALES WITH CHICK PEAS AND WALNUTS

1 cup couscous
2 teaspoons olive oil
1¼ teaspoons ground cumin
½ teaspoon salt, or to taste
1 can (8 ounces) garbanzo beans
   (chick peas), drained
   (¾ cup)
3 tablespoons fresh lemon juice
   (see page 11)

2 cups boiling water
⅓ cup finely chopped walnuts
   plus 8 walnut quarters or large
   pieces, toasted (see page 11)
8 (5-ounce) paper cups
4 green onions with tops, thinly
   sliced (½ cup)

To Make Couscous: In a 3-quart (12-cup) microwavesafe bowl stir together couscous, oil, cumin, salt, chick peas, lemon juice, and boiling water. Microwave, uncovered, on high (100%) for 2 to 3 minutes, or until most of the liquid is absorbed. Stir, cover, and let plump at room temperature for 15 minutes.

To Assemble: Place a large piece of walnut in the bottom of each paper cup. Sprinkle with a light layer of green onions. Stir remaining green onions and chopped walnuts into couscous. Place a scant ½ cup of the mixture into each cup, packing it down.

If serving immediately at room temperature, invert onto serving plates. (Timbales may be refrigerated overnight or frozen up to 1 month. Defrost in refrigerator. Bring to room temperature at least 1 hour before serving.)

Before Serving: Invert cups onto a microwavesafe plate, arranging them around the outer edge. Place plate in microwave and heat, uncovered, on high (100%) for 2 to 4 minutes, or until heated through, rotating the plate after each minute.

MAKES: 8 servings.

Leaner: Omit walnuts. The mixture will make only 7 timbales. Or substitute ½ cup finely chopped zucchini or yellow squash for the walnuts.

Couscous, a granular form of semolina wheat, is among the fastest pastas to prepare. To mold it (or cooked rice) into timbales, here's a trick I learned from the chef at The Boca Raton Hotel: Pack the cooked mixture into small paper cups, refrigerate them until firm, turn out onto a plate, and reheat in the microwave.

PREP TIME: 20 minutes

MICROWAVE TIME: 2 to 4 minutes

ADVANCE PREP: May be refrigerated up to 2 days or frozen.

NUTRITIONAL ANALYSIS

Per serving
148 calories
4 g fat
0 cholesterol
251 mg sodium

The Moroccan flavors of cayenne, cumin, and cinnamon, tempered with brown sugar and orange juice, melt into an enticing glaze for carrots, peas, and crookneck squash.

PREP TIME: 20 minutes

COOK TIME: About 15 minutes

ADVANCE PREP: Carrots may be partially cooked in glaze up to 4 hours ahead. Add squash and peas before serving.

VEGETABLES MARRAKESH

4 tablespoons (½ stick) butter or margarine
3 tablespoons (packed) light brown sugar
1 teaspoon ground cinnamon
½ teaspoon ground cumin
¼ teaspoon cayenne, or to taste
2 pounds baby carrots, peeled and trimmed
1¼ cups fresh orange juice
Salt and freshly ground black pepper
1 medium yellow crookneck squash (about 7 ounces), cut in half lengthwise and thinly sliced
2 cups fresh or frozen peas

To Cook Carrots: In a large skillet over low heat, melt butter or margarine. Stir in brown sugar, cinnamon, cumin, and cayenne and cook for 2 minutes. Stir in carrots and cook over medium heat until well coated and sugar is melted, about 3 minutes. Add orange juice and bring to a boil, stirring constantly. Reduce heat to a gentle boil, cover, and cook, stirring often, until carrots are nearly tender, about 6 to 8 minutes. Uncover and boil gently, stirring frequently, until liquid is reduced to a glaze. Season to taste with salt and pepper. (Carrots may be held at room temperature covered, up to 4 hours.)

Before Serving: Stir squash and peas into carrots and cook over medium-high heat, stirring, until vegetables are crisp-tender and heated through, about 4 minutes.

MAKES: 8 servings.

Leaner: Reduce butter or margarine to 2 tablespoons.

Change of Pace: To make Carrots Marrakesh, use only carrots. You will need 3 pounds to serve 8.

NUTRITIONAL ANALYSIS

Per serving
173 calories
6 g fat
16 mg cholesterol
135 mg sodium

ORANGE-PISTACHIO TORTE WITH RICOTTA AND FRESH FRUIT

Orange-pistachio Cake
1 medium-size orange
⅓ cup plus ⅓ cup sugar, divided
2 cups shelled, unsalted pistachio nuts, chopped (10½ ounces)
½ cup plus 1 tablespoon all-purpose flour
¾ teaspoon baking powder
⅛ teaspoon salt
9 large eggs, separated
¾ cup orange marmalade
1½ teaspoons vanilla extract

Ricotta Filling
2 cups whole milk or part skim ricotta cheese (about 1 pound)
¼ cup frozen orange juice concentrate, thawed
⅓ cup confectioners' sugar
Assorted fresh fruits, such as oranges, berries, sliced kiwi, sliced plums, sliced nectarines, red and green grapes, sliced papaya

To Make Cake: Preheat oven to 350°F. Grease or spray two 8½- or 9-inch layer cake pans. Cut a circle of parchment or wax paper to fit the bottom and grease or spray the paper.

Using a sharp vegetable peeler, peel the orange zest, cutting off any white pith, which may be bitter. Reserve fruit for the filling. Place zest in a food processor with the metal blade. Add ⅓ cup sugar and process until finely ground, scraping bottom and sides often. Add nuts and pulse until finely ground. Pulse in flour, baking powder, and salt.

In a large mixing bowl, beat egg yolks with ⅓ cup sugar until very thick and light, 3 to 5 minutes. Mix in marmalade and vanilla. On low speed, mix in nut mixture just until incorporated.

In a small mixing bowl with clean beaters, beat egg whites until stiff but moist peaks form. Partially fold a third of the whites into the nut mixture and then fold in the remainder. Divide the batter between the prepared pans. Bake for 25 to 30 minutes, or until a toothpick inserted in center comes out clean. Remove to racks and cool 20 minutes. Run a sharp knife around the sides and cool 30 minutes more. Invert onto racks to cool completely. (Cakes may be wrapped in foil and stored at room temperature overnight or frozen.)

To Make Filling: If the ricotta has excess liquid, pour it off. In a mixing bowl with electric mixer, beat ricotta until thick and light, about 2 minutes. Mix in orange juice concentrate and confectioners' sugar.

(continued)

With its jeweled crown of fresh fruit, this cake is as pretty as a still life. To whip ricotta, it is best to begin with a fresh package and drain off any excess liquid. (See color photo, page 10.)

PREP TIME: 1 hour

BAKE TIME: 20 to 24 minutes

CHILL TIME: 1 hour

ADVANCE PREP: Cake layers may be stored at room temperature overnight or frozen. Torte may be refrigerated up to 8 hours.

NUTRITIONAL ANALYSIS

Per serving (with low-fat ricotta)
575 calories
26 g fat
250 mg cholesterol
181 mg sodium

To Assemble: Up to 8 hours before serving, cut each cake layer in half horizontally. This is easiest to do on a turntable, marking the cake with toothpicks and using a serrated knife. Place 1 layer cut side up on cake plate. Spread with ½ cup filling. Top with second cake layer cut side up and spread with ½ cup filling. Halve the orange and slice it ¼ inch thick. Arrange a thick layer of orange and other fruit over filling. Top with third cake layer, spread with ½ cup filling, and top with final cake layer cut side down. Spread top with remaining filling and arrange fruit attractively on top. Cover with plastic wrap and refrigerate for at least 1 hour. Torte may be refrigerated up to 8 hours.

MAKES: 12 servings.

Change of Pace: Pecans, walnuts, or hazelnuts may be substituted for the pistachios.

Menu

◆

SORT-OF SUSHI

◆

PORK YAKIMONO WITH
GREEN AND YELLOW SQUASH
RIBBONS

◆

SPINACH AND CUCUMBER
SHREDS IN SWEET PEPPER
CUPS

◆

SHRIMP SALAD WITH
CELLOPHANE NOODLES

◆

UPSIDE-DOWN GINGER
CAKELETS

ROUND MOON
JAPANESE BOX SUPPER

*T*his is not run-of-the-mill picnic fare, and that's exactly why I recommend you try it. Yet even though the food is exotic, it still fits the most common picnic settings—sandy beaches, bleachers at a game, tailgate outings, moonlight on the bay, outdoor symphonies. Or maybe you'd prefer staying home and enjoying this as a romantic interlude.

This deluxe totable menu comes together so harmoniously because each dish is a self-contained entity, can be served at room temperature, and incorporates the pure and simple beauty of Japanese cuisine. The flavors are distinctive and irresistible.

Being a devotee of sushi but not one who enjoys duplicating dishes with hard-to-find ingredients and equipment, I created my own faux edition, which I call Sort-of Sushi. With astounding success, I've served these hors d'oeuvres to finicky eaters, some of whom wouldn't touch the authentic version.

Pork Yakimono, thin strips of pork and squash threaded on skewers, then marinated and grilled or broiled, are a movable treat on a stick. They are easy to pack, easy to eat, spillproof—and delicious.

In keeping with the Japanese affection for vegetables, the menu offers two salads, one of spinach and cucumber strips packed in sweet peppers; the other, translucent cellophane noodles or bean threads with shrimp. Although the Japanese would be happy to finish this feast with strawberries or slices of melon, I much prefer incorporating the fruit into moist and fragrant upside-down cakes. This picnic menu serves four.

GAME PLAN

1 Month Ahead	**Make sauce or sauces for sushi**
	Make and freeze cakelets
1 Week Ahead	**Make Jack Daniel's sauce for cakelets, if using**
2 Days Ahead	**Make dressing for spinach-cucumber salad**
	Make rice for sushi
1 Day Ahead	**Make Sort-of Sushi**
	Prepare pepper cups for spinach-cucumber salad
	Make marinade for pork
	Defrost cakelets
	Make cellophane noodle salad (without radishes and shrimp)
DAY OF PARTY	
4 Hours Ahead	**Marinate pork**
	Add shrimp and radishes to cellophane noodles
	Bring cakelets to room temperature
3 Hours Before Serving	**Complete spinach-cucumber salad**
Shortly Before Serving	**Slice sushi**
	Grill or broil pork

EXTRA POINTS

FOR TRANSPORTING

Look for boxes with handles or buckets at fast-food restaurants, paint stores, or paper goods shops. They can be sprayed with lacquer or covered with paper or appropriate stickers. Or use plastic storage boxes or totes with handles. Line your containers with rice paper (available from art supply stores), tissue paper, or Oriental-style wrapping paper and tie them with ribbon or natural string or sisal. Don't forget the chopsticks. (See color photo, page 12.)

SORT-OF SUSHI

Sticky Rice
1 cup uncooked medium- or short-grain rice, such as Arborio
2 tablespoons rice wine vinegar
2 tablespoons soy sauce

1 whole untorn leaf Chinese (napa) cabbage, the largest available, or 1 sheet dried seaweed (nori), about 7½ × 8½ inches, for each roll

Burbank Roll
1 to 2 slices ripe, but firm avocado
1 to 2 strips roasted red pepper, about ½ inch wide, blotted dry if canned
1 small green onion, cut in half lengthwise
1 to 2 tablespoons crabmeat

1 to 2 teaspoons toasted sesame seeds (see page 12)

Smoked Salmon Roll
1 to 3 teaspoons Honey Mustard (see page 149) or thick storebought honey mustard
1 small green onion, cut in half lengthwise
1 slice hothouse cucumber, about ½ inch thick × 7½ inches long
1 slice smoked salmon or lox, 1½ inches wide × 7½ inches long
1 to 2 teaspoons toasted sesame seeds (see page 12)
Ginger-Wasabi Sauce (recipe follows) or Asian Dipping Sauce (see page 158)

To Make Sticky Rice: Place rice in a medium bowl and cover with cold water. Rub with your fingers until water gets cloudy. Drain rice through a strainer and repeat the procedure 2 more times. Place rice, 1 cup water, vinegar, and soy sauce in a medium saucepan and stir to combine. Cover and cook over high heat until water reaches a vigorous boil and steam escapes around the lid, 3 to 5 minutes. Reduce heat to low and simmer for 8 to 10 minutes. The rice is done when the water is absorbed and the rice is tender. It should be sticky enough to hold together when pressed with your fingers. If not, remove from heat and let stand, covered, for 5 minutes. Uncover and cool to room temperature. (Rice may be refrigerated for several days.) This makes about 2 cups rice.

To Prepare Cabbage for Rolls: Soften the leaves by placing 3 or 4 on top of each other on a microwavesafe plate. Drizzle with water, cover with vented plastic wrap, and microwave on high (100%) for 1 minute, or until limp enough to roll. Cut off thick part of rib so leaf is same thickness throughout. Place a sheet of plastic wrap on work surface. Top with large cabbage leaf (or overlap smaller leaves) or seaweed.

After poring over numerous Japanese cookbooks with staggering instructions on how to make sushi, I've decided that the art is best left to the Japanese. My version doesn't call for raw fish or special equipment, uses ingredients available from most supermarkets, and can be refrigerated overnight before serving. Traditionally sushi is made with short-grain rice, but the more commonly found medium grain Arborio rice works well too. These rolls really are fun to make—you'll enjoy experimenting with your own fillings—and they always get raves. They can be wrapped with either napa cabbage leaves or sheets of seaweed (nori). If both are available, make some of each. Serve with Asian Dipping Sauce or Ginger-Wasabi Sauce, but use sparingly—the wasabi horseradish is very hot.

PREP TIME: 30 minutes

COOK TIME: Rice, 12 to 15 minutes

CHILL TIME: 2 hours

ADVANCE PREP: Sushi may be refrigerated overnight. Wasabi sauce may be refrigerated for 1 month.

Spoon ½ to ¾ cup rice into center. Cover with a sheet of plastic wrap and with your hands or rolling pin, press down firmly to spread rice evenly to the edges.

To Make 1 Burbank Roll: Beginning at a short end, arrange a row of avocado, red pepper, green onion, and crabmeat next to each other. Sprinkle with sesame seeds. Using plastic wrap as a guide, roll up tightly, taking care not to roll plastic wrap inside.

To Make 1 Smoked Salmon Roll: Beginning at a short end, spread rice with a thin coating of honey mustard. Arrange a row of smoked salmon near one edge. Top with a row of green onion and cucumber and sprinkle with sesame seeds. Using plastic wrap as a guide, roll up tightly, taking care not to roll plastic wrap inside.

Refrigerate rolls for at least 2 hours. (Sushi may be refrigerated overnight.)

Shortly Before Serving: Slice rolls about ½ inch thick. Serve with sauce for dipping.

EACH ROLL MAKES: 9 or 10 slices, depending on size of leaves.

GINGER-WASABI SAUCE

1 teaspoon wasabi powder
1 tablespoon grated peeled fresh ginger (see page 10)
2 tablespoons sake or dry sherry
2 tablespoons soy sauce
1 teaspoon rice wine vinegar

In a small bowl mix together the wasabi powder and 1 teaspoon water. Let stand for 5 minutes to develop flavor. Place the ginger and sake in a 2-cup microwavesafe measure. Cover and heat on high (100%) for 30 to 45 seconds or until mixture comes to a full boil. Cool and strain into a small bowl. Stir in the wasabi paste, soy sauce, and vinegar. (Sauce may be refrigerated for 1 month.)

MAKES: ¼ cup.

Most people are familiar with Yakitori. (Yaki means "to sear with heat"; *Tori* means "chicken.") Yakimono is a broader term that applies to any type of quickly cooked food, in this case pork. When you're looking for substantial finger food, it's hard to beat these savory skewered pick-ups. (See color photo, page 12.)

PREP TIME: 20 minutes

MARINADE TIME: 4 hours

COOK TIME: 3 minutes

ADVANCE PREP: May be grilled up to 2 hours before serving.

NUTRITIONAL ANALYSIS

Per serving
172 calories
2 g fat
39 mg cholesterol
550 mg sodium

PORK YAKIMONO WITH GREEN AND YELLOW SQUASH RIBBONS

Marinade
½ cup soy sauce
1 tablespoon grated peeled fresh ginger (see page 10)
2 garlic cloves, minced
3 tablespoons honey
Grated peel and juice of 1 medium orange (see page 11) (about ¼ cup juice)

6 ounces lean boneless pork, preferably from the loin or leg
1 medium zucchini
1 medium yellow crookneck squash
8 (6-inch) bamboo or metal skewers, soaked in cold water if bamboo
⅓ cup (packed) light brown sugar

To Marinate: Combine soy sauce, ginger, garlic, honey, orange peel, and orange juice in a heavy plastic zipper bag or glass bowl. (Marinade may be refrigerated overnight.)

Cut pork into ⅜-inch-thick strips, about 4 inches long and 1½ inches wide. Pound lightly to make even thickness. Cut zucchini and yellow squash into 4-inch pieces. Using food processor with ¼-inch (4 mm) slicing blade or a sharp knife, slice lengthwise into ¼-inch-thick strips. You will need 8 slices of each. Add pork and squash strips to marinade. Marinate for up to 4 hours in refrigerator, turning occasionally.

To Grill or Broil: As close to serving as possible, prepare coals, oil grill rack, and place it 3 to 4 inches from coals. Place a slice of zucchini and yellow squash on each slice of pork and thread onto skewers. When coals are hot, place brown sugar on small plate and dip each side of skewer into sugar. Grill over hot coals for 1½ minutes per side, or until cooked through. Or, if desired, the skewers may be broiled as close to the heat source as possible. Serve warm or at room temperature. To take on picnic, cool slightly and wrap in foil.

MAKES: 4 servings; 2 skewers each.

SPINACH AND CUCUMBER SHREDS IN SWEET PEPPER CUPS

4 small red, yellow, or orange
  bell peppers
2 cups fresh spinach leaves,
  washed, stemmed, and cut
  into ½-inch strips
½ hothouse or seedless
  cucumber, peeled (6-inch
  piece)

Dressing
½ cup rice wine vinegar
1 tablespoon sugar
¼ teaspoon wasabi powder
¼ teaspoon salt
1 tablespoon sesame seeds,
  toasted (see page 12)

To Make Salad: Cut a slice off top of each pepper to make a lid. Scoop out pulp and seeds to form a shell. (Hollowed peppers may be refrigerated, covered with plastic wrap, overnight.) Place spinach strips in medium bowl. Using a vegetable peeler, shave cucumber lengthwise into ribbons, stopping when you get to the seeds. Toss with spinach.

To Make Dressing: In a small bowl or glass jar, mix all ingredients together. (Dressing may be refrigerated up to 2 days.)

To Assemble: Up to 3 hours before serving, pour dressing over spinach and cucumbers and toss to coat. Spoon into peppers. Put tops on and serve immediately or refrigerate until serving. To transport, wrap each pepper in plastic wrap.

MAKES: 4 servings.

Change of Pace: Four medium red or yellow tomatoes may be substituted for the peppers.

Colorful pepper bowls filled to the brim with marinated cucumber and spinach strips are perfect picnic portables. (See color photo, page 12.)

PREP TIME: 25 minutes

ADVANCE PREP: Dressing may be refrigerated up to 2 days. Pepper cups may be refrigerated overnight. Salad may be refrigerated up to 3 hours.

NUTRITIONAL ANALYSIS

Per serving
66 calories
2 g fat
0 cholesterol
159 mg sodium

This refreshingly light salad can be served with or without shrimp. Although it is customary to soak cellophane noodles (bean threads) in hot water, microwaving gives them a plumper, softer texture. (See color photo, page 12.)

PREP TIME: 30 minutes

ADVANCE PREP: Dressed noodles may be refrigerated overnight. Add radishes and shrimp up to 4 hours ahead.

SHRIMP SALAD WITH CELLOPHANE NOODLES

1 package (3¾ ounces) cellophane noodles (bean threads)

Oriental Dressing
2 tablespoons oriental sesame oil
1 tablespoon grated peeled fresh ginger (see page 10)
2 medium garlic cloves, minced
⅓ cup rice wine vinegar
3 tablespoons chicken or vegetable broth

½ teaspoon sugar
½ teaspoon salt, or to taste

Salad
¾ cup shredded carrots (about 1½ medium)
½ cup green onions, sliced diagonally (about 4 medium)
½ cup sliced radishes (about 6)
¾ pound peeled and cooked bay or medium shrimp

To Cook Noodles: Pour 3 cups water into a 2-quart (8-cup) microwavesafe bowl. Microwave, covered, on high (100%) for 8 to 10 minutes, or until boiling. Add noodles and microwave, uncovered, on high for 2 minutes. Stir and microwave 2 to 3 minutes more. Remove from oven, stir, and let soak 5 to 10 minutes, or until very soft. If there is any water, drain it off. With scissors, cut the noodles into smaller pieces.

To Make Dressing: In a medium bowl or glass jar, mix all ingredients until well blended. (Dressing may be refrigerated up to 2 days.)

To Assemble Salad: Toss carrots and green onions into noodles. Pour dressing over and toss to coat. (Noodles may be refrigerated overnight.) Up to 4 hours before serving, toss in radishes and shrimp.

MAKES: 4 servings.

NUTRITIONAL ANALYSIS

Per serving
247 calories
8 g fat
81 mg cholesterol
544 mg sodium

UPSIDE-DOWN GINGER CAKELETS

4 tablespoons (½ stick) butter
  or margarine
¼ cup sugar
½ cup molasses
1 large egg
½ cup regular or chunky
  applesauce
1¼ cups all-purpose flour
2 teaspoons ground ginger
2 teaspoons ground cinnamon
¼ teaspoon baking soda

½ teaspoon baking powder
¼ teaspoon salt
1 cup fresh fruit, chopped or
  sliced, such as nectarines,
  pitted cherries, plums, pears,
  and grapes
Creamy Apricot Sauce (recipe
  follows) or Jack Daniel's
  Caramel-Mint Sauce (see
  page 216) (optional)

To Make Cakes: Place butter in a 2-quart (8-cup) microwavesafe bowl. Cover with paper towel and microwave on high (100%) for 45 to 60 seconds, or until melted. Stir in sugar and molasses. Whisk in egg. Stir in applesauce. Add flour, ginger, cinnamon, baking soda, baking powder, and salt. Stir until thoroughly blended.

Grease or spray four 10-ounce custard cups. (Check to be sure the cups hold 1¼ cups of water or the batter will spill over.) Arrange several pieces of fruit attractively in bottom of cups. Stir remaining fruit into batter. Pour ½ to ⅔ cup batter into each cup.

To Cook in Microwave: You need a microwave with 70% power. Place 2 cakes on an inverted dish or dishes to raise them off the oven floor. Microwave uncovered on high (100%) for 1 minute. Rotate and microwave on 70% power for 2 minutes, rotating after 1 minute. Cakes are done when they look damp on top, but feel springy when pressed with fingertips. If tops are still wet, microwave on 70% power for 30 to 90 seconds longer.

To Bake in Oven: Preheat oven to 375°F. Bake for 18 to 22 minutes, or until toothpick inserted in center comes out clean.

When cakes are done, go around edges with a knife and let sit 5 minutes. Invert onto racks, cool slightly and serve warm or at room temperature. (Cakes may be refrigerated up to 3 days or frozen. Defrost at room temperature.) Serve with sauce if desired.

MAKES: 4 cakelets.

(*continued*)

You'll be amazed how moist and flavorful these little cakes are. Aside from saving time, the microwave saves heating up the kitchen. Serve with either Creamy Apricot Sauce or Jack Daniel's Caramel-Mint Sauce, or give your guests a choice by offering both.

PREP TIME: 25 minutes

BAKE TIME: Microwave, 5 minutes; oven, 18 minutes

ADVANCE PREP: Cakes may be refrigerated up to 3 days or frozen. Apricot sauce may be refrigerated for 2 days.

NUTRITIONAL ANALYSIS

Per cakelet
455 calories
14 g fat
84 mg cholesterol
367 mg sodium

Faster: To make cake from a mix, mix 1 box (7 ounces) gingerbread mix with ½ cup applesauce, 1 egg, and 2 tablespoons water. Arrange fruit on bottom of cups and stir remainder into batter. Microwave for 3 minutes on high (100%) and 2 to 4 minutes on 70% power. Or bake at 375°F. for 18 to 22 minutes.

CREAMY APRICOT SAUCE

⅔ cup apricot jam or preserves   ½ cup heavy cream
¼ cup brandy   1 cup light sour cream

Stir jam and brandy in a 2-quart (8-cup) microwavesafe measure. Cover with wax paper and microwave on high (100%) for 2 minutes, or until jam is melted. Stir and cool to room temperature. In mixing bowl with electric mixer, beat heavy cream to soft peaks. Fold in sour cream and cooled jam. Use immediately or refrigerate. (Sauce may be refrigerated, covered, up to 2 days.)

MAKES: 2 cups.

Per 2 tablespoons sauce
36 calories
1 g fat
5 mg cholesterol
2 mg sodium

PEKING CHICKEN
On The
PATIO

From stir-frys to sombreros, chiles to chopsticks, it's a global merger when Peking meets Puerto Vallarta in this Oriental fiesta where anything goes—any time, any place, any where for any size group. When Mexican tortillas enfold strips of Chinese chicken and guacamole is enlivened with soy sauce and sesame oil, you know you're not in for a stuffy dinner. This menu is casual, unusual, and simple to make for four, but a great choice for forty. To multiply the menu, simply plan on two tortillas and one to one and a quarter chicken breast halves per person.

Grilling might be part of the fun during the party, but you can grill or broil the chicken ahead, slice it, and reheat it, covered, in a microwave. Or for greater flexibility, serve it at room temperature. The chicken is super for a picnic basket as well.

The guacamole may sound offbeat, but it has a perkier color and livelier taste than one made with avocado. I think you'll find your guests piling it up on their tortillas.

If you're having a small sit-down dinner, serve the Chinese salad as a first course. For a large gathering, you may wish to add the Two-Rice Salad with Shiitakes, Leeks, and Oranges (see page 60). With half a recipe of the scallops, the menu will serve four.

Menu

◆

CRUDITÉS WITH PEANUT DIPPING SAUCE:

SKEWERED SCALLOPS, ORANGES, AND SNOW PEAS
(See page 288)

•

PEKING CHICKEN IN TORTILLAS

◆

SWEET PEA GUACAMOLE

◆

CRISPY CHINESE SALAD WITH KIWI VINAIGRETTE

◆

FRESH SUMMER FRUIT IN JACK DANIEL'S CARAMEL-MINT SAUCE

GAME PLAN

1 Month Ahead	**Make and freeze guacamole**
1 Week Ahead	**Make Peanut Dipping Sauce** **Make Jack Daniel's Caramel-Mint Sauce**
3 Days Ahead	**Make kiwi vinaigrette**
1 Day Ahead	**Prepare vegetables for dip** **Marinate and cook scallops** **Blanch pea pods for scallops** **Marinate chicken** **Defrost guacamole** **Prepare greens and vegetables for salad**

DAY OF PARTY

4 Hours Ahead	**Prepare condiments for chicken**
1 Hour Ahead	**Prepare coals, if grilling** **Prepare fruit** **Assemble dip and vegetables**
10 Minutes Before Serving	**Grill or broil chicken**
Shortly Before Serving	**Heat tortillas** **Toss salad** **Toss fruit with caramel sauce**

· 211 ·

EXTRA POINTS

THE INVITATIONS

Write the information on paper of choice, wrap around chopsticks and insert into a paper towel tube. Secure the ends with masking tape, wrap, and mail.

THE SETTING

For summer entertaining, line your yard with lanterns. Wrap jade plants in tissue paper.

THE TABLE

Line a wok with plastic, wedge in a block of floral foam, and fill with flowers and chopsticks. (See color photo, page 11.)

I used to serve peanut sauce only with meat, until one day I inadvertently dipped a carrot into some leftovers and discovered a new predinner dip. (See color photo, page 11.)

PREP TIME: 15 minutes

ADVANCE PREP: Dipping sauce may be refrigerated up to 1 week. Vegetables may be prepared 1 day ahead.

CRUDITÉS WITH PEANUT DIPPING SAUCE

1 piece peeled fresh ginger, about 1 × 1½ inches
2 garlic cloves, peeled
½ cup peanut butter, preferably chunky
1 tablespoon oriental sesame oil
2 tablespoons soy sauce
2 tablespoons rice wine vinegar

½ to ¾ teaspoon Chinese chile sauce (see page 10) or chile oil, to taste
Vegetables, such as carrots, celery, jícama, red and yellow peppers, cut for dipping, radishes, cherry tomatoes, sugar snap peas, endive leaves

In a food processor with the metal blade, process ginger and garlic until minced. Add peanut butter, ⅓ cup water, sesame oil, soy sauce, and rice wine vinegar and process until blended, scraping down sides as needed. Stir in chile sauce or oil to taste. (Sauce may be refrigerated up to 1 week. If it becomes too thick, thin with additional water.) Serve with assorted vegetables.

MAKES: 1 cup sauce.

NUTRITIONAL ANALYSIS

Per 2 teaspoons sauce
38 calories
3 g fat
0 cholesterol
113 mg sodium

PEKING CHICKEN IN TORTILLAS

Marinade
¾ cup Chinese plum sauce
  (7- or 8-ounce jar)
½ cup hoisin sauce

4 to 6 skinless, boneless chicken
  breast halves (about 1¼
  pounds total)

8 flour tortillas, about 7 inches

Condiments
Sweet Pea Guacamole (recipe
  follows)
8 to 10 green onions, sliced
  lengthwise into halves or
  quarters
1 can (8 ounces) sliced water
  chestnuts, drained and cut
  into strips
1 cup cilantro leaves

To Marinate: In a small bowl, stir together plum and hoisin sauces. Cut all fat from chicken breasts, rinse, and pat dry. Place in a plastic zipper bag and pour half the marinade over. Marinate in the refrigerator for at least 4 hours, or preferably overnight, turning once to coat evenly. Refrigerate remaining marinade for sauce.

To Grill or Broil: Prepare coals. Oil grill rack and place it 3 to 4 inches from coals. When coals are hot, remove chicken from marinade. Grill for 3 to 4 minutes per side, or until cooked through. Or broil as close to heat source as possible. Remove to a cutting board and slice lengthwise into ¼-inch strips.

To Heat Tortillas: Divide tortillas in half and wrap in cloth napkins or towels to heat in microwave, or wrap in foil for conventional oven. Microwave 1 packet on high (100%) for 30 seconds, or until warm. (For a larger party, 8 tortillas can be wrapped together and microwaved on high for 1 to 2 minutes. Do not microwave more than 8 at a time or they will not heat evenly.) Or bake at 350°F. for 10 minutes, or until heated through.

To Serve: Offer each guest a warm tortilla. Spread with reserved marinade, top with chicken and assorted condiments, roll up, and enjoy. When guests have finished their first tortilla, microwave or bake second packet in the same manner.

MAKES: 4 servings, 2 tortillas per person.

I was inspired by Peking Duck but I've changed the bird, eliminated the skin, added different condiments, and substituted tortillas for the pancakes. But I kept the classic's incredibly great taste. The marinade combines two oriental sauces—Chinese plum, a sweet sauce resembling Major Grey chutney, and hoisin, a pungent bean paste, both widely available in supermarkets. (See color photo, page 11.)

PREP TIME: 20 minutes

MARINADE TIME: 4 hours or overnight

GRILL TIME: 6 to 8 minutes

ADVANCE PREP: Condiments may be refrigerated for several hours.

NUTRITIONAL ANALYSIS

Per serving (not including condiments)
457 calories
9 g fat
120 mg cholesterol
421 mg sodium

Creative chef Michael Roberts is to be credited with substituting peas for avocado in his guacamole. The Asian twist is my addition. Besides adding sweetness, peas don't turn brown when mashed ahead and can always be found ripe. (See color photo, page 11.)

PREP TIME: 10 minutes

ADVANCE PREP: May be refrigerated up to 2 days or frozen.

NUTRITIONAL ANALYSIS

Per tablespoon (with nonfat yogurt)
21 calories
1 g fat
0 cholesterol
90 mg sodium

SWEET PEA GUACAMOLE

1½ cups frozen peas, preferably not the petit variety
2 medium garlic cloves, peeled
1½ tablespoons oriental sesame oil
1½ tablespoons fresh lime juice
1½ tablespoons soy sauce

Several dashes hot chile oil or Tabasco, to taste
3 tablespoons chopped cilantro (optional)
3 tablespoons regular, low-fat, or nonfat plain yogurt or sour cream

Place peas in a medium microwavesafe bowl and microwave on high (100%) until hot, 2 to 4 minutes. In a food processor with the metal blade, mince garlic. Add peas, sesame oil, lime juice, soy sauce, chile oil, cilantro, if using, and yogurt or sour cream. Process until pureed, scraping sides, about 1 minute. Transfer to a bowl and refrigerate. (Guacamole may be refrigerated up to 2 days or frozen up to 1 month.) Bring to room temperature before serving.

MAKES: about 1¼ cups.

CRISPY CHINESE SALAD WITH KIWI VINAIGRETTE

Salad

1 small head (4 ounces) radicchio, torn into 1-inch pieces (1½ cups, packed)

8 to 10 large napa cabbage leaves, cut into 1-inch squares, thick stems discarded (3 cups, packed)

¼ small head romaine lettuce, torn into 1-inch pieces (1 cup, packed)

3 ounces bean sprouts, rinsed, dried, and cut into thirds

Kiwi Vinaigrette

1 piece fresh ginger, about the size of a quarter

2 large or 3 small kiwi, peeled and coarsely chopped

4 teaspoons fresh lime juice

Scant 1 teaspoon oriental sesame oil

1 tablespoon vegetable oil

3 tablespoons orange juice or water

¼ teaspoon salt, or to taste

2 to 3 teaspoons honey

1 cup peeled and chopped (½-inch pieces) jícama or apple

1 medium carrot, peeled and thinly sliced

To Make Salad: Refrigerate radicchio, cabbage, romaine, and bean sprouts in a plastic bag or bowl. (Greens may be refrigerated overnight.)

To Make Vinaigrette: In a food processor with the metal blade, process ginger until minced, scraping sides of bowl. Measure 1 teaspoon and return to processor. Add kiwi and process until pureed. Add lime juice, oils, orange juice, salt, and honey and process until mixture is smooth and creamy. Remove to small bowl or jar. (Dressing may be refrigerated up to 3 days.) This makes about ¾ cup.

To Serve: Add jícama and carrot to salad and toss with as much dressing as needed. Serve immediately.

MAKES: 4 to 5 servings.

What a surprise to find that kiwi makes a refreshing substitute for oil in a salad dressing. The pale green vinaigrette dressing is creamy and dotted with tiny black seeds resembling pepper. (See color photo, page 11.)

PREP TIME: 35 minutes

ADVANCE PREP: Greens may be refrigerated overnight. Vinaigrette may be refrigerated up to 3 days.

NUTRITIONAL ANALYSIS

Per serving salad (not including vinaigrette)
38 calories
less than 1 g fat
0 cholesterol
20 mg sodium

Per tablespoon vinaigrette
30 calories
2 g fat
0 cholesterol
45 mg sodium

When mint began taking over my herb garden, I must have stirred it into every dish I made. None fared better than this sauce, which makes a noteworthy adornment for seasonal fruit or plain cake.

PREP TIME: 20 minutes

COOK TIME: Microwave, about 6 minutes; top of stove, 10 minutes

CHILL TIME: Sauce, 30 minutes

ADVANCE PREP: Sauce may be refrigerated up to 1 week.

FRESH SUMMER FRUIT IN JACK DANIEL'S CARAMEL-MINT SAUCE

Caramel-Mint Sauce
2 tablespoons butter or margarine
½ cup sugar
Pinch salt
3 tablespoons orange juice
⅓ cup heavy cream
1 tablespoon Jack Daniel's or other whiskey

½ to 1 teaspoon finely minced fresh mint, or to taste

Fruit
4 fresh plums, sliced ¾ inch thick
4 nectarines, sliced ¾ inch thick
1 cup fresh blueberries
Mint sprigs, for garnish

To Make Sauce in Microwave: Place butter in a 4-cup glass measure. Cover with wax paper and microwave on high (100%) for 40 to 60 seconds, or until melted. With a rubber spatula, stir in sugar and salt. Microwave on high (100%), covered with wax paper for 1 minute, or until mixture comes to a full boil. Remove paper and microwave for 60 to 90 seconds, without stirring, until portions of the sugar turn golden. Watch carefully, it burns easily. Stir until mixture is smooth and uniformly caramel color; don't be concerned if some of the butter separates. Remove to a work surface and carefully stir in orange juice and cream. The mixture will bubble up and stiffen. Return to microwave and cook on high (100%), uncovered, for 1 to 2 minutes, stirring every 30 seconds, until caramel is melted and smooth. Stir in whiskey and mint.

To Make Sauce on Stove: Melt butter in heavy medium saucepan. Stir in sugar and salt. Cook over medium-high heat, stirring until the sugar melts into a syrup. Continue cooking without stirring until sugar caramelizes to a golden brown, about 6 minutes. If it begins to color in 1 section, swirl the pan to distribute the heat evenly. Remove from heat and carefully stir in the orange juice and cream. The mixture will bubble up and stiffen. Return to medium heat and cook, stirring, until caramel is dissolved and smooth. Remove from heat and stir in whiskey and mint.

Refrigerate sauce until it thickens, at least 30 minutes. (Sauce may be refrigerated up to one week.) This makes about ¾ cup sauce.

To Serve: Stir fruits together, add sauce, and toss to coat. Garnish with sprigs of mint.

MAKES: 4 servings.

Leaner: Substitute ⅓ cup evaporated skim milk for the cream.

Summer Seafood Sizzle

*T*his menu is ablaze with some of my favorite new American recipes, as good for a gala as for an intimate interlude. Both fish entrees are simple yet full of flavor. The crisp and creamy Potato–Mushroom–Blue Cheese Galette is a surefire accompaniment, but other choices might be Salad Bar Pasta (see page 132), Orzo with Broccoli Pesto (see page 108), or Roasted Red-Skin Potatoes with Rosemary (see page 119). Depending on the richness of the side dish you select, you might want to begin your dinner with Caramelized Onion, Walnut, and Blue Cheese Pizza (see page 151) instead of the tortellini.

Fresh Corn and Red Bell Pepper Salad is chock-full of summer's bounty; you might like to partner it with leafy greens in the Crispy Chinese Salad with Kiwi Vinaigrette (see page 215) or Garden Salad with Tortilla Strings and Grainy Mustard Vinaigrette (see page 172).

At the height of summer, when fresh fruit is at its peak, I offer no substitute for Nectarine-Raspberry Cobblers. But at other times of year, anything goes, from the refined Ebony, Ivory, and Milk Chocolate Torte (see page 122) to individual Peach Tortoni (see page 154). This menu serves six.

Menu

◆

TORTELLINI WITH PIMIENTO PEPPER DIP (See page 286)

◆

MESQUITE-GRILLED SALMON WITH CRISP CRUMB CRUST
OR
TUNA STUFFED WITH GUACAMOLE

◆

POTATO–MUSHROOM– BLUE CHEESE GALETTE

◆

FRESH CORN AND RED BELL PEPPER SALAD

◆

INDIVIDUAL NECTARINE- RASPBERRY COBBLERS

GAME PLAN

2 Weeks Ahead	**Make and freeze bread crumbs for salmon, if serving**
1 Day Ahead	**Make marinade for tuna, if serving** **Cook tortellini and make pimiento dip** **Make and microwave potato galette** **Make corn salad**
DAY OF PARTY 6 Hours Ahead	**Coat salmon with bread crumbs, if serving** **Make and bake cobblers**
4 Hours Ahead	**Stuff and marinate tuna, if serving**
1 Hour Ahead	**Prepare coals and soak wood chips** **Bring corn salad to room temperature**
35 Minutes Ahead	**Bake potato galette**
4 to 10 Minutes Ahead	**Grill tuna or salmon**
Shortly Before Serving	**Rewarm cobblers**

EXTRA POINTS

THE TABLE

Arrange groupings of vegetables, fruits, herbs, and flowers to reinforce the theme of summer.

What a treasure this recipe is. It comes from Michael James's book *Slow Food,* and I first made it, very successfully, for a party in his honor. I have since added the egg white to help the bread crumbs adhere. It may be necessary to call ahead and order center-cut fillets that are one inch thick and skinned.

PREP TIME: 15 minutes

GRILL TIME: 4 to 6 minutes

ADVANCE PREP: Bread crumbs may be frozen. Salmon may be refrigerated up to 6 hours before grilling.

NUTRITIONAL ANALYSIS

Per serving
278 calories
9 g fat
30 mg cholesterol
483 mg sodium

MESQUITE-GRILLED SALMON WITH CRISP CRUMB CRUST

5 cups fresh white or egg bread crumbs, made from slightly stale bread (see page 000)
6 salmon fillets, skin removed, and cut 1 inch thick (6 to 8 ounces each)
Salt and freshly ground black pepper
1 egg white, lightly beaten
1 to 2 tablespoons olive oil
Lemon wedges, for serving

Prepare coals, oil grill rack, and place it 3 to 4 inches from coals. Soak a handful of mesquite chips in water for at least 30 minutes, then drain.

Place bread crumbs in a shallow dish. Wipe salmon and season to taste with salt and pepper. Brush both sides with egg white and dip into crumbs, pressing so they adhere. Drizzle top lightly with olive oil. (Salmon may be refrigerated loosely covered with foil up to 6 hours. Bring to room temperature 1 hour before grilling.)

When coals are hot, add mesquite chips. Grill the salmon, covered with the lid of the grill to impart a smokier flavor and to keep the coals from flaring up, for 2 to 3 minutes on each side, until almost cooked through but still slightly translucent in the center. Fish will continue to cook after it's removed from the heat. Remove to plates and serve with lemon wedges.

MAKES: 6 servings.

TUNA STUFFED WITH GUACAMOLE

**6 tuna steaks, cut 1 inch thick
(8 to 10 ounces each)**

Guacamole Filling
**1 large shallot or ⅛ onion,
peeled (2 tablespoons minced)**
2 garlic cloves, peeled
**1 small avocado, peeled and pit
removed**
**1 tablespoon plus 1 teaspoon
fresh lemon juice**
**½ teaspoon Worcestershire
sauce**
**2 tablespoons butter or
margarine**
Salt to taste

Marinade
⅓ cup soy sauce
**3 tablespoons fresh lemon juice
(see page 11)**
1 garlic clove, minced
2 teaspoons Dijon mustard
3 tablespoons vegetable oil
3 tablespoons dry sherry

**Lemon wedges for garnish
(optional)**

To Prepare Fish: Holding the knife parallel to the work surface, make a pocket in the fish by cutting through the center as far back as possible, leaving back and sides attached.

To Make Filling: In a food processor with the metal blade, process shallot and garlic until minced. Add avocado, lemon juice, Worcestershire sauce, butter, and salt and process until pureed. Divide filling among fish, about 2 tablespoons per steak, spreading it towards the back and pressing gently on fish to make it even.

To Marinate: Mix all ingredients in a bowl or jar. Place fish close together in a shallow glass dish, pour marinade over, and turn to coat both sides. Cover and refrigerate for 4 or 5 hours.

To Grill: Prepare coals, oil grill rack, and place it 3 to 4 inches from coals. When coals are hot, remove fish from marinade and grill for 4 to 5 minutes per side, or until cooked through. Garnish with lemon wedges, if desired.

MAKES: 6 servings.

Change of Pace: Substitute swordfish or shark steaks for the tuna.

Cut a pocket in the middle of a tuna steak and fill it with guacamole. Besides tasting terrific, it reduces the risk of overcooking the fish.

PREP TIME: 20 minutes

MARINADE TIME: 4 hours

GRILL TIME: 8 to 10 minutes

ADVANCE PREP: May be stuffed and marinated up to 5 hours ahead.

NUTRITIONAL ANALYSIS

Per serving
514 calories
25 g fat
122 mg cholesterol
593 mg sodium

POTATO–MUSHROOM–BLUE CHEESE GALETTE

Filling
1 tablespoon olive oil
½ pound fresh mushrooms, thickly sliced
1 tablespoon all-purpose flour
½ cup regular, low-fat, or nonfat milk
⅓ cup crumbled blue cheese

Potatoes
No-stick cooking spray
3 medium baking potatoes (about 2 pounds)
6 tablespoons chicken or vegetable broth, divided
Salt and freshly ground black pepper
1 tablespoon butter (optional)

To Make Filling: In a medium skillet over medium heat, heat oil until hot. Sauté mushrooms until soft, 3 to 5 minutes. Stir in flour until incorporated. Slowly stir in milk, stirring constantly, until mixture comes to a boil and thickens. Stir in cheese until melted.

To Assemble: Spray bottom and sides of a microwavesafe 9-inch pie plate with cooking spray. Peel and thinly slice potatoes into ⅛- to ¼-inch slices by hand or in a food processor with 2 or 4 mm slicing blade. Working quickly so potatoes don't discolor, arrange half the potatoes in bottom of dish. Drizzle with 3 tablespoons chicken broth and sprinkle with salt and pepper. Top with mushroom filling, spreading evenly. Arrange remaining potatoes in overlapping circles over the top. Drizzle with 3 tablespoons chicken broth and salt and pepper. Spray with cooking spray or dot with butter, if desired.

To Microwave: Cover with plastic wrap and place in a microwave on a plate to catch possible drippings. Top with a plate or tray to compress the potatoes. Microwave on high (100%) for 9 to 14 minutes, or until crisp-tender when pierced with the tip of a sharp knife. Do not cook until soft because potatoes will finish baking in conventional oven. Clean edges of pie plate with damp paper towel. (Galette may be refrigerated overnight.)

To Bake: Preheat oven to 450°F.
Spray top of galette with cooking spray. Bake, uncovered, for 25 to 35 minutes, or until crisp and golden.

MAKES: 6 servings.

Most potato dishes need to be prepared at the last minute. Not this one. A piquant blue cheese and mushroom filling is sandwiched between thin layers of potatoes and microwaved—the dish can then be refrigerated overnight without the potatoes discoloring. Before serving, it is baked in a conventional oven until crisp and golden.

PREP TIME: 30 minutes

COOK TIME: Microwave, 9 to 14 minutes; oven, 25 to 35 minutes

ADVANCE PREP: Microwaved potatoes may be refrigerated overnight and baked before serving.

NUTRITIONAL ANALYSIS

Per serving (with nonfat milk)
227 calories
6 g fat
10 mg cholesterol
417 mg sodium

FRESH CORN AND RED BELL PEPPER SALAD

2 medium red bell peppers
1 tablespoon plus 1 tablespoon olive oil, divided
3 medium leeks, cleaned, cut in half lengthwise and sliced ½ inch thick (see page 11) (about 1 cup)
4 cups fresh uncooked corn cut off the cob (see page 10) (5 to 6 ears)

2 garlic cloves, minced
2 teaspoons fresh thyme leaves or ½ teaspoon dried thyme
5 teaspoons dry sherry
3 tablespoons raspberry vinegar
Salt and freshly ground black pepper

Halve, core, and seed peppers. Cut in half crosswise and then into ¼-inch strips. In a large skillet, heat 1 tablespoon olive oil over moderate heat. Add leeks and red peppers and sauté for 1 minute. Reduce heat to low, cover the pan with a sheet of wax paper and the lid, and cook until vegetables are soft but not brown, stirring occasionally, about 10 minutes. Remove to a medium bowl.

Increase heat to medium-high, add remaining tablespoon oil to skillet and heat until hot. Sauté corn and garlic, stirring often, until corn is barely tender, about 6 minutes. Add to peppers and stir in thyme, sherry, vinegar, and salt and pepper to taste. (Salad may be refrigerated overnight.) Serve at room temperature.

MAKES: 6 servings.

Faster: Substitute 4 cups frozen corn for the fresh. Do not defrost. Reduce cooking time to 2 to 3 minutes, or until tender but still crunchy.

This sunny salad is as at home on a buffet as it is in a picnic basket. It is well worth the little extra time it takes to cut fresh corn off the cob.

PREP TIME: 15 minutes

COOK TIME: 20 minutes

ADVANCE PREP: Salad may be refrigerated overnight.

NUTRITIONAL ANALYSIS

Per serving
169 calories
6 g fat
0 cholesterol
203 mg sodium

This summer cobbler is one of my very favorites. The topping is crunchy like a cookie and the filling is soft and perfumed with vanilla.

PREP TIME: 25 minutes

BAKE TIME: 25 to 35 minutes

ADVANCE PREP: May be baked up to 6 hours before serving.

INDIVIDUAL NECTARINE-RASPBERRY COBBLERS

Filling
6 to 8 medium nectarines, cut into ½-inch slices
½ cup peach or apricot preserves or fruit spread (reduced sugar preserves)
2 teaspoons vanilla extract
1 pint fresh raspberries

Topping
¼ pound (1 stick) butter or margarine, cold and cut into 8 pieces for food processor, at room temperature for mixer

1 cup sugar
1 large egg
½ teaspoon vanilla extract
½ cup all-purpose flour
½ teaspoon baking powder
⅛ teaspoon salt
Double Whipped Cream (see page 266), vanilla or cinnamon ice cream, or frozen yogurt for serving (optional)

Place rack in upper third of oven. Preheat oven to 375°F.

To Make Filling: In a medium bowl, toss nectarines with preserves and vanilla. Lightly mix in raspberries. Butter or spray six to eight 1- to 1½-cup gratin dishes or 10-ounce custard cups and divide fruit among dishes.

To Make Topping: In a food processor with the metal blade, or mixing bowl with electric mixer, process or mix butter and sugar until light and fluffy. Add egg and vanilla and process or mix until blended. Add flour, baking powder, and salt and pulse or mix until incorporated. Drop batter by tablespoonfuls over filling. It will not cover completely, but will spread during baking.

To Bake: Bake for 25 to 35 minutes, or until tops are golden brown. It may be necessary to rotate the dishes so they brown evenly. Cool at least 20 minutes before serving. (Cobblers may be baked up to 6 hours before serving. Leave at room temperature and reheat at 400°F. for 5 minutes before serving.) Serve with whipped cream, ice cream, or yogurt, if desired.

MAKES: 6 to 8 servings.

Change of Pace: To make 1 large cobbler, butter or spray 7 × 11-inch baking dish and mix fruit in it. Spoon topping over and bake for 35 to 40 minutes. Cool 45 minutes before serving.

HAPPY HOLIDAYS
and
CELEBRATIONS

Pages fall from the calendar as weeks turn into months and seasons pass. Take time to capture life's most precious moments with these treasured menus. Gather with family and friends around the Easter or Passover table to celebrate the holiday's religious traditions and the rebirth of Spring with new contemporary dishes. Invite the gang to get together in your backyard for a Southwestern-style flag-raising Fourth of July. Greet loved ones with a bountiful Thanksgiving feast that evokes memories of the past and hopes for the future. For large group gatherings, stage an on-the-run cocktail party, where you can enjoy the luxury of relaxing with your guests. And for life's most joyous occasions—a wedding, birthday, shower, or anniversary—offer an elaborate but very manageable buffet.

Menu

SHRIMP MOUSSE WITH
DILL-PISTACHIO
PESTO (See page 283)

◆

SPIRAL-SLICED STOREBOUGHT
BAKED HAM WITH THREE-
STAR SAUCES:

GARNET DOUBLE-CHERRY
SAUCE

•

PEACH-RHUBARB SAUCE

•

MUSTARD SAUCE WITH GREEN
PEPPERCORNS

◆

GRATINÉED FARINA-PESTO
GNOCCHI

◆

ASPARAGUS SALAD WITH
HAZELNUT VINAIGRETTE

◆

HONEY GRAHAM–SWEET
POTATO ROLLS (See page 274)

◆

LIGHT AND LUSH LEMON
CAKE

EXTRA-SPECIAL EASTER DINNER

Eating ham for Easter is a very old rural custom. Pigs were fattened and slaughtered in the fall, so the meat could hang and cure over the cold winter months. By spring the hams were ready to eat, just in time for the Easter celebration.

Today's cooks can happily forget about raising, hanging, soaking and cooking pigs. In fact, you can buy one of those wonderful honey-glazed ready-to-eat hams and, instead of hovering over the stove for hours, concentrate on sauces to go with it. I offer three—serve them all and let your family vote for their favorite.

Yesterday's country cooks may have based their Easter dumplings on cornmeal, but I prefer farina, or Cream of Wheat, in mine. In Italy, these are called gnocchi, and they are made from potatoes, flour, cornmeal, semolina, or farina. Serve the dumplings with any meat, fish, or poultry dish that does not have a creamy or cheese-laden sauce.

Asparagus Salad with Hazelnut Vinaigrette continues in the spring mode. When I compared cooking asparagus in the microwave with steaming and with simmering bunches in a skillet, the skillet technique won hands down. The spears cook more evenly with brighter color and flavor. Pencil-thin asparagus tied in bundles with blanched green onion tops instead of string are ready to be chilled, dressed, and served.

Light and Lush Lemon Cake is baked in a bundt pan and served either warm, chilled, or at room temperature. Decorated with daisies, lemon slices, and sprigs of fresh mint, it makes a fitting finale for this spring-time feast. This menu serves eight.

G A M E   P L A N

1 Month Ahead	**Make and freeze gnocchi** **Make and freeze pesto** **Make and freeze lemon cake** **Make and freeze rolls**
2 Weeks Ahead	**Make mustard sauce** **Infuse hazelnut oil for 36 hours, strain, and** **refrigerate**
4 Days Ahead	**Make cherry and peach-rhubarb sauces** **Make hazelnut vinaigrette**
2 Days Ahead	**Make sour cream sauce, if using**
1 Day Ahead	**Defrost gnocchi, pesto, rolls, and cake** **Cook asparagus** **Make shrimp mousse**

DAY OF PARTY

8 Hours Ahead	**Assemble gnocchi**
1 Hour Ahead	**Unmold shrimp mousse** **Bring gnocchi to room temperature**
20 Minutes Ahead	**Bake gnocchi**
Shortly Before Serving	**Assemble asparagus salad** **Rewarm cake, if desired** **Rewarm rolls**

· EXTRA · POINTS

THE TABLE

Spread shredded cellophane grass down the center of your table and scatter candy, chocolate, and/or real dyed eggs and small pots of flowers in it. Or collect various size and shape baskets, line them with pastel netting, excelsior, or tissue and fill with colored eggs and pots of hyacinths, tulips, or lilies of the valley.

THE PLACE CARDS

Write names with colored markers on dyed eggs. Nestle them in grass nests in tiny baskets or small paper bowls. Colorful stickers make eggs and baskets easy to decorate.

Popular with all ages, this sauce—reminiscent of the raisin sauce grandma served with ham—is so good I've even spooned it over ice cream, frozen yogurt, and plain cakes.

PREP TIME: 5 minutes

COOK TIME: Microwave, 6 to 9 minutes; stovetop, 3 to 4 minutes

ADVANCE PREP: May be refrigerated up to 4 days.

GARNET DOUBLE-CHERRY SAUCE

1 can (16 ounces) dark sweet cherries, drained, reserving ½ cup juice
1 can (16 ounces) tart cherries, drained, reserving ¼ cup juice
½ cup whole-berry cranberry sauce or Cran-Fruit
1 tablespoon plus 1 teaspoon cornstarch

2 tablespoons currant jelly
1 tablespoon balsamic vinegar
2 teaspoons fresh chopped mint or ½ teaspoon dried mint (optional)

In a 4-cup (1-quart) microwavesafe bowl or saucepan, stir together cherries and juice, cranberry sauce, cornstarch, jelly, and vinegar. Microwave, covered, on high (100%) for 6 to 9 minutes, stirring every 3 minutes, or cook on top of the stove over moderate heat, stirring occasionally, until sauce comes to a boil and thickens. Stir in mint to taste, if using. Serve warm or at room temperature. (Sauce may be refrigerated up to 4 days.)

MAKES: 3½ cups.

NUTRITIONAL ANALYSIS

Per 2 tablespoons
34 calories
less than 1 g fat
0 cholesterol
3 mg sodium

PEACH-RHUBARB SAUCE

1 piece peeled fresh ginger, about 1 inch wide × ⅜ inch thick
1½ cups plus ¾ cup frozen peach slices, partially thawed and very coarsely chopped, divided
1 cup fresh or frozen rhubarb, partially thawed and very coarsely chopped
5 tablespoons honey
2 tablespoons fresh lime juice

In a food processor with the metal blade, process ginger until minced. Add 1½ cups peaches and the rhubarb and pulse until coarsely chopped. Remove to a medium microwavesafe bowl and stir in honey and lime juice. Microwave, uncovered, on high (100%) for 14 to 18 minutes, without stirring, to the consistency of thick applesauce. Cool to room temperature and stir in remaining ¾ cup peaches. (Sauce may be refrigerated up to 4 days.) Serve warm or at room temperature.

MAKES: 2 cups.

Although this chutney-like sauce can be made year round with frozen fruits, it's a welcome harbinger of spring when made with fresh rhubarb. To save time, partially thaw frozen fruit in the microwave.

PREP TIME: 10 minutes

MICROWAVE TIME: 14 to 18 minutes

ADVANCE PREP: May be refrigerated up to 4 days.

NUTRITIONAL ANALYSIS

Per 2 tablespoons
56 calories
less than 1 g fat
0 cholesterol
3 mg sodium

MUSTARD SAUCE WITH GREEN PEPPERCORNS

⅔ cup regular or light sour cream
2 tablespoons grainy mustard, such as Moutarde de Meaux
1 tablespoon Dijon mustard
2 teaspoons creamy horseradish, preferably white
2 tablespoons beef broth
½ teaspoon coarsely crushed green peppercorns
2 tablespoons madeira wine

In a medium bowl, stir together all the ingredients. Cover and refrigerate until serving. (Sauce may be refrigerated up to 2 weeks.) Serve chilled or at room temperature.

MAKES: 1 cup.

Here you have a sophisticated creamy sauce accented with the bite of horseradish and green peppercorns.

PREP TIME: 10 minutes

ADVANCE PREP: May be refrigerated up to 2 weeks.

NUTRITIONAL ANALYSIS

Per 2 teaspoons (with light sour cream)
13 calories
1 g fat
3 mg cholesterol
51 mg sodium

arina is just a fancy name for Cream of Wheat, and for years Italians have been turning it into gnocchi (pronounced NOH-kee), or dumplings. It bears little resemblance to breakfast cereal when cooked until thick, flavored with parmesan cheese, and cut into squares or other shapes— for Easter, try bunnies. Although farina takes a little longer to cook in the microwave than on top of the stove, you don't have to stir constantly, and you won't be left with a scorched saucepan to scrub out.

PREP TIME: 30 minutes including cooking farina

CHILL TIME: 1 hour

BAKE TIME: 15 to 20 minutes

ADVANCE PREP: Gnocchi may be refrigerated up to 3 days or frozen. Pesto may be refrigerated up to 1 week or frozen. Assemble up to 8 hours before baking.

NUTRITIONAL ANALYSIS

Per serving
371 calories
21 g fat
37 mg cholesterol
575 mg sodium

GRATINÉED FARINA-PESTO GNOCCHI

Gnocchi
4 cups whole milk
¾ teaspoon salt, or to taste
1½ cups regular farina (Cream of Wheat), not instant
3 tablespoons butter or margarine
⅓ cup plus ⅓ cup grated parmesan cheese, divided
1 tablespoon grainy mustard, such as Moutarde de Meaux
½ teaspoon freshly ground rainbow or black pepper

Basil Pesto
1 medium garlic clove, peeled
1 cup (packed) fresh basil leaves (1 ounce) or ¼ cup dry basil and ½ cup (packed) spinach leaves
¼ cup grated parmesan cheese
¼ cup pine nuts or walnuts
¼ cup olive oil
⅛ teaspoon salt, or to taste

To Make Gnocchi in Microwave: Pour milk into a 3 to 4-quart microwavesafe bowl or casserole. Whisk in salt and farina. Cover with plastic wrap and microwave on high (100%) for 13 to 18 minutes, stirring well every 4 minutes, until the mixture is very stiff and a wooden spoon stands up straight. Stir in butter, ⅓ cup parmesan, mustard, and pepper.

To Make Gnocchi on Stove: In a heavy large saucepan over medium heat, bring milk to a simmer. Lower the heat, add salt, and slowly pour in the farina in a slow, steady stream, whisking constantly to avoid lumps. Continue to cook, stirring vigorously over medium-high heat, until the mixture comes to a boil. Continue cooking and stirring for another 3 to 5 minutes until the mixture is very thick and the sides pull away from the pan. Remove from heat and stir in butter, ⅓ cup parmesan, mustard, and pepper.

Butter or spray a rimmed 15½ × 10½ × 1-inch baking sheet (jelly-roll pan) and spread mixture into a 10 × 12-inch rectangle about ⅝ inch thick. Cover with foil, cool to room temperature and refrigerate for at least 1 hour. Gnocchi may be refrigerated up to 3 days or frozen up to 1 month. Defrost covered in refrigerator.)

To Make Pesto: In a food processor with the metal blade, process garlic until minced. Add basil, ¼ cup parmesan, and nuts and pulse until ground. Add olive oil and salt and process until pureed. Makes ½ cup sauce. (Pesto may be refrigerated up to one week or frozen.)

To Assemble: Up to 8 hours before serving, butter or spray a rimmed baking sheet or gratin dish. Spread top of gnocchi with pesto and sprinkle with remaining ⅓ cup parmesan. Cut into 2-inch squares with a knife or into other shapes with a cookie cutter. Place close together or slightly overlapping in prepared pan. (Gnocchi may be refrigerated covered with foil up to 8 hours. Remove from refrigerator 1 hour before baking.)

To Bake: Preheat oven to 450°F.

Bake, uncovered, in middle or upper third of oven for 15 to 20 minutes, or until lightly golden.

MAKES: 8 side-dish servings

Leaner: For a less creamy version, substitute lowfat (2%) milk for whole milk. Reduce parmesan cheese in gnocchi to 3 tablespoons and top with 3 tablespoons.

Faster: Substitute ½ cup storebought pesto.

My frugal side resists buying expensive hazelnut oil, especially when it's so easy to make your own by steeping toasted hazelnuts in vegetable oil. The homemade version is less concentrated, but the nuts are a bonus. Refrigerate them separately to toss on salads, vegetables, or grilled fish that you've drizzled with the infused oil.

PREP TIME: 15 minutes

COOK TIME: About 4 minutes

STEEP TIME: Hazelnut oil, 24 to 36 hours.

ADVANCE PREP: Vinaigrette may be refrigerated for several days. Asparagus may be cooked 1 day ahead.

NUTRITIONAL ANALYSIS

Per serving salad (not including vinaigrette, with 2 teaspoons nuts)
82 calories
6 g fat
0 cholesterol
4 mg sodium

Per tablespoon vinaigrette
120 calories
14 g fat
0 cholesterol
89 mg sodium

ASPARAGUS SALAD WITH HAZELNUT VINAIGRETTE

Hazelnut Oil
¾ cup vegetable oil
½ cup finely chopped hazelnuts, toasted (see page 11)

2 pounds thin asparagus
4 green onions
2 tablespoons raspberry vinegar
Salt and freshly ground black pepper
Greens, such as romaine or butter lettuce, to line plates

To Make Hazelnut Oil: At least 24 hours before using, heat vegetable oil on top of stove or in microwave until very hot. Place nuts in a small bowl or glass jar and pour hot oil over. Cover and steep at room temperature for 24 to 36 hours. Pour through strainer, pressing down lightly on the nuts. Refrigerate oil and nuts separately until ready to use. (Nuts and oil may be refrigerated up to 2 weeks.)

To Prepare Asparagus Bundles: Cut off the woody bottoms of asparagus, leaving spears about 5 inches long. Separate into bundles of 6 to 8 thin spears each, with tips pointing in the same direction. Cut off green onion tops where the white ends and cut green tops in half lengthwise. (Reserve white parts for another use.) Place tops in a microwavesafe pie dish, add ¼ inch water and microwave, covered, on high (100%) for 1 to 2 minutes, or until wilted. Cool slightly. Tie green strips of onion around asparagus bundles.

To Cook: In a large skillet, bring about 1 inch of salted water to a boil. Add asparagus bundles and boil gently, uncovered, until just tender, about 4 minutes. Remove bundles and run under cold water to stop the cooking. Blot dry. (Asparagus may be refrigerated overnight on a double thickness of paper towels covered with plastic wrap.)

To Make Vinaigrette: In a small bowl or jar, whisk or shake vinegar and hazelnut oil. Season to taste with salt and pepper. (Dressing may be refrigerated for several days.)

To Assemble: Shortly before serving, line salad plates with greens. Place 1 asparagus bundle on each plate, whisk vinaigrette, and drizzle over each serving. Sprinkle with chopped hazelnuts.

MAKES: 8 servings.

LIGHT AND LUSH LEMON CAKE

Cake
1 tablespoon melted butter, for coating pan
Confectioners' sugar
2 to 3 lemons
½ cup plus ¾ cup granulated sugar, divided
¾ cup whole milk, not low or nonfat
¼ pound (1 stick) butter or margarine
⅔ cup cake flour
6 large eggs, separated
Salt

Lemon Sour Cream Sauce (optional)
1 cup regular or light sour cream
2 tablespoons heavy cream
½ cup granulated sugar
3 to 4 tablespoons fresh lemon juice, or to taste

Garnish (optional)
Lemon slices
Mint leaves
Fresh daisies

Brush a 12-cup bundt pan with melted butter. Sprinkle with confectioners' sugar and shake out the excess; set aside. Fill a 3-inch-deep baking pan that is large enough to hold the bundt pan with 1 to 2 inches of water. Place in center of oven and preheat to 325°F.

To Make Cake: Using a sharp vegetable peeler, remove peel from 1 large or 2 small lemons. Cut off all white pith from inside peel. Squeeze lemons to make ⅓ cup juice (see page 11) and set aside. Place peel in a food processor with the metal blade, add ½ cup granulated sugar, and process until peel is minced as fine as the sugar, about 1 minute. Transfer to an 8-cup (2-quart) microwavesafe measure. Add milk and butter and microwave covered on high (100%) for 2 to 3 minutes, or until butter is melted. Return to food processor with metal blade, add flour and process 20 seconds to combine. With machine running, add egg yolks through the feed tube and process until blended, about 20 seconds. Pour in lemon juice and process until incorporated.

In a large mixing bowl with electric mixer, beat egg whites with a pinch of salt until soft peaks begin to form. Beating continuously, mix in ¾ cup granulated sugar, 2 tablespoons at a time, until stiff but not dry peaks form. Partially fold a third of the yolk mixture into whites; then fold in the remainder until incorporated. Spoon into prepared pan, spreading top evenly.

To Bake: Place pan in hot water in oven and bake for 50 to 55 minutes, or until top is golden and cracked. Transfer to a rack and cool 15 minutes; cake will fall to the top of the pan. Go around sides with a

(continued)

This isn't a soufflé, but it rises and falls like one. And it isn't a mousse, but it has the cloudlike consistency of one. And it's not really a cake, but it cuts like one. When I brought it to a dinner party and asked what to call it, my friend Lynn responded instantly, "Lemon Lust."

PREP TIME: 35 minutes

BAKE TIME: 50 to 55 minutes

ADVANCE PREP: Cake may be refrigerated for 2 days or frozen. Sauce may be refrigerated for 2 days.

NUTRITIONAL ANALYSIS

Per serving cake
227 calories
12 g fat
132 mg cholesterol
127 mg sodium

Per 2 tablespoons sauce (with light sour cream)
66 calories
3 g fat
11 mg cholesterol
9 mg sodium

small knife and invert onto a platter (microwavesafe if you plan to reheat cake) or sheet of heavy-duty foil if you plan to freeze it. (Cake may be refrigerated up to 2 days or frozen up to 1 month. Defrost at room temperature.)

To Make Sauce: While cake bakes, stir sour cream, heavy cream, sugar, and lemon juice together in a medium bowl. Refrigerate until serving. (Sauce may be refrigerated up to 2 days. Stir well before using.) This makes 1½ cups.

To Serve: To serve warm, reheat the cake in the microwave, covered with plastic wrap, for 40 to 60 seconds, or until warm. Or serve at room temperature or chilled. If serving sauce, spoon a small amount onto each plate, swirling to coat the bottom. Top with a slice of cake and garnish with lemon slices, mint sprigs, and daisies, if desired.

MAKES: 12 servings.

shalom

Menu

◆

**HAROSET WITH ORANGES,
PEARS, AND DRIED
CRANBERRIES**

◆

GEFILTE FISH TORTE

◆

**ROAST BREAST OF TURKEY
STUFFED WITH MATZO
FARFEL AND SPINACH**

◆

ONION SOUFFLÉ SQUARES

◆

**ASPARAGUS, CARROTS, AND
RED BELL PEPPERS WITH
CAULIFLOWER-LEEK PUREE**

◆

**ALMOND MACAROON–
APPLE CAKE**

◆

**FLOURLESS COCOA-
CINNAMON-CARROT CAKE**

CEREMONIAL PASSOVER SEDER

Passover is a distinctive holiday full of beautiful symbolic rituals, which have been handed down from generation to generation for over three thousand years. Part of the Passover tradition is the custom of eating foods made without flour, yeast, or other leavening agents during the eight-day holiday period, to commemorate the Hebrews' heroic flight from Egyptian enslavement. History has it that in their hasty departure, the Jews had no time to let their bread rise, and the resulting flatbread became the first matzos. Today, matzo meal, matzo cake meal, and potato starch are used in place of flour in all Passover baking and cooking.

When I was asked by a large charity group to give a demonstration with new renderings of favorite dishes for the Seder, the ceremonial Passover dinner, it was quite a challenge to develop kosher-for-Passover recipes that were low in fat and cholesterol, could be prepared in advance, would serve a crowd, and yet still retain the traditional flavors people look forward to in their holiday meal.

Most families serve a succession of time-honored dishes—haroset, a mixture of fruit, spices, and nuts to recall the mortar the Jews made as slaves; fish or chopped liver; soup; meat; vegetables; and dessert—that with today's dietary restraints can be a real test of a cook's creativity.

To modernize gefilte fish, a mixture of ground white fish conventionally shaped into ovals or balls, simmered in stock, and served with horseradish and cooked carrots, I've devised Gefilte Fish Torte, with alternate layers of fish soufflé, horseradish, carrots, and beets.

For the main dish, I found stuffing a turkey breast and tying it into a roast solves myriad problems commonly associated with cooking for large groups. This can be made and roasted a day ahead, can be doubled or tripled, is effortless to carve, and doesn't need to be served piping hot. Another excellent holiday choice is Sweet and Sticky Cornish Hens with Tart Cherry Sauce (see page 131). Although Onion Soufflé Squares make a great side dish for both of these entrees, you might prefer to bake Roasted Red-Skin Potatoes with Rosemary (see page 119) in the same oven with the hens. They will take about ten to fifteen minutes longer if baked at 425°F. instead of 450°F. as directed in the recipe.

You'll want to remember the steamed Asparagus, Carrots, and Red Bell Peppers throughout the year, whenever you need a vibrant vegetable medley to dress up a plate. Reheating the vegetables in the oven instead of sautéing them on top of the stove frees you for other chores, but do be careful not to overcook them. Cranberry-glazed Baby Carrots (see page 272), with four tablespoons nondairy margarine substituted for the butter, would also be good for a Passover meal.

For dessert, I offer two choices. Sponge cake has become the customary dessert, but instead of serving it plain or shortcake style, crumble it up and layer it with sautéed apples and macaroons in a showy torte. Nuts and coconut make a great substitute for flour as you'll see when you taste the light and airy Flourless Cocoa-Cinnamon-Carrot Cake. This menu serves twelve.

GAME PLAN

1 Month Ahead	**Make and freeze Onion Soufflé Squares** **Make and freeze Cocoa-Cinnamon-Carrot Cake** **Make and freeze apple cake**
3 Days Ahead	**Make Haroset**
1 Day Ahead	**Defrost and frost Cocoa-Cinnamon-Carrot Cake** **Make Gefilte Fish Torte** **Make and roast turkey and sauce** **Defrost onion squares and apple cake** **Cook vegetables and cauliflower-leek puree**
DAY OF PARTY 45 Minutes Ahead	**Reheat turkey**
15 Minutes Ahead	**Reheat onion squares** **Reheat vegetables in oven**
Shortly Before Serving	**Slice and garnish Gefilte Fish Torte** **Carve turkey and reheat sauce**

EXTRA POINTS

Let the kids help decorate by drawing pictures of the ten plagues—blood, frogs, gnats, flies, murrain, boils, hail, locusts, darkness, and slaying of the firstborn—on pieces of construction paper, using colored markers, paints, glitter, yarn, and scraps of fabric. Glue them onto Popsicle sticks (they can paint and glitter the sticks, too) and insert them into a flower arrangement or small squares of Styrofoam for place cards.

My mother's recipe for haroset was like everyone else's—the same as her mother's and her grandmother's. To give it a contemporary touch, I've added dried cranberries and varied the fruits. It's so good I use it year round as a strudel filling.

PREP TIME: 15 minutes

CHILL TIME: 8 hours

ADVANCE PREP: May be refrigerated up to 3 days.

NUTRITIONAL ANALYSIS

Per tablespoon
23 calories
less than 1 g fat
0 cholesterol
less than 1 mg sodium

You may find it hard to believe that a fish dish can look as glamorous as a showy dessert, but this one does. It's also much easier, faster, and less expensive to make than traditional gefilte fish, though it tastes very similar. (See color photo, page 2.)

PREP TIME: 45 minutes

BAKE TIME: 16 to 18 minutes

CHILL TIME: 1 hour

ADVANCE PREP: May be refrigerated overnight.

HAROSET WITH ORANGES, PEARS, AND DRIED CRANBERRIES

¼ cup pitted chopped dates
¼ cup finely chopped dried apricots
¼ cup chopped walnuts or pecans
½ cup dried cranberries or cherries
1 fresh ripe pear, peeled, cored, and chopped
1 navel orange, peeled and chopped
½ teaspoon ground ginger
½ teaspoon ground cinnamon
½ cup dry red wine
2 teaspoons honey

Stir all the ingredients together in a medium bowl. Cover and refrigerate at least 8 hours for the flavors to blend and the cranberries to soften. (Haroset may be refrigerated up to 3 days.)

MAKES: 2 cups.

GEFILTE FISH TORTE

Gefilte Fish Torte
2 tablespoons unsalted nondairy margarine
½ cup plus ¼ cup finely chopped onion, divided
4 tablespoons potato starch
1¾ cups homemade chicken broth or 1 can (10¼ ounces) condensed chicken broth and ¾ cup water
1 pound white fish fillets (preferably cod or a mixture of whitefish and halibut)
5 egg yolks
6 egg whites
½ teaspoon salt
¼ teaspoon freshly ground black pepper

Horseradish-Beet Filling
1 can (8¼ ounces) sliced carrots
1 can (8¼ ounces) sliced beets
4 tablespoons red horseradish
Salt and freshly ground black pepper to taste

Garnish (optional)
Lettuce leaves
Carrot and beet roses (recipe follows)
Green onion tops, cut into thin strips and soaked in ice water for 10 minutes

To Make Torte: Line a 15½ × 10½ × 1-inch rimmed baking sheet (jelly-roll pan) with parchment or foil, letting 1 inch extend over each short end. Grease or spray the paper. Preheat the oven to 400°F. Melt margarine in a medium saucepan and sauté ½ cup onion until soft. Stir in potato starch. Whisk in broth and stir over moderate heat until mixture just comes to a boil and thickens. Remove from heat.

Cut fish into 2-inch pieces and process with remaining ¼ cup onion in food processor with the metal blade until ground. Add egg yolks, 1 cup of the sauce, salt, and pepper and pulse until well blended. In a large mixing bowl with electric mixer, beat egg whites until stiff but not dry peaks form. Fold fish mixture into whites. Spread into prepared pan. Bake for 16 to 18 minutes, or until top springs back when pressed and toothpick inserted in center comes out clean. Cool in pan.

To Make Filling: Drain carrots, chop into ¼-inch dice, and stir into sauce in pan. Stir in 2 tablespoons beet juice. Drain remaining beet juice, chop beets into ¼-inch dice, and stir into sauce. Stir in horseradish and salt and pepper.

To Assemble: Lift paper with fish on it out of the pan and place on work surface. Cut lengthwise into 3 equal strips. Using 2 spatulas, place 1 strip on large platter. Spread with half the filling. Top with second strip. Spread with remaining filling. Top with third strip. Cover with plastic wrap and refrigerate at least 1 hour or overnight.

To Garnish and Serve: Line salad plates with lettuce. If desired, garnish torte with carrot and beet roses and green onions. Or, using small canapé cutters, cut shapes from sliced carrots and beets. Slice torte into ¾- to 1-inch slices, place on lettuce leaves, and garnish with carrots and beets.

MAKES: 15 servings.

Leaner: Reduce egg yolks to 3 and increase egg whites to 7.

CARROT AND BEET ROSES

Use largest carrots available, or substitute orange sweet potatoes or yams. Slice as thinly as possible. (A mandoline works well.) Place slices in a small bowl of hot water. Add 1 to 2 tablespoons salt. Soak until slices are soft enough to bend. Roll 1 slice up tightly for center of rose. Overlap slices around center to form petals. Insert toothpicks to secure petals; snip off ends so they sit flat. Make beet roses in same manner but do not peel. Soak slices in a separate bowl. Roses may be wrapped in plastic wrap and kept at room temperature for several hours. Do not refrigerate. (See color photo, page 2.)

NUTRITIONAL ANALYSIS

Per serving
93 calories
4 g fat
82 mg cholesterol
396 mg sodium

This stuffing is made with matzo farfel, a packaged matzo dough that comes crumbled in small pieces. Part of the stuffing is rolled up inside a boneless turkey breast and the rest is baked on top, to make a crisp crust. I developed this recipe for a Passover demonstration and the turkey was served to over 200 guests. It was such a hit that the next Thanksgiving I modified the recipe for a year-round version.

PREP TIME: 45 minutes

MARINADE TIME: 18 to 24 hours

BAKE TIME: 1 hour 30 minutes

ADVANCE PREP: Turkey may be roasted a day ahead. Sauce may be refrigerated overnight.

NUTRITIONAL ANALYSIS

Per serving
511 calories
23 g fat
119 mg cholesterol
412 mg sodium

ROAST BREAST OF TURKEY STUFFED WITH MATZO FARFEL AND SPINACH

1 whole turkey breast, skinned, boned, and butterflied (5½ to 7 pounds with bones, 4 to 5 pounds without)

Marinade
Juice and grated peel of 3 oranges (about 1 cup juice), (see page 11)
⅓ cup red wine vinegar
⅓ cup dry red wine
⅓ cup olive oil
⅓ cup honey
1 teaspoon salt

Stuffing
2 tablespoons olive oil
2 onions, chopped
3 cups chopped fresh spinach (bite-size pieces)
2 cups matzo farfel, pounded lightly to resemble oatmeal

2 cups coarsely chopped pecans
1 cup coarsely chopped dried apricots
3 eggs, lightly beaten
Salt and freshly ground black pepper

1 cup dry red wine
¾ cup chicken or beef broth
¼ cup honey
1 egg white, mixed with 1 teaspoon water, for brushing on turkey
1 to 2 tablespoons (packed) potato starch, mixed with equal parts water
Salt and freshly ground black pepper

Garnish (optional)
Greens, such as spinach or parsley
Orange slices

Rinse and dry turkey breast. Pound lightly to make as even as possible. Place in a shallow nonaluminum dish.

To Marinate: Mix all the ingredients in small bowl. Pour over turkey, turning to coat both sides. Cover and refrigerate overnight, turning once or twice.

To Make Stuffing: In a large skillet, heat oil over moderate heat until hot. Sauté onion, stirring often, until tender, about 10 minutes. Stir in spinach and sauté until wilted. Remove to a large bowl and stir in farfel, pecans, apricots, eggs, and salt and pepper to taste.

To Prepare Turkey: Remove turkey from marinade, dry well, and place on work surface, skin side down. Pour marinade into deep 4-quart saucepan and set aside. Sprinkle meat with salt and pepper and spread with half the stuffing. Beginning with a short end, roll up like a jelly roll; do not be concerned with torn or uneven pieces of meat. Tie with string at 1-inch intervals. Sprinkle with salt and pepper.

To Roast: Preheat oven to 375°F. Place turkey in a shallow roasting pan, add about ½ inch water, and roast for 50 to 60 minutes, or until a meat thermometer reaches 120°F., basting with pan drippings every 15 minutes and adding more water to pan as needed. While turkey roasts, begin sauce by adding wine and broth to reserved marinade. Simmer over moderate heat until reduced by about half. Set aside.

Remove turkey from pan to a cutting board. Pour drippings into sauce. Stir 1 tablespoon into honey. Cut strings off turkey, brush the top and sides with egg white and press remaining stuffing firmly over top and sides. Drizzle with half the honey mixture. Return to oven and roast for 15 minutes. Drizzle with remaining honey and roast for 15 minutes more, or until brown and crusty and thermometer inserted into center of roast reaches 145° to 150°F. Remove roast to carving board and let sit 20 minutes. (Turkey may be cooled to room temperature, wrapped in foil and refrigerated overnight. To reheat, bring to room temperature, return to roasting pan, add ½ inch broth or water, cover loosely with foil, and roast at 375°F. for 30 minutes, or until heated through.)

To Complete Sauce: Deglaze the roasting pan by placing it over medium-high heat. Add a little of the sauce and bring to a boil, scraping the bottom of the pan and stirring constantly. Strain into remaining sauce in saucepan, remove from heat, and whisk in potato starch. Return to heat and cook, whisking, until the sauce comes to a boil and thickens slightly. Season to taste with salt and pepper and more wine and/or honey if needed. (Sauce may be refrigerated overnight. Reheat before serving.)

To Serve: Carve the roast into ⅜-inch slices, arrange overlapping on a serving platter, drizzle with sauce, and, if desired, garnish with greens and oranges. Pass remaining sauce.

MAKES: 8 to 12 servings.

Leaner: In the stuffing, substitute ¾ cup frozen egg substitute, thawed, for the 3 eggs. Decrease nuts to 1 cup or omit altogether; increase matzo farfel to 3 cups.

Spongy, moist, airy, and redolent with the sweet aroma of sautéed onions, here's a casserole to accompany any full-flavored or saucy entree, any time of year.

PREP TIME: 30 minutes

BAKE TIME: 35 to 40 minutes

ADVANCE PREP: Baked soufflé may be refrigerated up to 2 days or frozen.

NUTRITIONAL ANALYSIS

Per serving
160 calories
10 g fat
137 mg cholesterol
196 mg sodium

ONION SOUFFLÉ SQUARES

6 large garlic cloves, peeled
5 large onions, peeled and cut into eighths (2½ pounds)
3 tablespoons plus ¼ cup vegetable oil, divided
9 eggs, separated
1 teaspoon salt, or to taste
Freshly ground black pepper to taste
½ teaspoon ground nutmeg
½ cup matzo meal

To Make Soufflé: In a food processor with the metal blade, process garlic until minced. Add half the onions and pulse until finely chopped. Remove to a bowl and chop remaining onions. In a large skillet over medium-high heat, heat 3 tablespoons oil until hot. Sauté onion and garlic, stirring often, until very soft and transparent, about 15 minutes. Set aside to cool slightly. In same processor bowl, process egg yolks until thick and creamy. Pulse in onion, ¼ cup oil, nutmeg, salt, pepper and matzo meal.

In a large mixing bowl, beat egg whites until stiff but not dry peaks form. Scrape yolk mixture over whites and fold in until incorporated.

To Bake: Preheat oven to 350°F. Grease a 9 × 13-inch baking dish. Pour soufflé mixture into casserole. Bake for 35 to 40 minutes, or until puffed and brown and a knife inserted in the center comes out clean. Soufflé will fall as it cools. (Soufflé may be cooled and refrigerated up to 2 days or frozen up to 1 month. Bring to room temperature and reheat, uncovered, at 400°F. for 15 minutes or until heated through.) To serve, cut into squares.

MAKES: 12 to 14 servings.

Leaner: Reduce egg yolks to 5; whites remain the same.

Change of Pace: For a year-round version, substitute dried bread crumbs for the matzo meal.

ASPARAGUS, CARROTS, AND RED BELL PEPPERS WITH CAULIFLOWER-LEEK PUREE

Cauliflower-Leek Puree
1 head cauliflower
1 cup chopped leeks, white part only (see page 11)
1 cup chicken or vegetable broth plus up to ¼ cup more if needed
Salt and freshly ground black pepper

Vegetables
3 large red bell peppers
1½ pounds fresh thin asparagus spears
1½ pounds fresh baby carrots, peeled and trimmed
1 tablespoon olive oil

To Make Puree: Chop cauliflower florets into 1-inch pieces. Measure out 6 cups and save rest for another purpose. Place in a microwavesafe pie plate with leeks and 1 cup broth. Microwave, covered, on high (100%) for 10 to 15 minutes, or until very soft. With slotted spoon, remove vegetables to a food processor with the metal blade and process until pureed. Add broth and puree until smooth, about 1 minute. If too thick to spoon, add additional chicken broth until mixture is the consistency of mashed potatoes. Season to taste with salt and pepper. (Puree may be refrigerated overnight.)

To Cook Vegetables: Halve, seed, and slice peppers into strips, ⅜ inch wide by 1½ inches long. Break tough stems off asparagus and cut diagonally into thirds. In a large skillet, bring 1 inch salted water to a boil. Add carrots, cover, and cook over high heat for 4 to 5 minutes or until barely tender. Place pepper strips over carrots and top with asparagus. Cover and cook 3 minutes more, or until asparagus are crisptender. Remove from heat to a colander. Sprinkle with ice and run under cold water to stop the cooking. Blot dry. (Vegetables may be refrigerated overnight. Bring to room temperature before reheating.)

Before Serving: To reheat vegetables in oven, preheat oven to 400°F. Place vegetables in a shallow baking pan, sprinkle with oil and salt, and bake, covered with foil, for 10 to 15 minutes, or until heated through. Or stir-fry in wok or large skillet in 1 tablespoon oil until hot.

Place puree in a microwavesafe bowl and microwave, covered, on high (100%) for 2 to 5 minutes, or until hot, stirring once. Or heat on top of stove. Spoon vegetables onto platter or serving plates and top with puree.
MAKES: 12 servings.

You'll have to try this to believe how vibrant the colors are and how terrific it tastes. And it's made in a jiffy. The vegetables all cook in the same saucepan by what I call the "layered steam method," one on top of the other, with the slowest cooking ones on the bottom. And the puree is so mild, no one can guess what it is.

PREP TIME: 30 minutes

COOK TIME: 8 to 10 minutes

ADVANCE PREP: Vegetables and puree may be refrigerated overnight.

NUTRITIONAL ANALYSIS

Per serving
83 calories
2 g fat
less than 1 mg cholesterol
186 mg sodium

This recipe dates back to my early days as a cooking teacher. In the sixties, the landmark Los Angeles restaurant Scandia shared their signature apple cake with me, and I adapted and taught it to one of my first cooking classes for the Lanai Road School P.T.A. gourmet club. Through the years I've rearranged the layers of cake and macaroon crumbs, apples, almonds, and raspberry preserves to stay within the restrictions of Passover. When dietary restrictions permit, frost the cake with whipped cream.

PREP TIME: 45 minutes

BAKE TIME: 25 to 35 minutes

CHILL TIME: 4 hours

ADVANCE PREP: May be refrigerated for 2 days or frozen.

NUTRITIONAL ANALYSIS

Per serving
573 calories
25 g fat
95 mg cholesterol
92 mg sodium

ALMOND MACAROON–APPLE CAKE

3 cups Passover sponge cake crumbs (about half a 9-inch cake)
2 cups almond macaroon cookie crumbs (16 canned soft macaroons)
6 tablespoons plus 4 tablespoons unsalted nondairy margarine, divided
4 pounds tart apples (about 9 large apples)
½ cup (packed) light brown sugar
2 teaspoons (packed) potato starch
⅓ cup seedless red raspberry preserves
¾ cup sliced almonds (about 3 ounces)

To Prepare Crumbs: Preheat the oven to 375°F. Break cake into small pieces, place in a food processor with the metal blade, and pulse into crumbs. Pour onto rimmed baking sheet. Break macaroons into pieces, place in food processor, and pulse into crumbs. Mix together with cake crumbs. Bake for 12 to 15 minutes, stirring every 3 to 5 minutes, until golden brown. Cool. Melt 6 tablespoons margarine and stir into crumbs. Leave oven at 375°F.

To Cook Apples: Peel, core, and thinly slice apples. In a 12-inch skillet or sauté pan, melt 4 tablespoons margarine with the brown sugar. Add apple slices and cook over medium-high heat, turning often, until apples are barely tender, about 8 minutes. Sprinkle with potato starch and cook, stirring, until juices thicken. Immediately remove from heat and cool slightly.

To Assemble: Grease a 9-inch springform pan. Layer 1¾ cups toasted crumbs in bottom of springform and press down firmly with a spatula. Top with half the apples and press down firmly. Spoon preserves over the apples and spread lightly to within ½ inch of side of pan. Sprinkle with half the almonds and top with 1 cup crumbs, pressing down firmly. Spoon remaining apples with their juices over crumbs, spread evenly, and press down firmly. Mix remaining almonds with crumbs, sprinkle over top of cake, and press down firmly.

To Bake: Place pan on a baking sheet and bake at 375°F. for 25 to 35 minutes, or until top is golden brown. Cool to room temperature, cover, and refrigerate for at least 4 hours or up to 2 days. (Torte may be frozen up to 1 month. Defrost overnight in the refrigerator.) Before serving, bring to room temperature. Run a sharp knife around inside edge of the pan and remove sides of springform.

MAKES: 10 servings.

Faster: Substitute 2 cans (21 ounces each) apple pie filling for the sautéed fresh apples. Omit the 4 tablespoons margarine and ½ cup brown sugar.

To quickly peel, core, and slice apples, use an apple peeler-corer-slicer, available from cookware shops.

Frosted with a silky cinnamon-scented chocolate glaze, this cake is like a European torte, where nuts replace flour to give it lightness and character.

PREP TIME: Cake, 30 minutes; frosting, 10 minutes

BAKE TIME: 40 to 50 minutes

ADVANCE PREP: Unfrosted cake may be refrigerated up to 3 days or frozen. Frosted cake may be stored at room temperature overnight.

NUTRITIONAL ANALYSIS

Per serving
262 calories
16 g fat
128 mg cholesterol
279 mg sodium

FLOURLESS COCOA-CINNAMON-CARROT CAKE

Cake
1 cup chopped walnuts (about 4 ounces)
4 medium carrots, peeled and cut into 2-inch pieces (about 2 cups)
6 large eggs, separated
¾ cup plus ¼ cup sugar, divided
2 teaspoons vanilla extract
1¼ teaspoons ground cinnamon
¼ cup unsweetened cocoa powder
½ teaspoon salt
¾ cup shredded coconut, toasted (see page 12)
1 teaspoon finely grated orange peel (see page 11)

Chocolate-Cinnamon Glaze
6 ounces semisweet chocolate chips
3 tablespoons unsalted nondairy margarine
½ teaspoon ground cinnamon
Orange slices, for garnish (optional)

Preheat oven to 375°F. Grease a 9-inch springform pan. Line the bottom with a round of parchment or wax paper and grease the paper.

To Make Cake: In a food processor with the metal blade, pulse nuts until finely ground. Remove to a bowl. Change to shredding disk and shred carrots. Remove to sheet of wax paper. In same processor bowl, (no need to wash it), process egg yolks and ¾ cup sugar until very thick and creamy, about 1 minute. Scrape down sides and pulse in vanilla. Add cinnamon, cocoa, and salt and pulse until mixed. Add carrots and pulse 6 to 8 times, or until chopped but not pureed. Add nuts, coconut, and orange peel and pulse 8 to 10 times until incorporated.

In a large mixing bowl with electric mixer, beat egg whites until very soft peaks form. Slowly add ¼ cup sugar, beating continuously, until stiff but moist peaks form. Fold cocoa batter into whites. Pour batter into prepared pan.

To Bake: Bake for 40 to 50 minutes, or until the sides begin to pull away and a toothpick inserted in the center comes out clean. Remove to rack and cool 15 minutes. Go around sides with a sharp knife, remove springform sides, and invert cake onto rack. Remove springform bottom and paper. Cool completely. (Cake may be refrigerated up to 3 days or frozen.)

To Glaze: Place cake on a rack set over a baking sheet to catch the drippings. In a 4-cup microwavesafe measure, microwave chocolate, margarine, corn syrup, and cinnamon, uncovered, at 70% power for 2 to 4 minutes, or until melted, stirring every minute. Stir smooth. Or melt in a heavy saucepan over low heat, stirring until smooth. If too thin to coat, let stand until thickened slightly. Pour over center of cake, tilting the cake so the glaze runs down the sides. Use a knife to help smooth the sides, but do not try to touch up the top or the knife marks will show. If desired, garnish with twisted orange slices. Let set for at least 1 hour. (Cake may be held at room temperature uncovered overnight.)

MAKES: 10 servings.

Change of Pace: Omit coconut and increase nuts to 1½ cups.

CELEBRATION BUFFET BASH

*Y*our parents are celebrating their fiftieth anniversary. Your best friend is turning thirty. You're hosting a wedding rehearsal supper. Your spouse is promoted. When the occasion calls for a special dinner for a crowd, here is a feast for both the eye and the palate. The food is exquisite, but not temperamental — easy to prepare ahead and reheat, and sturdy enough to sit out without collapsing. Nothing needs cutting, so guests can balance their plates on their laps if table space is limited.

If you're having sixteen or more guests, offer an assortment of three or four different kinds of hors d'oeuvres, allowing four to five per person. For fewer guests, a selection of one to three will do. For this menu I suggest Savory Scotch Biscotti with or without Canadian Bacon and Mustard Seed Spread (see pages 114–115), Potato Nachos with Roasted Garlic (see page 179), Mini Thai Crab Cakes (see page 158), and Eggplant Rolls with Garlic-Herb Cheese (see page 148).

Most casseroles are too casual for important events, but not Veal and Orzo. It bridges the culinary generation gap by appealing to the meat-and-potatoes crowd as well as the trendier set. And to please the cook, it can be assembled (even frozen), baked, and served in the same dish. Gratin of Polenta, Tomatoes, and Wild Mushrooms (see page 164) offers the same advantages.

A monochromatic main dish begs for glowing accompaniments and both the rosy Beet and Carrot Swirl and the Garden-Fresh Vegetable Platter bring vibrant color to the menu. As an alternative, try Asparagus, Carrots, and Red Bell Peppers with Cauliflower-Leek Puree (see page 243).

In recent years, I have come to value the merits of serving lightly cooked vegetables instead of raw ones for dipping and as a salad replacement.

Flash-cooking intensifies their flavor and color, and it also prevents them from drying out. Rather than marinating the vegetables in the Garden Fresh Vegetable Platter in the Caesar vinaigrette, serve it on the side and let guests help themselves. If you prefer another tossed salad to the Spinach Grapefruit Salad with Blue Cheese and Pine Nuts, try Crispy Chinese Salad with Kiwi Vinaigrette (see page 215).

No other dessert causes the furor of Flaming Chocolate Volcanoes, an idea sparked at a food conference by Robbin Smolka, executive chef at the Paradox Brasserie and Taverne in Washington, D.C. Chocolate liqueur cups are embedded in chocolate-coated ice cream, filled with liquor, and ignited. Your guests will be blown away! If they'll be eating on their laps, consider purchasing or renting snack sets with an indentation for the coffee cup. This menu serves twelve, but the recipes can be multiplied for any size crowd.

GAME PLAN

1 Month Ahead	**Make and freeze Veal and Orzo** **Make and freeze Beet and Carrot Swirl** **Make and freeze biscotti** **Make and freeze Canadian bacon spread, if using**
2 Weeks Ahead	**Make and freeze chocolate volcanoes**
1 Week Ahead	**Make Caesar vinaigrette for vegetable platter**
2 Days Ahead	**Make vinaigrette for spinach salad** **Defrost Veal and Orzo** **Make sauce for Beet and Carrot Swirl, if using** **Remove paper cups from volcanoes and return to freezer**
1 Day Ahead	**Prepare greens for spinach salad** **Cook vegetables for garden platter**
DAY OF PARTY 4 Hours Ahead	**Bring veal to room temperature**
40 Minutes Ahead	**Sprinkle crumbs over veal and bake** **Arrange vegetable platter**
Shortly Before Serving	**Reheat Beet and Carrot Swirl** **Toss salad**

I love this as a freshly tossed crisp salad, but it's equally good when it becomes slightly wilted, making it ideal buffet fare.

PREP TIME: 30 minutes

ADVANCE PREP: Vinaigrette may be refrigerated up to 2 days. Greens may be refrigerated overnight.

SPINACH-GRAPEFRUIT SALAD WITH BLUE CHEESE AND PINE NUTS

15 ounces stemmed and trimmed spinach (about 3 to 4 pounds untrimmed)
4 heads Belgian endive, sliced ½ inch thick (about 1¼ pounds)
2 medium grapefruit, preferably pink (about 1 pound each)
⅔ cup blue cheese, frozen and crumbled (3 ounces)
⅓ cup pine nuts toasted (see page 12)

Grapefruit-Honey Vinaigrette
2 medium grapefruit, preferably pink (about 1 pound each)
2 tablespoons fresh lemon juice
4 to 6 tablespoons honey
2 tablespoons vegetable oil
Freshly ground black pepper

To Prepare Salad: Tear spinach into bite-size pieces and toss with endive. Wrap in paper towels and a plastic bag and refrigerate. (Greens may be refrigerated overnight.) Cut ends off grapefruit and with a sharp knife, remove peel. Separate into segments, cut each into 2 or 3 pieces, and refrigerate.

To Make Vinaigrette: Peel grapefruits and separate into sections, cutting between the membranes to remove only the fruit. Place in a food processor with the metal blade and process until pureed. Measure out 1½ cups and discard the rest. Return to processor and add lemon juice and honey to taste. Process until blended, about 1 minute. With machine running, slowly pour oil through feed tube. (Vinaigrette may be refrigerated up to 2 days.)

To Assemble: Toss spinach, endive, grapefruit, blue cheese, and pine nuts in a large bowl. Add as much vinaigrette as needed to coat, sprinkle with pepper to taste, and toss well.

Faster: Substitute 2 jars (26 ounces each) grapefruit segments for the fresh in the salad and vinaigrette. Use 2 cups segments, well-drained and blotted dry, in the salad and puree 1½ cups for the vinaigrette.

Leaner: Substitute ⅔ cup croutons for the pine nuts. Reduce cheese to ⅓ cup.

MAKES: 12 servings.

Change of Pace: Substitute crumbled goat cheese for the blue cheese.

NUTRITIONAL ANALYSIS

Per serving salad (not including vinaigrette)
90 calories
5 g fat
9 mg cholesterol
211 mg sodium

Per tablespoon vinaigrette
20 calories
less than 1 g fat
0 cholesterol
less than 1 mg sodium

GARDEN-FRESH VEGETABLE PLATTER WITH CAESAR VINAIGRETTE

Caesar Vinaigrette
1 large garlic clove, peeled
4 anchovy fillets, rinsed (optional)
¼ cup fresh lemon juice (see page 11)
1 tablespoon plus 1 teaspoon Worcestershire sauce
2 teaspoons Dijon mustard
⅓ cup grated parmesan cheese
⅓ cup olive oil
⅓ cup orange juice
⅓ cup regular, low-fat, or nonfat plain yogurt

Salt and freshly ground black pepper

Vegetables
1 large zucchini, ends trimmed
3 large carrots, peeled
1 large red bell pepper
1 large yellow bell pepper
1 pound green beans, stem ends trimmed
1 large bunch broccoli, cut into florets
1 large head cauliflower, cut into florets

To Make Vinaigrette: In a food processor with the metal blade, process garlic until minced and anchovies, if using. Add lemon juice, Worcestershire sauce, mustard, parmesan, oil, and orange juice. Pulse to combine. Transfer to a bowl and whisk in yogurt. (Do not process yogurt or it will break down.) Season with salt and pepper. (Vinaigrette may be refrigerated up to 1 week.) This makes 1½ cups.

To Cook Vegetables: With a serrated cutter or knife, cut zucchini and carrots into ¼-inch diagonal slices. Cut peppers in half, remove seeds, and cut into ½-inch strips. Bring 1 inch of water to a boil in a 12-inch Dutch oven or skillet with lid. Add green beans, cover, and steam for 1 minute. Top with broccoli, cauliflower, and zucchini, cover and steam over medium-high heat until crisp-tender, 5 to 6 minutes. Remove from heat, sprinkle with ice and rinse under cold water to stop the cooking. Meanwhile, place carrots in a shallow microwavesafe dish with about ¼ inch water. Cover with vented plastic wrap and microwave on high (100%) for 1 to 3 minutes, or until crisp-tender. Remove to a plate and cool to room temperature. Microwave pepper strips in same manner for 1 to 2 minutes. Or the carrots and peppers may be steamed or blanched in boiling water on top of the stove. (Vegetables may be refrigerated overnight. Serve chilled or at room temperature.)

To Assemble: As close to serving as possible, cluster cauliflower in center of a large round platter. Arrange concentric circles of each of the vegetables around cauliflower. Serve with vinaigrette.

MAKES: 12 servings.

Crudités dry out, delicate greens collapse, but vegetables cooked until crisp-tender and then chilled remain lively and fresh on a buffet. In this technique, adapted from the Asian multi-level steaming method, the vegetables are tiered in a skillet or Dutch oven with the ones that require the longest cooking time on the bottom.

PREP TIME: 40 minutes

ADVANCE PREP: Vinaigrette may be refrigerated up to 1 week. Vegetables may be refrigerated overnight.

NUTRITIONAL ANALYSIS

Per serving vegetables (not including vinaigrette)
47 calories
less than 1 g fat
0 cholesterol
20 mg sodium

Per tablespoon vinaigrette
38 calories
3 g fat
1 mg cholesterol
96 mg sodium

I f you've relegated stew to family-only dinners, here's a rendition that's sophisticated enough for your loftiest parties. Savory cubes of veal, simmered in a delicate white wine sauce, are enfolded in layers of rice-shaped orzo pasta (sometimes called *seme di melone* or melon seeds) and blanketed under crisp garlic-scented bread crumbs. The first time I made this, Hal was so impressed he said he could eat it every night for a week. By the time I perfected it, he had. Funny, he's never said that again.

PREP TIME: 1 hour

COOK TIME: Stew, 1 hour; casserole, 40 minutes

ADVANCE PREP: May be refrigerated up to 2 days or frozen.

NUTRITIONAL ANALYSIS

Per serving
408 calories
13 g fat
123 mg cholesterol
857 mg sodium

VEAL AND ORZO WITH A GARLIC CRUMB CRUST

Veal Stew
4 pounds veal stew meat, cut into 1½-inch cubes
Salt and freshly ground black pepper
3 to 5 tablespoons vegetable or olive oil, divided
2 tablespoons instant beef soup base or 2 beef bouillon cubes
2 tablespoons tomato paste
¼ cup all-purpose flour
½ cup imported dry vermouth or dry white wine
2 cups chicken broth
1 tablespoon currant jelly
1 package (10 ounces) frozen pearl onions, thawed on paper towels, or 1 jar (about 15 ounces) pearl onions, well drained

1 pound medium or large mushrooms, cleaned with stems cut even with the caps

2 cups uncooked orzo pasta

Bread Crumb Crust
3 tablespoons olive oil
2 large garlic cloves, minced
2½ cups sourdough, Italian, or egg bread crumbs (page 9) (about 5 slices)
½ cup chopped parsley

To Prepare Stew: Rinse meat, blot dry, trim fat, and sprinkle generously with salt and pepper. Heat 1 tablespoon oil in a Dutch oven or wide saucepan over medium-high heat. Sauté the veal in batches until lightly browned, adding more oil as needed. If the oil begins to burn, reduce heat. As meat browns, remove with a slotted spoon to a plate. Remove the pan from the heat and if dry, stir in another tablespoon oil. Stir in the soup base, tomato paste, and flour; the mixture will be grainy. Return to heat and whisk in the wine, broth, and jelly, scraping up all brown bits from the bottom of the pan. Cook, stirring and whisking, until the mixture comes to a boil. Return meat to pan. The meat should be almost covered with the sauce. If not, transfer to a smaller pan.

Preheat oven to 350°F.

Bake, covered, for 40 minutes, stirring after 20 minutes. If juices are boiling rapidly, reduce heat to 325°F. Stir in onions and mushrooms and continue to cook, covered, for 20 to 40 more minutes, stirring every 15 minutes, until meat is tender when pierced with a knife. The timing will depend on the cut of the meat.

To Cook Orzo: While stew bakes, bring a large pot of salted water to a boil. Add orzo and cook until tender to the bite, about 8 to 10 minutes. Drain well, remove to a bowl, and toss with 1 tablespoon oil. Sprinkle with salt to taste.

To Make Crumb Crust: In a large skillet over medium heat, heat oil. Add garlic and sauté until soft, about 1 minute. Add crumbs and cook, stirring often, until golden, about 10 minutes. Remove to a bowl and stir in parsley. (Crumbs may be refrigerated up to 2 days or frozen.)

To Assemble: Grease or spray a 9 × 13-inch baking dish. With a slotted spoon, spoon veal into bottom. Spoon over half the sauce. Spread with orzo and pour over remaining sauce. (Casserole may be covered with plastic wrap and heavy foil and refrigerated up to 2 days or frozen up to 1 month. Defrost in refrigerator for at least 36 hours. Bring to room temperature before baking.)

To Bake Casserole: Preheat oven to 375°F.

Sprinkle crumbs evenly over orzo. Cover with foil and bake in middle of oven for 20 minutes. Remove foil and bake, uncovered, for 20 minutes, or until edges are bubbling and veal is heated through.

MAKES: 12 servings.

Originally I created this marbling of pureed beets and carrots to add color to the plate, but it's won the hearts of so many skeptical guests — and converted so many non-beet-eaters among them — that it's become one of my most frequently served vegetables.

PREP TIME: 20 minutes

COOK TIME: 25 to 35 minutes

ADVANCE PREP: May be refrigerated up to 2 days or frozen.

NUTRITIONAL ANALYSIS

Per serving (not including sauce)
72 calories
less than 1 g fat
0 cholesterol
224 mg sodium

Per 2 teaspoons horseradish sauce
14 calories
1 g fat
4 mg cholesterol
9 mg sodium

BEET AND CARROT SWIRL

Carrot Puree
2 pounds carrots (about 14 medium)
¼ cup orange marmalade
Heaping ⅛ teaspoon ground nutmeg
½ teaspoon salt, or to taste

Beet Puree
6 large beets (about 1½ pounds)
Scant ½ teaspoon salt, or to taste

2 tablespoons amaretto liqueur
¼ teaspoon ground cinnamon
4 teaspoons lemon juice

Horseradish Sauce (optional)
½ cup sour cream
1 teaspoon creamy-style red or white horseradish

Carrot and beet roses for garnish (optional) (see page 239)

To Make Carrot Puree: Scrub carrots (it's not necessary to peel them), cut off stems, and cut into 2-inch pieces. Place in a 9- or 10-inch microwavesafe deep-dish pie plate or casserole. Add ½ cup water and microwave, covered with vented plastic wrap, on high (100%) for 18 to 25 minutes, or until soft. Or cook carrots on top of stove in water to cover. Drain and reserve several tablespoons liquid. Remove carrots to a food processor with the metal blade. Add orange marmalade, nutmeg, and salt and puree until smooth. Slowly add as much cooking liquid as needed to make a thick puree.

To Make Beet Puree: Scrub beets, remove stems, and cut unpeeled beets into 2-inch chunks. Add to same deep-dish pie plate or casserole with ¾ cup water. Cover with vented plastic wrap and microwave on high (100%) for 15 to 20 minutes, or until very tender when pierced with a fork. Or cook on top of stove in water to cover. Drain and reserve liquid for puree. Place beets in food processor with metal blade and process until smooth. Add salt, amaretto, cinnamon, lemon juice, and enough cooking liquid to make a thick puree.

To Make Horseradish Sauce: Stir sour cream and horseradish together in small bowl. (Sauce may be refrigerated up to 2 days.) Serve chilled.

To Assemble: Alternate heaping tablespoons of carrot and beet purees in a 9- or 10-inch quiche dish or pie plate. You will have more carrots than beets. (Vegetables may be refrigerated overnight or frozen. Defrost in refrigerator overnight or at room temperature for several hours. To reheat, microwave, covered, on high (100%) for 5 minutes or bake, covered, with foil at 375°F. for 20 minutes or until heated through.) Serve warm or at room temperature. If desired, serve with Horseradish Sauce, and garnish with carrot and beet roses.

MAKES: 12 servings.

Faster: Substitute 2 cans (16 ounces each) sliced beets, well drained, for the fresh. Process until pureed, put into a strainer and drain, stirring to extract juices. Remove to a bowl and stir in amaretto, cinnamon, and lemon juice. Fresh carrots are preferred to frozen or canned.

FLAMING CHOCOLATE VOLCANOES

For Each Serving
1 chocolate liqueur cup
1 (5-ounce) paper cup
   (not Styrofoam)
2 ounces semisweet chocolate or
   scant ½ cup semisweet chips

½ cup desired flavor ice cream
   or frozen yogurt
1 chocolate wafer cookie
151-proof liquor

Place liqueur cup in bottom of paper cup with open side down. Melt chocolate in microwave or over hot water in a double boiler until warm enough to stir smooth but not so hot as to melt the chocolate cup. With a butter knife or small spatula, spread inside of paper cup with chocolate, dabbing around liqueur cup to hold it in place. Freeze firm. If necessary, repeat with a second layer of chocolate to make an even coating and freeze firm.

Stir ice cream to soften and spoon into chocolate-lined paper cup. Top with a cookie, pressing it down gently. Freeze solid. (Volcanoes may be frozen well covered up to 2 weeks.)

Several hours or even days before serving, remove paper cup from chocolate by gently pulling away and tearing off the paper. Return volcano to freezer until ready to serve.

Before Serving: Place volcano, cookie side down, on dessert plate. Dim lights, fill liqueur cup half full of liquor, ignite, and serve.

MAKES: 1 serving.

Dim the lights and brace yourself for gasps from your guests when they receive their own flaming chocolate mountain. To light these dessert volcanoes, you need a liquor that can be ignited without heating (heat will melt the chocolate). I recommend either a previously unopened bottle of 151 proof liquor (alcohol evaporates once the bottle is opened) such as Trader Vic's rum, Sambuca, or Rumple Minze.

PREP TIME: About 10 minutes per volcano

FREEZE TIME: 24 hours

ADVANCE PREP: Volcanoes may be frozen up to 2 weeks.

NUTRITIONAL ANALYSIS

Per serving (with 1 tablespoon liquor)
544 calories
32 g fat
45 mg cholesterol
100 mg sodium

Menu

GUACAMOLE AND CORN
SALSA (See page 170)

❖

ROLLED STUFFED FLANK
STEAK SANTA FE

❖

CHICKEN BREASTS SANTA FE

❖

TEX-MEX BAKED BEANS

❖

RED-SPANGLED SLAW WITH
DRIED CRANBERRIES

❖

CORNBREAD PUDDING

❖

SHORTCAKE SAMPLER:

MANGO-PINEAPPLE
SHORTCAKES WITH
GINGERBREAD BISCUITS

•

RED, WHITE, AND BLUEBERRY
SHORTCAKES WITH
CHOCOLATE BISCUITS

•

WARM CARAMEL-PEACH
SHORTCAKES WITH ALMOND
BISCUITS

SOUTHWESTERN FOURTH of JULY

*A*s wise and prophetic as our founding fathers were, chances are they did not plan the signing of the Declaration of Independence around a particular time of year. How fortunate for us, though, that it happened to be during the most dependable weather for picnicking, watching parades and fireworks, and outdoor grilling.

Barbecuing is believed to have originated with the Indians of the Caribbean, who dried meat on woven green wood strips over slow coals. The Spanish dropped anchor, discovered this form of cooking, adopted it, and called it *barbecoa*. They transported the idea to Mexico, added their own distinctive touches, and barbecue became a regional specialty. In celebration of our country's independence and barbecue history, here is a menu with a Southwestern signature.

You can marinate flank steak in the jalapeño-spiked lime dressing from five hours to overnight, depending on your schedule. Because the marinade and the salsa include many of the same ingredients, it is convenient to make both at the same time. One steak serves four to six people; for a large gathering make two or more. Or offer your guests a choice of entrees by doubling the marinade and using half for the steak and the remainder for Chicken Breasts Santa Fe.

Add thickly glazed Tex-Mex Baked Beans, Cornbread Pudding, coleslaw with a star-spangled twist and tip your toque to our sagacious ancestors, our great Southwestern heritage, and over two hundred years of freedom.

For dessert, choose one of the shortcakes or present a shortcake buffet by putting out a variety of biscuits, sauces, toppings, frozen yogurt or ice cream and letting guests help themselves. Plan on one to one and a half biscuits and one cup filling per person. This menu serves ten if you serve both the flank steak and chicken breasts or two flank steaks.

GAME PLAN

1 Month Ahead	**Make and freeze beans** **Make and freeze Cornbread Pudding** **Make and refrigerate Fatless Fudge Sauce**
2 Weeks Ahead	**Make and freeze gingerbread, chocolate, and/or almond biscuits**
2 Days Ahead	**Make Zucchini Salsa** **Make marinade for steak and/or chicken**
1 Day Ahead	**Marinate flank steak** **Defrost beans, Cornbread Pudding, and biscuits** **Make slaw** **Make Double Whipped Cream** **Make Mango-Pineapple Filling, if serving** **Make Guacamole Corn Salsa**
DAY OF PARTY 4 Hours Ahead	**Stuff and roll flank steak** **Marinate chicken, if serving** **Prepare Red and Blueberry Filling, if serving**
1 Hour Ahead	**Prepare coals** **Prepare Caramel-Peach Filling, if serving**
20 Minutes Ahead	**Grill steak** **Reheat beans** **Reheat Cornbread Pudding**
8 Minutes Ahead	**Grill chicken, if serving**
Shortly Before Serving	**Assemble shortcakes** **Reheat fudge sauce, if serving**

EXTRA POINTS

THE INVITATIONS

For each invitation you will need a 4- to 5-inch cardboard tube cut from a paper-towel roll or the inside of a roll of gift wrap. Write a message on a sheet of paper. Tape curly ribbon to the back of the paper, roll up, and insert into the cardboard tube with the ribbon extending over the top. Wrap in colored tissue. Mail in box or padded envelope. (See color photo, page 4.)

THE TABLE

Cover your table with a blue and white striped cloth and decorate it with strings of red chile peppers and pots of cactus tied with red and blue bandanas. Flower shops and party stores sell sprays or coils of foil or metallic star garlands that you can insert into cactus pots or weave around the table like barbed wire. Use bandanas for napkins. (See color photo, page 5.)

THE KICKER

Ask your guests to wear red, white, and blue.

Flank steak, one of the lowest in fat, most economical, and most flavorful cuts of beef, is greatly underused. To ensure that it's tender enough to cut with a fork, ask the butcher to run it through a tenderizing machine twice and pound it a quarter inch thick. (Or pound it yourself; it takes only a few good whacks with a meat pounder.) After the steak has marinated, it's layered with zucchini salsa, cheese, and roasted red peppers, rolled up, grilled, and sliced into pretty spirals. It's every bit as delicious at room temperature as hot. (See color photos, pages 4 and 5.)

PREP TIME: 45 minutes

MARINADE TIME: 5 hours or overnight

GRILL TIME: 13 minutes plus 15 minutes standing time

ADVANCE PREP: Salsa and marinade may be refrigerated up to 2 days. Steak may be assembled up to 5 hours before grilling.

NUTRITIONAL ANALYSIS

Per serving with low-fat provolone
273 calories
15 g fat
72 mg cholesterol
299 mg sodium

ROLLED STUFFED FLANK STEAK SANTA FE

1 flank steak, put through the butcher's tenderizing machine twice and pounded ¼ inch thick (about 1½ pounds)

Jalapeño-Lime Marinade
2 garlic cloves, peeled
1 pickled, or fresh seeded jalapeño (1 to 1½ inches) (see page 10)
2 tablespoons cilantro leaves
¼ cup chicken broth
¼ cup fresh lime juice (see page 11)
2 tablespoons honey

Zucchini Salsa
2 garlic cloves, peeled
1 pickled or fresh seeded jalapeño (about 1 to 1½ inches), quartered

¼ cup (lightly packed) cilantro leaves
2 green onions with tops, cut into 1-inch pieces
¼ cup pimiento-stuffed green olives
1 medium zucchini, cut into 1-inch pieces (about 6 ounces)
Salt

4 ounces regular or low-fat sliced provolone cheese, at room temperature
1 roasted red pepper (jarred or fresh), cut into 2-inch strips
3 tablespoons jalapeño jelly, hot or mild, melted

To Marinate: Place meat in a large, nonmetal dish. In a food processor with the metal blade, process garlic and jalapeño until minced. Add cilantro, broth, lime juice, and honey and process until well blended. Reserve 2 tablespoons marinade for salsa and set aside. Pour the remainder over the meat. (Steak may be folded over, if needed; just make sure all surfaces are coated.) Cover with plastic wrap and marinate in the refrigerator for 5 hours or overnight, turning once or twice.

To Make Salsa: In a food processor with metal blade, process garlic and jalapeño until minced, scraping sides. Add cilantro, green onions, olives, zucchini, and 2 tablespoons reserved marinade and pulse until finely minced. Season to taste with salt. (Salsa may be refrigerated up to 2 days.)

To Assemble: Up to 5 hours before grilling, remove meat from marinade, place on work surface, and blot dry with paper towels. Sprinkle with salt and spread with salsa. Top with overlapping slices of cheese. Place strips of red pepper down 1 long end. Beginning with end with red peppers, roll up tightly, jelly-roll fashion. Using metal skewers and/

or turkey lacers, skewer seam and both ends closed. If not grilling immediately, cover and refrigerate.

To Grill: Prepare coals, oil grill rack, and place it 3 inches from coals.

When coals are hot, blot meat dry, brush seam side with jelly, and grill, seam side down, for 4 minutes. Turn and grill on other 3 sides, brushing with jelly, for 3 minutes per side, for a total cooking time of 13 minutes. Let stand at least 15 minutes. Remove skewers and carve into ⅜-inch slices.

MAKES: 4 to 6 servings.

Faster: Substitute 1 cup thick and chunky prepared salsa, well drained, for the Zucchini Salsa.

CHICKEN BREASTS SANTA FE

8 skinless, boneless chicken
   breast halves (about 4 pounds
   net weight)
Jalapeño-Lime Marinade
   (see page 258)

Salt and freshly ground black
   pepper
⅓ cup jalapeño pepper jelly, hot
   or mild, melted
Zucchini Salsa (see page 258)

Cut fat from chicken and place beasts in a large heavy plastic zipper bag. Reserve 2 tablespoons marinade for salsa and pour the rest over chicken. Marinate in the refrigerator 2 to 4 hours, turning several times. Do not marinate more than 4 hours or the texture will break down. Make salsa as directed in recipe.

Prepare coals, oil grill rack, and place it 3 inches from coals. Remove breasts from marinade and blot dry with paper towels. Sprinkle with salt and pepper. When coals are hot, brush 1 side of chicken with jelly. Grill, jelly side down, for 3 minutes. Brush top with jelly, turn, and grill for 3 to 4 minutes more, or until cooked through. Do not overcook. Chicken will continue cooking off the heat. Serve with salsa.

MAKES: 8 servings.

This is a first cousin to the flank steak recipe. Here chicken breasts are permeated with the same Jalapeño-Lime Marinade, and the Zucchini Salsa is served as a sauce. If you double the recipe for the marinade and salsa, you can make both the steak and chicken and offer your guests a choice.

PREP TIME: 20 minutes

MARINADE TIME: 2 to 4 hours

GRILL TIME: 6 to 7 minutes

ADVANCE PREP: Salsa may be refrigerated up to 2 days. Marinade may be refrigerated up to 2 days.

NUTRITIONAL ANALYSIS

Per serving chicken
429 calories
10 g fat
193 mg cholesterol
170 mg sodium

Per 2 tablespoons salsa
8 calories
less than 1 g fat
0 cholesterol
65 mg sodium

To bring my family's favorite barbecue bean recipe up to date, I replaced regular bacon with Canadian, substituted canned beans for dried, and eliminated hours of cooking time and lots of fat. The result? No one noticed the difference. (See color photos, pages 4 and 5.)

PREP TIME: 25 minutes

BAKE TIME: 45 minutes

ADVANCE PREP: May be refrigerated up to 2 days or frozen.

NUTRITIONAL ANALYSIS

Per serving (with reduced-fat Canadian bacon)
209 calories
3 g fat
5 mg cholesterol
865 mg sodium

TEX-MEX BAKED BEANS

1 tablespoon vegetable oil
6 ounces regular or reduced-fat Canadian bacon, chopped into ½-inch pieces
1 large onion, chopped (2 cups)
1 can (8 ounces) tomato sauce
1 cup (packed) light brown sugar
2 tablespoons Worcestershire sauce
2 tablespoons molasses
2 tablespoons apple cider vinegar
½ teaspoon liquid smoke
½ teaspoon salt, or to taste

1 teaspoon chile powder, hot or mild to taste
½ teaspoon hot-pepper sauce, such as Tabasco, or to taste
1 can (15 ounces) kidney beans, rinsed and well drained
1 can (15 ounces) butter beans, rinsed and well drained
1 can (15 ounces) black beans, rinsed and well drained
1 can (15 ounces) garbanzo beans (chick peas), rinsed and well drained

Preheat the oven to 375°F.

Heat oil in a medium skillet. Sauté bacon, stirring frequently, until browned. Add onion and sauté over medium-high heat, stirring often, until soft and lightly browned, about 10 minutes. Transfer to a 3-quart baking dish or bean pot. Stir in tomato sauce, brown sugar, Worcestershire sauce, molasses, vinegar, liquid smoke, salt, chile powder, pepper sauce, and beans until well mixed.

Bake in center of oven, uncovered, stirring every 15 minutes, for 45 minutes, or until sauce has thickened slightly and beans are nicely glazed. They will appear slightly soupy, but will thicken up substantially in about 5 minutes. (Beans may be refrigerated up to 2 days or frozen up to 1 month. Bring to room temperature and reheat, covered, in microwave or in oven at 350°F. for 20 to 30 minutes or until heated through.)

MAKES: 10 servings.

Leaner: Reduce Canadian bacon to 3 ounces or less. Although the bacon adds a smoky flavor, the beans are still excellent with a smaller amount.

RED-SPANGLED SLAW WITH DRIED CRANBERRIES

9 cups thinly sliced green
  cabbage (about 1½ pounds)
3 cups thinly sliced red cabbage
1 cup dried cranberries
2 medium tart apples, peeled,
  cored, and chopped into ½-
  inch cubes

Dressing
¾ cup frozen margarita mix,
  thawed
¼ cup cider vinegar
¼ cup vegetable oil
¾ teaspoon celery seed
¾ teaspoon salt, or to taste

**Red cabbage leaves for garnish
(optional)**

In a medium bowl, toss together green and red cabbage, cranberries, and apple.

To Make Dressing: In a small bowl, stir together margarita mix, vinegar, oil, celery seed, and salt. Pour over slaw and toss well. Cover and refrigerate for at least 2 hours for flavors to blend. (Slaw may be refrigerated overnight.)

Before Serving: Line a salad bowl with red cabbage leaves, if desired, and fill with slaw.

MAKES: 10 to 12 servings.

Faster: Purchase presliced cabbage or coleslaw mix from the supermarket produce section or refrigerator case. A 16-ounce package yields about 10 cups.

When you glance down this list of ingredients, it's not the cranberries that will cause the double take. It's the margarita mix. As unexpected as this is in coleslaw, when you consider it's made with lime juice and sweeteners, it seems less surprising. The cranberries were my friend Marion Cunningham's contribution. (See color photos, page 5.)

PREP TIME: 15 minutes

CHILL TIME: 2 hours

ADVANCE PREP: Slaw may be refrigerated overnight.

NUTRITIONAL ANALYSIS

Per serving
125 calories
5 g fat
0 cholesterol
145 mg sodium

Experimenting with cornbread is great fun, because everyone loves corn and its derivatives. In this version I've eliminated the flour to produce a custardy cornmeal pudding. For a patriotic twist, make the pudding ahead, let it cool, and cut out stars with a cookie cutter. Reheat them on a greased baking sheet at 375°F. for five to eight minutes. (See color photos, pages 4 and 5.)

PREP TIME: 15 minutes

BAKE TIME: 35 to 45 minutes plus 10 minutes standing time

ADVANCE PREP: May be refrigerated overnight or frozen.

NUTRITIONAL ANALYSIS

Per serving (with nonfat milk)
104 calories
6 g fat
64 mg cholesterol
457 mg sodium

CORNBREAD PUDDING

4 tablespoons (½ stick) butter or margarine
3 large eggs
1½ cups regular, low-fat, or nonfat buttermilk
½ teaspoon baking soda
¾ teaspoon baking powder

2 tablespoons sugar
½ teaspoon salt, or to taste
¼ teaspoon hot-pepper sauce, such as Tabasco
1 cup yellow cornmeal
2 cans (4 ounces each) green chiles, undrained and chopped

Place butter or margarine in a 9 × 13-inch glass baking dish. Preheat oven to 375°F. Place baking dish in oven until butter melts and sizzles.

Meanwhile, in a large bowl, whisk eggs and buttermilk until blended. Mix in baking soda, baking powder, sugar, salt, pepper sauce, cornmeal, and chiles. Swirl butter in dish to coat bottom and sides; pour remainder into batter, whisk to combine and pour into baking dish.

Bake in center of oven for 35 to 45 minutes, or until top is lightly golden and knife inserted in the center comes out clean. Let stand 10 minutes before serving; it will fall as it cools. (Pudding may be held at room temperature up to 4 hours, refrigerated overnight, or frozen up to 1 month. Bring to room temperature and reheat, uncovered, at 400°F. for 10 minutes or until heated through.) Cut into squares or desired shapes and transfer to a serving platter.

MAKES: 10 to 12 servings.

MANGO-PINEAPPLE SHORTCAKES WITH GINGERBREAD BISCUITS

Mango-Pineapple Filling
2 mangoes
6 tablespoons fresh lime juice
   (see page 11)
⅔ cup pineapple or white grape
   juice
¾ to 1 cup sugar, depending on
   sweetness of fruit
2 cups fresh pineapple cut into
   ¾-inch pieces

Gingerbread Biscuits
2 cups all-purpose flour
½ cup (packed) light brown
   sugar

½ teaspoon baking soda
2 teaspoons baking powder
¼ teaspoon salt
¼ teaspoon ground nutmeg
1 teaspoon ground cinnamon
1 tablespoon ground ginger
⅓ cup shortening, butter, or
   margarine
2 tablespoons molasses
½ cup plus 1 tablespoon regular,
   low-fat, or nonfat buttermilk
1 tablespoon sugar, for
   sprinkling on top

1 recipe Double Whipped Cream
   (see page 266)

To Make Filling: Peel mangoes with vegetable peeler. Cut off fruit, removing as much from around the pit as possible, and place in food processor with the metal blade. Process until pureed. Remove to a small bowl and stir in remaining ingredients. Refrigerate at least 1 hour for flavors to blend. (Fruit may be refrigerated overnight.)

To Make Biscuits: Place rack in upper third of oven. Preheat oven to 400°F. In food processor with metal blade or mixing bowl with a fork, pulse or mix flour, brown sugar, baking soda, baking powder, salt, nutmeg, cinnamon and ginger. Add shortening and pulse or cut in until the consistency of coarse meal. Stir molasses into buttermilk and pour, all at once, into batter. Pulse or stir until the dough is thoroughly moistened and begins to hold together; it should feel sticky.

Drop by tablespoons about 2 inches apart onto ungreased baking sheet, making 8 mounds about 1½ inches high. Sprinkle tops with sugar. Bake for 12 to 15 minutes, or until tops are set and lightly browned. Biscuits will spread out. Immediately remove from baking sheets to racks. (Biscuits may be stored loosely covered overnight or frozen up to 2 weeks. Reheat, uncovered, at 350°F. for 8 to 12 minutes.)

To Assemble: Cut biscuits in half horizontally. Place bottom half on plate, spoon fruit over, and top with other half of biscuit, more fruit, and a dollop of whipped cream.

MAKES: 8 servings.

A felicitous blending of the old and new, these gingerbread biscuits are sandwiched with a modern mango filling to make an avant garde but homey dessert.

PREP TIME: Biscuits, 10 minutes; filling, 10 minutes

BAKE TIME: 12 to 15 minutes

CHILL TIME: Filling, 1 hour

ADVANCE PREP: Biscuits may be stored at room temperature overnight or frozen. Filling may be refrigerated overnight.

NUTRITIONAL ANALYSIS

Per serving (with nonfat buttermilk, not including whipped cream)
400 calories
9 g fat
0 cholesterol
226 mg sodium

or all of you who believe a dessert is not worth its sugar unless it's crammed with chocolate, here's a soft chocolate biscuit loaded with chocolate chips, sandwiched with berries, then smothered in a fudgy chocolate sauce. (See color photo, page 4.)

PREP TIME: Biscuits, 10 minutes; filling, 10 minutes

BAKE TIME: 12 to 15 minutes

ADVANCE PREP: Biscuits may be stored at room temperature overnight or frozen. Filling may be refrigerated up to 4 hours.

NUTRITIONAL ANALYSIS

Per serving (with nonfat buttermilk, not including toppings)
365 calories
12 g fat
less than 1 mg cholesterol
299 mg sodium

RED, WHITE, AND BLUEBERRY SHORTCAKES WITH CHOCOLATE BISCUITS

Chocolate Biscuits
1⅔ cups all-purpose flour
1 tablespoon baking powder
¾ teaspoon baking soda
3 tablespoons unsweetened cocoa powder
¼ teaspoon salt
½ cup sugar
⅓ cup shortening, butter, or margarine, cut into pieces
1 teaspoon vanilla extract
⅔ cup regular, low-fat, or nonfat buttermilk
½ cup chocolate chips

Red and Blueberry Filling
2 pints fresh strawberries, divided (about 4 cups)

1 pint fresh raspberries, divided (about 2 cups)
½ cup sugar
1½ teaspoons fresh lemon juice
½ cup fresh blueberries
2 tablespoons Chambord liqueur (optional)

Double Whipped Cream substituting crème de cacao for peach schnapps (see page 266)
Fatless Fudge Sauce (see page 66) or storebought fudge sauce

To Make Biscuits: Place rack in upper third of oven and preheat to 425°F. Combine flour, baking powder, soda, cocoa, salt, and sugar in a food processor with the metal blade or in a medium bowl with a fork. Add shortening and pulse or cut in until the consistency of coarse meal. Stir vanilla into buttermilk. Add to flour mixture. Add chocolate chips. Pulse or stir until the dough is thoroughly moistened and begins to mass together; it should feel sticky.

Drop by tablespoons about 2 inches apart onto ungreased baking sheet, making 8 mounds about 1½ inches high. Bake for 12 to 15 minutes, or until tops are set and dry. Immediately remove to racks to cool. (Biscuits may be stored at room temperature overnight or frozen up to 2 weeks. Reheat at 350°F. for 8 to 10 minutes.)

To Make Filling: Hull and slice strawberries. Place half in a food processor with the metal blade. Add half the raspberries and process until pureed. Place a medium mesh strainer over a bowl and strain mixture through it, stirring and scraping puree from underneath the strainer. Stir in sugar, lemon juice, blueberries, and Chambord, if using. (Filling may be refrigerated up to 4 hours.) Up to 2 hours before serving, stir in remaining berries and refrigerate.

To Assemble: Cut biscuits in half horizontally. Place bottom half on plate, top with spoonfuls of filling, other half of biscuit, more filling, a heaping tablespoon of fudge sauce and a dollop of whipped cream.

MAKES: 8 servings.

SOUTHWESTERN FOURTH OF JULY

WARM CARAMEL-PEACH SHORTCAKES WITH ALMOND BISCUITS

Almond Biscuits
1 cup slivered almonds
½ cup sugar plus 1 tablespoon,
   for sprinkling on top
2 cups all-purpose flour
1 tablespoon baking powder
½ teaspoon baking soda
½ teaspoon salt
1 tablespoon grated lemon peel
   (see page 11)
⅓ cup shortening, butter, or
   margarine
½ teaspoon almond extract
1 cup reguiar, low-fat, or
   nonfat buttermilk

Caramel-Peach Filling
3 pounds firm ripe peaches,
   peeled (see page 12)
   (about 8 medium)
4 tablespoons (½ stick) butter or
   margarine
1 cup (packed) light brown sugar
2 tablespoons fresh lemon juice
2 tablespoons dark rum
   (optional)

Double Whipped Cream
   (recipe follows)

To Make Biscuits: Place oven rack in top third of oven and preheat to 400°F. Proccss almonds in a food processor with the metal blade until finely chopped. Add ½ cup sugar and process until ground. Add flour, baking powder, soda, salt, and lemon peel, and pulse to mix. Pulse in shortening until mixture resembles coarse meal. Stir almond extract into buttermilk and pour into batter. Pulse until thoroughly moistened and it begins to mass together; it should feel sticky.

   Drop by tablespoons 2 inches apart onto ungreased baking sheet, making 8 mounds about 1½ inches high. Sprinkle tops with sugar. Bake until set and golden brown, about 12 to 15 minutes. Immediately remove to racks to cool. (Biscuits may be stored loosely covered overnight or frozen up to 2 weeks. Reheat at 350°F. for 8 to 10 minutes.)

To Make Filling: Cut peaches in half, remove pits, and slice. (Cover and refrigerate up to 2 hours.) Melt butter in large skillet over medium-high heat. Add brown sugar and stir until blended, about 4 minutes. Stir in lemon juice and rum, if using, and cook over high heat about 5 minutes. (Sauce may be held up to 2 hours. Reheat before adding peaches.) Add peaches and sauté, stirring often, for 5 minutes, or until slightly softened.

To Assemble: Cut biscuits in half horizontally. Place bottom half on plates. Spoon warm peaches over and top with upper half of biscuit on a jaunty angle. Top with a dollop of whipped cream.

MAKES: 8 servings.

I can't take the credit for developing this noteworthy recipe. I found it in *Bon Appétit* magazine in an article by Edna Sheldon. The only change I've made is to reduce some of the fat.

PREP TIME: Biscuits, 10 minutes; filling, 20 minutes

BAKE TIME: 12 to 15 minutes

ADVANCE PREP: Biscuits may be stored at room temperature overnight or frozen. Peaches may be peeled and sliced and filling prepared up to 2 hours ahead.

NUTRITIONAL ANALYSIS

Per serving (with nonfat buttermilk, not including whipped cream or rum)
564 calories
22 g fat
16 mg cholesterol
410 mg sodium

DOUBLE WHIPPED CREAM

1 cup heavy cream, chilled
1 cup light sour cream, chilled
⅓ cup confectioners' sugar

1 teaspoon vanilla extract
1 tablespoon peach schnapps,
apricot brandy, Grand Marnier,
or other liqueur (optional)

In a mixing bowl with electric mixer, beat heavy cream until soft peaks form. Add sour cream, sugar, vanilla, and liqueur, if using, and continue beating until soft peaks form. (Cream may be refrigerated in a covered container overnight.)

MAKES: 4 cups.

E ver since I discovered this combination of flavored sweet and sour cream, I use it in place of whipping cream for everything but decorating. If you plan to whip it ahead and refrigerate it, use light sour cream instead of regular; it holds up better.

PREP TIME: 5 minutes

ADVANCE PREP: May be refrigerated overnight.

NUTRITIONAL ANALYSIS

Per 2 tablespoons (not including liqueur)
40 calories
4 g fat
13 mg cholesterol
6 mg sodium

Mango Pineapple

Red, White & Blueberry

Caramel Peach

THANKSGIVING FEAST

The Pilgrims may have cooked a whole wild turkey rather than stuffing and roasting only the breast of a domestic tom, but they didn't share the concerns of the health-conscious and harried modern-day cook. Of the original 102 settlers who arrived at Plymouth in the winter of 1620, only fifty-five were still alive by the spring of 1621, and as far as we know, none of them perished from high cholesterol or saturated fats.

You won't need to be up at daybreak to stuff and truss this bird; the rolled breast can be roasted a day ahead, leaving you and your oven free. Just be sure to allow eighteen to twenty-four hours for the meat to marinate.

If boning a turkey breast is not high on your list of accomplishments, call ahead and ask the butcher to bone and butterfly a large breast. You might also ask to have it pounded, but it's easy enough to do yourself. A round metal pounder with a handle in the center is more efficient to work with than the hammer type, but even a rolling pin will do the job.

Here you'll find traditional ingredients incorporated into dishes in new ways. Cranberry sauce adds a rosy glaze to baby carrots and sweet potatoes heighten the flavor of the dinner rolls. Wild Rice Pilaf with Leeks and Dried Pears makes an ideal complement to this fall feast. Wild rice does not grace our Thanksgiving table as often as it should, especially when you consider it is a native seed, harvested on North American soil long before white men stepped foot on it. If you wish to add a green vegetable, consider Crisp Garlic Green Beans (see page 121) or Sugar Snap Peas (see page 98).

Even if your family insists on conventional pumpkin pie, go ahead and serve Harvest Patchwork Cake as well. This marbled cake made with two batters, cheesecake and pumpkin-carrot, may begin a new tradition. This menu serves ten to twelve, if you double the soup.

G A M E   P L A N

1 Month Ahead	**Make and freeze soup** **Make and freeze cake** **Make and freeze rolls**
2 Days Ahead	**Make Wild Rice Pilaf**
1 Day Ahead	**Make and roast turkey and make sauce** **Cook carrots** **Defrost cake, soup, and rolls**
DAY OF PARTY 8 Hours Ahead	**Make garnish for soup**
30 Minutes Before Serving	**Reheat turkey**
Shortly Before Serving	**Reheat soup and garnish** **Slice turkey and reheat sauce** **Glaze carrots** **Reheat Wild Rice Pilaf** **Rewarm rolls**

EXTRA ◆ POINTS ◆

THE TABLE

Arrange groupings of various size and shape squashes, gourds, fruits, fall leaves, dried flowers, and vines in the center and down the length of the table. Carve out little pumpkins and set them aglow with votive candles. (See color photo, page 14.)

THE PLACE CARDS

For each guest, cut a small slice off the top of a small acorn squash or pumpkin. Scoop out enough of the pulp to make room for a three-ounce paper cup. Fill the cup with assorted raw vegetables. If not serving immediately, cover the vegetables with wet paper towels and plastic wrap and refrigerate for up to eight hours. Glue a name card on to the squash or pumpkin top. Insert a wooden skewer into the back and insert it in the cup. (See color photo, page 14.)

By marinating and stuffing a boneless breast and using the marinade for the sauce, you eliminate the fatty skin and dark meat, the butter and oil for basting, and the calorie-laden gravy. Besides tasting terrific, this rolled-up roast can be baked a day ahead and is a breeze to carve. (See color photo, page 15.)

PREP TIME: 45 minutes

MARINADE TIME: 18 to 24 hours

BAKE TIME: 1 hour and 30 minutes

ADVANCE PREP: Turkey may be roasted 1 day ahead. Sauce may be refrigerated overnight.

NUTRITIONAL ANALYSIS

Per serving
489 calories
25 g fat
102 mg cholesterol
308 mg sodium

ROAST BREAST OF TURKEY WITH CORNBREAD, SPINACH, AND PECANS

1 whole turkey breast, skinned, boned, and butterflied (5½ to 7 pounds with bones, 4 to 5 pounds without bones)

Marinade
Juice and grated peel of 3 medium oranges (about 1 cup juice) (see page 11)
⅔ cup balsamic vinegar
¼ cup olive oil
¼ cup honey

Stuffing
1 tablespoon olive oil
2 onions, chopped
2 cups chopped fresh spinach (bite-size pieces)
1½ cups packaged cornbread stuffing, such as Pepperidge Farm

2½ cups coarsely chopped pecans, toasted (see page 11)
1 tablespoon prepared mustard
¼ cup chicken broth
2 large eggs, lightly beaten

Salt and freshly ground black pepper
1 cup dry red wine
¾ cup chicken broth
¼ cup honey
1 egg white, mixed with 1 teaspoon water, for brushing on turkey
1 tablespoon cornstarch, mixed with 1 tablespoon water

Garnish (optional)
Greens, such as spinach or parsley
Orange slices

Rinse and dry turkey breast. Pound lightly to make as even as possible. Place in a shallow nonaluminum dish.

To Make Marinade: Mix juice, peel, vinegar, oil, and honey in small bowl. Pour over turkey, turning to coat both sides. Cover and refrigerate overnight, turning once or twice.

To Make Stuffing: In a large skillet, heat oil over moderate heat until hot. Sauté onion until tender, about 10 minutes. Stir in spinach and sauté until wilted. Remove to a large bowl and stir in cornbread stuffing, pecans, mustard, broth, and eggs.

To Prepare Turkey: Remove turkey from marinade. Dry well and place on work surface, skin side down. Pour marinade into a deep saucepan and set aside. Sprinkle meat with salt and pepper and spread with half the stuffing. Beginning with a short end, roll up like a jelly roll; do not be concerned about torn or uneven pieces of meat. Tie with string at 1-inch intervals. Sprinkle with salt and pepper.

To Roast: Preheat oven to 375°F.

Place turkey in a shallow roasting pan, add about ½ inch water, and roast for 50 to 60 minutes, or until a meat thermometer reaches 120°F., basting with pan drippings every 15 minutes and adding more water to pan as needed. While turkey roasts, pour wine and broth into marinade for sauce. Simmer over moderate heat until reduced by about half. Set aside.

Remove turkey from pan to a cutting board. Pour drippings into sauce. Stir 1 tablespoon into honey. Cut strings off turkey, brush the top and sides with egg white and press remaining stuffing firmly over top and sides. Drizzle with half the honey mixture. Return to oven and roast 15 minutes. Drizzle with remaining honey and roast for 15 minutes more, or until brown and crusty and thermometer inserted into center reaches 145° to 150°F. Remove roast to cutting board and let rest 20 minutes before carving. (Turkey may be cooled to room temperature, wrapped in foil and refrigerated overnight. To reheat, bring to room temperature, return to roasting pan, add ½ inch broth or water, cover loosely with foil and roast at 375°F. for 30 minutes or until heated through.)

To Complete Sauce: Deglaze the roasting pan by placing it over medium-high heat. Add a little of the sauce and bring to a boil, scraping the bottom of the pan and stirring constantly. Strain into remaining sauce in saucepan. Remove from heat and whisk in cornstarch. Return to heat and cook, whisking, until sauce comes to a boil and thickens. Season to taste with salt and pepper, and more wine and/or honey, if needed. (Sauce may be refrigerated overnight. Reheat before serving.)

To Serve: Carve the roast into ⅜-inch slices, arrange overlapping on a platter, drizzle with sauce, and, if desired, garnish with greens and oranges. Pass remaining sauce.

MAKES: 8 to 12 servings.

Leaner: In the stuffing, substitute ½ cup frozen egg substitute, thawed, for the 2 eggs. Decrease the pecans to 1 cup or omit altogether. Increase cornbread stuffing to 2½ cups.

Glazing carrots in butter and brown sugar is a classic preparation, but adding cranberry sauce makes a great dish even better. (See color photo, page 15.)

PREP TIME: 15 minutes

ADVANCE PREP: May be cooked a day ahead. Glaze before serving.

CRANBERRY-GLAZED BABY CARROTS

3 pounds fresh baby carrots, peeled and trimmed
6 tablespoons (¾ stick) butter or margarine
¾ cup whole berry or jellied cranberry sauce
⅓ cup packed light brown sugar
1 tablespoon plus 1 teaspoon fresh lemon juice
Salt
Freshly ground black pepper

To Cook Carrots: Bring a saucepan of salted water to a boil, add carrots, and boil gently, covered, until crisp-tender, about 8 to 10 minutes. Drain and run under cold water to stop the cooking. (Carrots may be refrigerated overnight. Bring to room temperature before continuing.)

To Glaze: Before serving, in a large skillet over medium-high heat, melt butter, cranberry sauce, brown sugar, lemon juice, and salt to taste, stirring until smooth. Simmer 2 minutes. Add carrots and cook, stirring occasionally, until glazed and heated through, about 5 minutes. Season with salt, pepper, and lemon juice, if needed.

MAKES: 12 servings.

Faster: Substitute frozen carrots. Line baking sheets with several layers of paper towels. Defrost carrots in a single layer until they reach room temperature. Blot dry. Cook in glaze, stirring, for 6 to 8 minutes, or until cooked through.

Change of Pace: Add 1½ pounds cooked sugar snap peas (see page 98) or snow peas into the carrots before serving and toss in the glaze until heated through.

NUTRITIONAL ANALYSIS

Per serving
149 calories
6 g fat
16 mg cholesterol
194 mg sodium

WILD RICE PILAF WITH LEEKS AND DRIED PEARS

1½ cups uncooked wild rice
(6 ounces)
¾ teaspoon salt
6 teaspoons olive oil
¾ cup chopped lean smoked
ham (½-inch pieces)
1½ cups cleaned and chopped
leeks, white part only
(see page 11)

1 cup chopped dried pears
(½-inch pieces)
1¾ cups chicken or vegetable
broth
½ cup heavy cream

Rinse and drain rice. Place in a medium saucepan, add 4½ cups water and salt, and bring to a boil. Reduce heat and simmer, covered, until rice is tender, but still slightly crunchy, about 40 to 50 minutes. If all the water is not absorbed, drain off excess. (Rice may be refrigerated overnight.)

In a large skillet over medium heat, heat olive oil until hot. Add ham and sauté for about 4 minutes or until golden. Add leeks and pears and sauté, stirring for 3 to 5 minutes until leeks are soft but not brown. Stir in cooked rice, broth, and cream. Bring to a boil, lower heat, and cook, uncovered, stirring occasionally, until thickened and most liquid has evaporated, about 7 minutes. Season with salt to taste. (Pilaf may be refrigerated up to 2 days. Reheat on top of stove or covered in microwave.)

MAKES: 12 servings.

Leaner: Omit the cream.

Change of Pace: Substitute dried apples for the pears.

The idea for this dynamic combination of nutty wild rice, sweet pears and salty ham comes from Dean Fearing, chef at The Mansion on Turtle Creek in Dallas. Be careful not to overcook the rice in the initial cooking or the grains will split open when they absorb the broth and cream. (See color photo, page 15.)

PREP TIME: 20 minutes

COOK TIME: About 1 hour

ADVANCE PREP: May be refrigerated up to 2 days.

NUTRITIONAL ANALYSIS

Per serving
192 calories
7 g fat
18 mg cholesterol
363 mg sodium

akers know that potatoes in bread dough produce an extremely light texture. Sweet potatoes add fragrance as well. Coating the batter balls in honey-butter and graham cracker crumbs gives these whole wheat rolls a tasty crust. (See color photo, page 15.)

PREP TIME: 40 minutes

RISE TIME: Microwave, about 30 minutes; room temperature, about 1 hour

BAKE TIME: 25 to 30 minutes

ADVANCE PREP: May be refrigerated overnight or frozen.

NUTRITIONAL ANALYSIS

Per serving
250 calories
9 g fat
16 mg cholesterol
248 mg sodium

HONEY GRAHAM– SWEET POTATO ROLLS

1 cup all-purpose flour
1½ cups whole wheat flour
¾ teaspoon salt
1 package quick-rising yeast
½ cup cooked mashed sweet potatoes, canned or fresh
⅓ cup honey
2 tablespoons vegetable oil
1 egg white

⅓ cup syrup from canned sweet potatoes, or water
Butter, for serving (optional)

Coating
⅓ cup melted butter or margarine
2 tablespoons honey
1½ cups graham cracker crumbs

To Make Dough: Place flours, salt, and yeast in a food processor with the metal blade and pulse to combine. Add sweet potatoes, honey, vegetable oil, and egg white and process until blended. Heat syrup or water to 125° or 130°F., or until very hot to the touch. With the motor running, slowly pour the hot liquid through the feed tube, holding back a little to see if the dough forms a ball. Process until the dough begins to leave the sides of the bowl and forms a ball. Add the last liquid only if necessary. Process 1 minute to knead. Dough should be sticky. Remove to a lightly floured surface and knead lightly. Shape into a ball.

To Rise in Microwave: You need a machine with 10% power. Make a hole in the center of the dough like a doughnut and return to food processor bowl without the blade. Spray top with no-stick spray or brush lightly with oil. Cover loosely with plastic wrap and a damp towel. Place an 8-ounce glass of water in back of oven. Place bowl in center. Microwave at 10% power for 5 minutes, then let rest for 5 minutes. Rotate bowl and microwave 5 minutes more and rest 5 minutes more. Repeat 1 more time for a total of 30 minutes rising time. The dough should be double in bulk and when you poke it with your finger, a hole should remain. If it isn't double, cover and let rise at room temperature until doubled in bulk.

To Rise at Room Temperature: Coat a large bowl with oil and place dough in bowl, turning to coat all sides. Cover with a damp towel. Let rise in a warm place (see page 9) for about 1 hour, or until double in size and a hole remains when dough is poked with your finger.

To Shape and Coat: Grease or spray a 9-inch cake pan. Punch dough down and turn out onto lightly floured surface and knead a few times

· 274 ·

until smooth. Divide dough into 12 equal portions and roll each piece into a ball.

To make coating, in a small bowl, mix butter and honey. Place graham cracker crumbs in a plastic bag. Roll each ball in butter-honey mixture and then shake in graham cracker crumbs to coat. Place close together in prepared pan. Let stand 10 minutes.

To Bake: Preheat oven to 400°F.

Bake for 25 to 30 minutes, or until golden brown. Let stand 10 minutes. Invert onto serving plate or sheet of foil and turn right side up. (Cooled rolls may be refrigerated overnight or frozen up to one month. Reheat, uncovered, at 400°F. for 8 to 10 minutes.) Serve warm with butter, if desired.

MAKES: 12 rolls.

Get wrapped up in this alluring dessert as homey, comforting, and attractive as a snuggly quilt. The patchwork design comes from alternating spoonfuls of carrot-pumpkin and cheesecake batters. (See color photo, page 14.)

PREP TIME: 40 minutes

BAKE TIME: 1 hour and 15 minutes

ADVANCE PREP: May be refrigerated up to 3 days or frozen.

NUTRITIONAL ANALYSIS

Per serving (with low-fat cream cheese)
363 calories
15 g fat
109 mg cholesterol
429 mg sodium

HARVEST PATCHWORK CAKE

Carrot-Pumpkin Batter
2 large carrots, peeled
1½ cups all-purpose flour
1¼ cups sugar
1 teaspoon baking powder
1 teaspoon baking soda
½ teaspoon salt
1¼ teaspoons ground cinnamon
¼ teaspoon ground cloves
½ teaspoon ground nutmeg
⅓ cup vegetable oil
3 large eggs
½ cup cooked mashed pumpkin, canned or fresh
1 can (8 ounces) crushed pineapple, drained, ½ cup juice reserved for glaze

Cheesecake Batter
2 packages (8 ounces each) regular or low-fat cream cheese, softened
2 large eggs, separated
¼ cup sugar
1 tablespoon lemon juice

Pineapple Glaze
1 cup confectioners' sugar, for glaze
1½ to 2 tablespoons reserved pineapple juice

Marbleized Chocolate Leaves (optional)
24 nonpoisonous leaves (see page 10)
3 ounces white chocolate chips
3 ounces butterscotch chips

To Make Carrot-Pumpkin Batter: Preheat oven to 325°F. In a food processor with the shredding disk or with a hand grater, shred carrots. Measure 1½ cups and set aside. In same workbowl (no need to wash it) with the metal blade, pulse flour, sugar, baking powder, baking soda, salt, cinnamon, cloves, and nutmeg. Add oil, eggs, and pumpkin and pulse until blended, about 20 seconds. Add carrots and pineapple and pulse 5 or 6 times until incorporated.

To Make Cheesecake Batter: In a large mixing bowl with electric mixer, beat cream cheese until fluffy. Add egg yolks, sugar, and lemon juice and mix until well blended. Set aside. In a small mixing bowl with clean beaters, beat egg whites until stiff peaks form. Fold into cheesecake batter.

To Bake: Grease or spray a 9-inch springform pan. Alternate spoonfuls of each batter in pan, putting more cheesecake batter toward the outside rim. (It tends to fall toward the center while it bakes.) Marble with a knife two or three times to swirl. Bake for 1 hour and 15 to 1 hour and 25 minutes, or until a toothpick inserted into the center comes out free of carrot-pumpkin batter. Remove to a rack and cool 30 minutes. Invert, then turn right side up to cool completely. Cake will sink as it cools.

To Make Glaze: In a medium bowl, stir together confectioners' sugar and enough pineapple juice to make a thick glaze. Place cooled cake over a sheet of wax paper and drizzle glaze over top and sides. (Cake may be refrigerated up to 3 days or frozen.) Serve chilled or at room temperature.

MAKES: 12 servings.

Leaner: Substitute ¾ cup frozen egg substitute, thawed, for the 3 eggs in the carrot-pumpkin batter. Substitute 2 tablespoons frozen egg substitute, thawed, for the egg yolks in the cheesecake batter; egg whites remain the same.

MARBLEIZED CHOCOLATE LEAVES

Wash and dry 24 nonpoisonous leaves. Line a small baking sheet with wax paper. Melt white chocolate and butterscotch chips in separate bowls in microwave at 70% power. Using a small brush or knife, spread a portion of underside of each leaf with butterscotch. Place on baking sheet and refrigerate or freeze until firm. Spread a layer of white chocolate over leaf and butterscotch to cover completely. Chill until firm. To remove leaf from chocolate, grasp leaf's stem and gently pull back until separated. Discard garden leaves. Chocolate leaves may be refrigerated, covered, for several weeks. (See color photo, page 14.)

Menu

◆

CONSTANT COMMENT
CHAMPAGNE PUNCH WITH
FROSTED FRUIT MOLD

◆

SAVORY PICK-UPS:

SHRIMP MOUSSE WITH DILL-
PISTACHIO PESTO

•

YAM SLICES WITH SMOKED
TURKEY AND CRANBERRY-
GINGER RELISH

•

CHUNKY ITALIAN SALSA WITH
TUSCANY TOASTS

•

TORTELLINI WITH PIMIENTO
PEPPER DIP

•

ON-*The*-RUN COCKTAIL PARTY

riginally, cocktail parties were a prelude to an evening's activities. Guests would gather for drinks and hors d'oeuvres before the theater, dinner, or an outing. But in my philosophy, if you're doing all that work, you might as well make it a full-fledged event. Add some sandwich fixings and dessert and call it a cocktail buffet party. If you don't put an ending time on your invitation, guests will assume it's for the entire evening.

An On-the-Run Cocktail Party calls for on-the-run food. Instead of hot and cold hors d'oeuvres, serve tidbits at room temperature. Instead of passing them on trays, put them out on a buffet. Instead of cooking everything yourself, let friends pitch in. Instead of using your good dishes, purchase high-quality paper ones. ''Anything goes'' is the credo for the eclectic nineties. Regardless of the dress and ambience, the versatile appetizers and desserts I'm proposing will be right at home.

THE FOOD: Here is a broad selection of party morsels that can be made fully or partially ahead, require a minimum of last-minute preparation, can sit out with little attention, and can be picked up and popped in the mouth without a utensil (that's why I call them pick-ups). If your party doesn't include dinner, plan on ten to fourteen hors d'oeuvres per person. If they are predinner, allow four to six. Regardless of the number of guests, select an assortment of five or six hors d'oeuvres, more are not really necessary, but fewer get boring. For a light supper, supplement them with thinly sliced roasts, such as turkey, ham, pork, or beef (allow about three ounces per person), sandwich breads and rolls, and some Mustard Sauce with Green Peppercorns (see page 229).

If your dishes will be sitting out for several hours, don't put out large quantities all at once — replenish the platters so they always look fresh. Instead of molding the Shrimp Mousse in one large dish, use two smaller ones. Other hors d'oeuvres in the book which meet the "prepare ahead/room temperature" criteria are: Asparagus Spears with Smoked Salmon (see page 149), Confetti-capped Mushrooms (see page 150), Eggplant Rolls with Garlic-Herb Cheese (see page 148), Potato Nachos with Roasted Garlic (see page 179), Savory Scotch Biscotti (or Thumb-prints) with Canadian Bacon and Mustard Seed Spread (see pages 114–115), Artichokes with Romesco Sauce (see page 178), crudités with Peanut Dipping Sauce (see page 212), and Guacamole and Corn Salsa (see page 170).

When the party is planned for the entire evening, dessert is appropriate. Set up a separate table or sideboard with petit sweets, coffee, and tea. Allow three to four pastries per person and offer a variety of at least two or more. Besides the ones suggested here, you may also wish to consider Biscotti with Dried Fruits (see page 54).

THE BEVERAGES: To quench the thirst, supplement Constant Comment Champagne Punch with wine and a nonalcoholic punch, club soda, or fashionable sparkling and still waters. One bottle of wine yields six drinks; one case (twelve fifths) yields seventy-two drinks. One liter of spirits yields thirty drinks. Plan on one to one and a half pounds ice per person.

THE EQUIPMENT: As soon as you decide to throw the party, assess what you'll need, inventory what you have, and beg, borrow or rent the rest. There are so many marvelous paper goods on the market, keep things simple by using them. Luncheon or dessert plates are ideal for the main meal as well as dessert, and luncheon-size napkins are more practical than cocktail ones — the average person will go through four to five napkins in an evening. Glasses and cups present a greater challenge. Plastic punch cups are adequate for punch, but the stemmed plastic glasses for wine and champagne are so flimsy, you may prefer to rent the real thing. For a three- to four-hour party, plan on two to three cocktail glasses per person. You might also want to rent coffee mugs. They're easier to handle than cups and saucers and safer than paper cups. Forget the silverware. With this on-the-go menu, you won't need anything but serving utensils.

THE HELP: Even when serving room-temperature food on paper plates, consider getting someone to replenish platters, remove empty plates and glasses, and help with the cleanup. Think of it as a night out when you hire a baby-sitter.

PUREE OF WHITE BEANS WITH VEGETABLES
SKEWERED SCALLOPS, ORANGES, AND SNOW PEAS
SWEET POTATO PANCAKES WITH SOUR CREAM AND CHUTNEY
SESAME CHICKEN WITH CRANBERRY-PLUM DIPPING SAUCE
TOSTADA CUPS WITH SAUSAGE AND BLACK BEANS

SWEET PICK-UPS:
ESPRESSO FUDGE CUPS
ALABASTER CHEESECAKE BITES
LEMON STREUSEL SQUARES
RITA CALVERT'S SHORTBREAD ALMOND FLORENTINES
MINI MERINGUES WITH CHOCOLATE TRUFFLES

EXTRA POINTS

THE INVITATIONS

For a holiday open house, purchase small Christmas stockings, tuck a note inside, and drop them into berry-red envelopes from a party shop. Or purchase frosted white Christmas balls and using a gold marker, write your message on them, wrap in bubble wrap, tuck in a box, and mail.

THE THEME

Plan a black, white, and sparkle party. Add glitz to black-and-white invitations with glitter or foil confetti. Decorate with black and white and add sparkle with crystal, candles, gold or silver balloons, spray-painted leaves or branches. Ask guests to wear black and/or white and let them interpret the sparkle.

GAME PLAN

1 Month Ahead
- **Prepare and freeze Tuscany Toasts**
- **Make and freeze Puree of White Beans**
- **Make and freeze Espresso Fudge Cups**
- **Make and freeze Alabaster Cheesecake Bites**
- **Make and freeze Lemon Streusel Squares**
- **Make and freeze Shortbread Almond Florentines**

2 Weeks Ahead
- **Make and freeze ice mold for punch**
- **Make and freeze Sweet Potato Pancakes**
- **Make and freeze Tostada Cups**
- **Make and freeze Mini Meringues**

1 Week Ahead
- **Make and freeze Sesame Chicken**
- **Make Cranberry-Plum Dipping Sauce for chicken**

3 Days Ahead
- **Make cranberry-ginger relish for yam slices**

1 Day Ahead
- **Make punch**
- **Defrost Tuscany Toasts**
- **Cook tortellini and prepare pimiento dip**
- **Defrost Puree of White Beans and prepare vegetables for dipping**
- **Defrost Espresso Fudge Cups and Florentines**
- **Cut cheesecake into squares and refreeze**
- **Make Shrimp Mousse**
- **Make Chunky Italian Salsa**
- **Blanch snow peas for scallops**
- **Marinate and cook scallops**

DAY OF PARTY

Morning of Party
- **Defrost Tostada Cups**
- **Defrost Lemon Streusel Squares**

6 Hours Ahead
- **Make turkey salad and microwave yams**
- **Assemble scallops on skewers**

2 Hours Ahead
- **Assemble yam slices**

1 Hour Ahead
- **Unmold Shrimp Mousse**
- **Remove cheesecake squares from freezer**
- **Bring chicken and sauce to room temperature**

10 Minutes Before Serving	**Bake chicken** **Bake Tostada Cups** **Reheat and garnish Sweet Potato Pancakes**
Shortly Before Serving	**Put punch and ice mold in bowl** **Remove Mini Meringues from freezer**

EXTRA POINTS

THE TABLE

If you like your dining room table, don't cover it with a tablecloth — a pretty punch bowl and platters laden with food may be all the embellishment it needs. Or just lay a table runner down the center. An assortment of paired or unmatched candlesticks with different height candles adds atmosphere and costs a lot less than flowers. Intersperse sprigs of greenery around their base. Votive candles are an inexpensive way to get lots of glow. For candleholders, use an assortment of different shapes and heights of stemmed aperitif glasses.

For a punch that provokes constant comment, serve this combination of orange-and-spice tea, orange liqueur, and sparkling champagne, which I created for a segment on *Good Morning America*. It was such a big hit with the staff, they made it for their annual Christmas party. A tea-flavored ice mold crowned with jeweled fruit looks terrific and ensures the punch is never diluted.

PREP TIME: Ice mold, 15 minutes; punch, 10 minutes plus steeping

CHILL TIME: Ice mold, 24 hours; punch, 2 hours

ADVANCE PREP: Ice mold, may be frozen up to 2 weeks. Tea may be refrigerated overnight.

NUTRITIONAL ANALYSIS

Per 4-ounce serving
58 calories
0 fat
0 cholesterol
2 mg sodium

CONSTANT COMMENT CHAMPAGNE PUNCH WITH FROSTED FRUIT MOLD

Ice Tea Mold
4 Constant Comment tea bags
6 cups boiling water
Assorted fruit, such as red and green seedless grapes, cut into small clusters; sliced navel oranges; sliced lemons; strawberries; sliced starfruit (carambola); sliced kiwi; garden leaves (see page 10)

Punch
4 Constant Comment tea bags
4 cups boiling water
⅓ cup sugar
⅓ cup Grand Marnier
1 bottle extra dry Champagne, chilled

To Make Mold: Place tea bags in a heatproof bowl, pitcher, or nonaluminum saucepan. Pour boiling water over and steep until tea reaches room temperature. Remove tea bags. Pour enough tea into a 6-cup ring, tree, heart, or other shape mold to fill about two thirds full. Refrigerate remaining tea. Freeze mold until firm. Arrange fruits over top. Pour in enough of the remaining tea to come within ¼ inch of top of mold (you may not use it all). Freeze firm. To unmold, dip briefly in cool water, invert onto sheet of heavy foil, turn right side up, wrap in foil, and freeze until serving. (Mold may be frozen up to 2 weeks.)

To Make Punch: Place tea bags in a heatproof bowl, pitcher, or nonaluminum saucepan. Pour boiling water over and stir in sugar. Let steep until tea reaches room temperature. Remove tea bags. Refrigerate until chilled. (Tea may be refrigerated overnight.) Before serving, pour tea into punch bowl. Stir in Grand Marnier. Pour in champagne. Add ice tea mold. Serve in punch cups, champagne glasses, or goblets.

MAKES: 16 (4-ounce) servings.

SHRIMP MOUSSE
WITH DILL-PISTACHIO PESTO

Shrimp Layer
½ medium onion, coarsely
  chopped
6 ounces regular or light cream
  cheese
¾ pound peeled cooked shrimp,
  blotted very dry (about 1¼
  pounds with shell)
2 teaspoons finely grated lemon
  peel (see page 11)
3 tablespoons fresh lemon juice
1¼ teaspoons hot-pepper sauce,
  such as Tabasco
1 tablespoon plus 1 teaspoon
  Dijon mustard
½ teaspoon salt, or to taste

Dill-Pistachio Pesto
3 garlic cloves, peeled
¾ cup (lightly packed) dill sprigs
¾ cup (lightly packed) parsley
  sprigs
¾ cup natural unsalted
  pistachios
½ teaspoon salt
3 to 5 tablespoons olive oil

2 to 4 ounces peeled cooked
  shrimp, for garnish
Dill sprigs, for garnish
Crackers, bread rounds, and/or
  cucumber slices, for serving

To Make Shrimp Layer: In a food processor with the metal blade, pulse onion into small pieces. Add cream cheese, shrimp, lemon peel, lemon juice, hot-pepper sauce, mustard, and salt and pulse until incorporated. Process until smooth. Remove to a bowl.

To Make Pesto: In a clean processor bowl with the metal blade, process garlic, dill, and parsley until minced. Add pistachios and process until finely chopped. Add salt and enough oil to make a spreadable paste.

To Assemble: Line a 3- to 4-cup mold with plastic wrap. Spoon half the shrimp mixture into the bottom, pushing it into the sides and smoothing the top with a knife. Spread with half the pesto. Top with remaining shrimp mixture, smoothing the top. Cover with plastic wrap and refrigerate for at least 2 hours or until firm. (Mold may be refrigerated overnight. Refrigerate shrimp garnish and pesto separately.)

To Serve: Invert the mold onto a plate and remove plastic wrap. Spread remaining pesto over the top and garnish with shrimp and sprigs of dill. Serve with crackers, bread rounds, or cucumber slices.

MAKES: 3 cups.

Change of Pace: Pecans or hazelnuts may be substituted for the pistachios.

Food fads come and go, but a good shrimp spread remains the most popular hors d'oeuvre at a cocktail party. This one is enhanced with a layer of emerald dill pesto, which also decorates the top. To carry through a holiday theme, choose a Christmas tree or bell mold and multiply or divide the recipe as needed. (See color photo, page 6.)

PREP TIME: 20 minutes, not including cooking shrimp

CHILL TIME: 2 hours

ADVANCE PREP: May be refrigerated overnight.

NUTRITIONAL ANALYSIS

Per tablespoon (with low-fat
cream cheese)
34 calories
2 g fat
16 mg cholesterol
96 mg sodium

YAM SLICES WITH SMOKED TURKEY AND CRANBERRY-GINGER RELISH

These tiny nibbles capture all the flavors of a full-blown holiday feast in a single bite.

PREP TIME: 30 minutes

ADVANCE PREP: Relish may be refrigerated up to 3 days. Yams and turkey salad may be refrigerated up to 6 hours. Assemble up to 2 hours ahead.

2 small yams or sweet potatoes, peeled (about 8 ounces each)
1¼ cups orange juice

Turkey Salad
2 green onions with tops
1¾ cups smoked turkey, cut into 1-inch cubes (about 6 ounces)
½ cup regular or light sour cream
Freshly ground freshly ground black pepper

Cranberry-Ginger Relish
1 piece peeled fresh ginger, about the size of a quarter
3 tablespoons fresh or frozen cranberries
1 can (8 ounces) crushed pineapple, well drained and patted dry (⅓ cup)
3 tablespoons hot jalapeño jelly

Fresh cranberries, for garnish (optional)

To Prepare Yams: Slice yams into ¼-inch rounds; you should have about 40 slices. Place in a 9-inch microwavesafe pie plate or square baking dish. (They may overlap.) Pour in orange juice, cover, and microwave on high (100%) for 4 minutes. Rotate pan and microwave for 3 to 5 minutes more, or until crisp-tender. Remove to paper towels to drain. Reserve 2 tablespoons poaching liquid. (Yams may be refrigerated wrapped in paper towels up to 6 hours.)

To Prepare Turkey Salad: In a food processor with the metal blade, pulse green onions until finely minced. Remove to a bowl. Add turkey to food processor and pulse until minced. Remove to bowl with onions and stir in sour cream, 2 tablespoons reserved poaching liquid, and pepper to taste. (Salad may be refrigerated up to 6 hours.)

To Make Relish: In a food processor with the metal blade, process ginger until minced. Remove, measure 1 teaspoon, and return it to processor. Add cranberries and pulse until minced. Remove to bowl and stir in pineapple and jelly. (Relish may be refrigerated up to 3 days.)

To Assemble: Up to 2 hours before serving, place yam slices on plate and sprinkle lightly with salt. Spread with turkey salad and top with a dollop of relish. Refrigerate until serving. If desired, line a platter with a layer of fresh cranberries as a bed for the yam slices.

MAKES: 35 to 40 yam slices.

Faster: Substitute ⅓ cup Cran-Fruit or whole berry cranberry sauce, well drained in a strainer, for the Cranberry-Ginger Relish. If desired, stir in 1 teaspoon grated fresh ginger or ½ teaspoon ground ginger.

NUTRITIONAL ANALYSIS

Per slice (with light sour cream)
20 calories
less than 1 g fat
2 mg cholesterol
35 mg sodium

CHUNKY ITALIAN SALSA WITH TUSCANY TOASTS

2 garlic cloves peeled
1 pickled or fresh seeded jalapeño (¾ to 1 inch) (see page 10)
1 medium carrot, peeled and cut into 1-inch pieces
½ medium red onion, peeled and quartered
1 medium red or yellow bell pepper, seeded and very coarsely chopped

2 medium tomatoes, seeded and very coarsely chopped (see page 12)
½ cup (loosely packed) fresh basil leaves
1 can (15 ounces) garbanzo beans (chick peas), drained
1 tablespoon plus 2 teaspoons fresh lemon juice
3 tablespoons raspberry vinegar
1 teaspoon salt, or to taste
Tuscany Toasts, for serving (recipe follows)

In a food processor with the metal blade, process garlic and jalapeño until finely minced. Add carrot and onion, and pulse until finely chopped. Remove to a medium bowl. Pulse bell pepper, tomatoes, and basil until finely chopped. Add to carrots. Pulse garbanzo beans until finely chopped. Add to carrots. Stir in lemon juice, vinegar, and salt. Refrigerate 30 minutes for the flavors to blend. (Salsa may be refrigerated up to 2 days.)

Before serving, drain off excess liquid. Serve with a spoon to top Tuscany Toasts.

MAKES: 3½ cups.

TUSCANY TOASTS

½ cup olive oil
2 large garlic cloves, minced

1 baguette (about 1 pound)
3 to 4 tablespoons grated parmesan cheese

Preheat oven to 375°F.

In a small bowl, stir together oil and garlic. Slice bread as thin as possible. Place slices on baking sheet and spread with garlic oil. Sprinkle with parmesan cheese. Bake for 10 minutes or until lightly browned. (Toasts may be stored airtight for several days or frozen.)

MAKES: about 50 toasts.

Leaner: Omit olive oil and spray bread with olive or regular oil cooking spray. Omit garlic. Sprinkle lightly with cheese.

This "I don't know what-I'd-do-without-it" recipe is virtually a garden in a salsa. It's simple to prepare in the food processor and goes with almost everything—meats, fish, poultry, and omelets. Serve it with a spoon and let guests top their own crispy toasts or tortilla chips, or slices of cucumber and jícama.

PREP TIME: Salsa, 15 minutes; toasts, 10 minutes

CHILL TIME: 30 minutes

BAKE TIME: Toasts, 10 minutes

ADVANCE PREP: Toasts may be stored at room temperature up to 2 days or frozen. Salsa may be refrigerated up to 2 days.

NUTRITIONAL ANALYSIS

Per 2 teaspoons salsa (not including toasts)
7 calories
less than 1 g fat
0 cholesterol
46 mg sodium

Per toast
47 calories
3 g fat
0 cholesterol
58 mg sodium

Ideveloped this recipe for the American pimiento growers and was delighted to learn that in taste tests with four-star ratings, it garnered five. Look for fresh tortellini in the refrigerator section of your supermarket. The recipe will feed a crowd, but for a small gathering, you can cut it in half.

PREP TIME: 20 minutes

ADVANCE PREP: Tortellini and dip may be refrigerated overnight.

NUTRITIONAL ANALYSIS

Per 4 tortellini (not including dip)
88 calories
3 g fat
14 mg cholesterol
112 mg sodium

Per 2 teaspoons dip
13 calories
less than 1 g fat
3 mg cholesterol
34 mg sodium

TORTELLINI WITH PIMIENTO PEPPER DIP

1 to 1½ pounds fresh spinach-, meat-, or cheese-filled tortellini
2 tablespoons olive oil
3 tablespoons chopped fresh basil or 1 tablespoon dried basil
Salt

Pimiento Pepper Dip
1 garlic clove, peeled
2 jars (4 ounces each) pimientos, drained and patted dry
1 package (4 ounces) regular or low-fat soft garlic-herb cheese
1 teaspoon balsamic vinegar
Salt

Cook tortellini according to package directions. Drain, run under cold water, and drain well. Place in a large bowl and toss with olive oil, basil, and salt to taste.

To Make Dip: In a food processor with the metal blade, mince garlic. Add pimientos and process until pureed. Add cheese, vinegar, and salt to taste and process until smooth, about 1 minute. Refrigerate until chilled. (Tortellini and dip may be refrigerated, covered, overnight. Remove from refrigerator at least 15 minutes before serving.)

To Serve: Place tortellini on end of frilled toothpicks or short skewers, 2 per pick. Arrange on a platter around a bowl of dip.

MAKES: about 72 hors d'oeuvres, depending on package size.

PUREE OF WHITE BEANS WITH VEGETABLES

1 garlic clove, minced
⅓ cup chopped fresh cilantro
    leaves
1 can (16 ounces) lima grands
    (also called butter beans and
    California large limas), rinsed
    and well drained
¾ teaspoon ground cumin
1 tablespoon plus 1 teaspoon
    fresh lemon juice

3 to 4 tablespoons olive oil
Salt and freshly ground black
    pepper
Vegetables for dipping, such as
    sliced carrots, celery, blanched
    green beans (see page 121),
    Belgian endive leaves, or crisp
    dried vegetable chips (Terra
    chips)
Cilantro sprigs, for garnish

Place garlic and cilantro in a food processor with the metal blade and process until minced. Add beans, cumin, lemon juice, oil, and salt and pepper to taste. Pulse until mixture is almost pureed, but still slightly chunky. Refrigerate for at least 1 hour. (Puree may be refrigerated up to 4 days or frozen up to 1 month.)

Before serving, arrange vegetables around dip. Garnish with cilantro.

MAKES: 1⅓ cups.

Change of Pace: Substitute 1 can (19 ounces) cannellini beans, rinsed and drained, for the limas.

If you're looking for a creamy yet low-fat dip for vegetables, stop here. Everyone will be guessing—wrong—the mystery ingredient. This is also delicious as a spread for Tuscany Toasts (see page 285).

PREP TIME: 15 minutes

CHILL TIME: 1 hour

ADVANCE PREP: Puree may be refrigerated up to 4 days or frozen up to 1 month.

NUTRITIONAL ANALYSIS

Per tablespoon puree
32 calories
2 g fat
0 cholesterol
110 mg sodium

For a guiltless, colorful hors d'oeuvre, permeate scallops with a soy-ginger-orange marinade, wrap in snow peas and serve on sticks with orange wedges. (See color photo, page 6.)

PREP TIME: 30 minutes

MARINADE TIME: 2 to 4 hours

ADVANCE PREP: Marinade may be refrigerated up to 2 days. Snow peas and scallops may be cooked and refrigerated overnight. Skewers may be assembled up to 6 hours ahead.

SKEWERED SCALLOPS, ORANGES, AND SNOW PEAS

Orange Marinade
⅔ cup orange juice
6 tablespoons soy sauce
5 tablespoons orange marmalade
1 tablespoon plus 1 teaspoon oriental sesame oil
1 tablespoon minced fresh ginger (see page 10)
3 garlic cloves, minced
¼ to ½ teaspoon chile oil or Tabasco sauce, or to taste

1 pound sea scallops, rinsed and patted dry
½ pound snow peas
½ teaspoon vegetable oil
1½ teaspoons cornstarch
2 large seedless oranges
Toothpicks or short wooden skewers

To Marinate: In a large plastic zipper bag, stir together orange juice, soy sauce, marmalade, sesame oil, ginger, garlic, and chile oil. Add scallops and toss to coat. Refrigerate 2 to 4 hours.

To Prepare Snow Peas: Cut ends off snow peas and remove strings. Fill a small saucepan half full of water. Add oil and bring to a boil. Add snow peas and boil for 1 to 2 minutes until crisp-tender. Run under cold water to stop the cooking. Pat with paper towels. (Snow peas may be refrigerated wrapped in paper towels and plastic wrap overnight.)

To Cook Scallops: Preheat broiler. Remove scallops to a foil-lined broiler pan. Broil as close to heat as possible for about 2 to 3 minutes, or until cooked. Do not overcook or they will be tough. (Scallops may be refrigerated overnight.)

For Sauce: Pour marinade into a small saucepan. Stir in cornstarch until dissolved. Bring to a boil, stirring constantly. Cool. (Sauce may be refrigerated overnight.) Serve at room temperature.

To Assemble: Peel oranges and slice ½ inch thick. Cut each slice into 6 wedges. Insert 1 orange wedge onto toothpick. Wrap a snow pea around a scallop. Thread onto one end of pick so it will be easy to dip. Repeat for remaining skewers. (Skewers may be refrigerated, covered, up to 6 hours.) Arrange on platter with sauce for dipping.

MAKES: about 30 skewers.

SWEET POTATO PANCAKES WITH SOUR CREAM AND CHUTNEY

1 pound sweet potatoes or yams
1 piece peeled fresh ginger, about the size of a quarter
2 large eggs
1 tablespoon all-purpose flour
¾ teaspoon salt, or to taste
¼ teaspoon freshly ground black pepper

Vegetable oil
About ⅓ cup regular, low-fat, or nonfat sour cream, for serving
About ⅓ cup chutney, pieces chopped if large, for serving
Garden leaves, for garnish (see page 10) (optional)

To Make Pancakes: Peel potatoes and shred in a food processor with the shredding disk or with a hand grater. Measure 4 cups, discarding rest, and place in a bowl. In same processor bowl with the metal blade, process ginger until minced. Remove, measure 1 teaspoon, and return it to processor. Add eggs, flour, salt, and pepper and pulse until blended. Add potatoes and pulse 3 or 4 times until incorporated; do not puree.

To Cook: Pour about ¼ inch oil into a large skillet. Heat over medium-high heat until it reaches 365°F. on a thermometer or sizzles instantly when a small amount of batter is added. Using a tablespoon measure, drop sweet potato mixture into oil, without crowding, flattening the tops slightly. Fry until golden on the bottom, turn, and brown on the other side, about 2 minutes per side. If potatoes brown too fast, reduce the heat. Remove to paper towels to drain. (If not serving immediately, pancakes may be cooled, layered with wax paper in an airtight container, and refrigerated up to 2 days or frozen. Reheat, without defrosting, at 400°F. for 6 to 10 minutes or until hot and crisp.)

To Serve: Top each pancake with a small dollop of sour cream and chutney. Although best served hot, potatoes may also be served at room temperature. If desired, garnish platter with garden leaves.

MAKES: about 24 pancakes.

Doesn't everyone love a potato pancake? How sweet it is when crisp shreds of orange spuds replace the ubiquitous white tuber.

PREP TIME: 45 minutes

ADVANCE PREP: May be refrigerated up to 2 days or frozen.

NUTRITIONAL ANALYSIS

Per serving
48 calories
2 g fat
19 mg cholesterol
75 mg sodium

SESAME CHICKEN WITH CRANBERRY-PLUM DIPPING SAUCE

When hors d'oeuvres are intended as dinner, you want something a bit substantial, like these chicken brochettes. They were so popular with the students in my holiday classes, many adapted the recipe to whole breasts and served them as an entree. Because the marinade and the dipping sauce use many of the same ingredients, it is convenient to make them at the same time.

PREP TIME: 20 minutes

MARINADE TIME: 2 to 6 hours

COOK TIME: 7 to 8 minutes

ADVANCE PREP: Marinated skewers may be frozen up to 1 week before baking. Sauce may be refrigerated up to 1 month.

NUTRITIONAL ANALYSIS

Per skewer (not including sauce)
51 calories
2 g fat
21 mg cholesterol
42 mg sodium

Marinade
1 piece peeled fresh ginger, about the size of a quarter
4 garlic cloves, peeled
2 green onions, cut in quarters
⅓ cup dry sherry
3 tablespoons soy sauce
1 tablespoon plus 2 teaspoons oriental sesame oil
2 tablespoons hoisin sauce
2 tablespoons Chinese plum sauce
½ teaspoon Chinese chile sauce (see page 10)

2 pounds skinless, boneless chicken breasts

36 (4-inch) wooden skewers or toothpicks
4 tablespoons sesame seeds, toasted (see page 12)
Cranberry-Plum Dipping Sauce (recipe follows)
Watercress or parsley sprigs, for garnish

To Marinate: Place ginger and garlic in a food processor with the metal blade. Process until minced. Add green onions, sherry, soy sauce, sesame oil, hoisin, plum, and chile sauces and process until blended. Remove fat and any cartilage from chicken, cut into 1-inch pieces, and place in a heavy plastic zipper bag. Pour marinade over chicken and marinate in the refrigerator for 2 to 6 hours, turning once or twice. Thread 2 pieces of chicken on each skewer. (Skewers may be frozen up to one week. Defrost in the refrigerator.)

To Bake: Before serving, preheat the oven to 425°F. Line a rimmed baking sheet with heavy-duty foil.

Place sesame seeds in a shallow dish. Dip 1 side of chicken into seeds and place, seed side up, on foil. Bake for 7 to 9 minutes, or until cooked through. Place dipping sauce in bowl on platter, arrange skewers like spokes around it, and garnish with watercress or parsley sprigs.

MAKES: about 36 skewers.

CRANBERRY- PLUM DIPPING SAUCE

2 garlic cloves, peeled
2 slices peeled fresh ginger, each
    about the size of a quarter
2 tablespoons soy sauce
1 tablespoon cider vinegar
½ teaspoon oriental sesame oil
1 can (8 ounces) whole berry
    cranberry sauce

2 tablespoons Chinese plum
    sauce
¼ to ½ teaspoon Chinese chile
    sauce, to taste (see page 10)

In a food processor with the metal blade, process garlic and ginger until minced. Add remaining ingredients and process until combined. Remove to a bowl and refrigerate several hours for the flavors to blend. (Sauce may be refrigerated up to 1 month.)

MAKES: 1 cup.

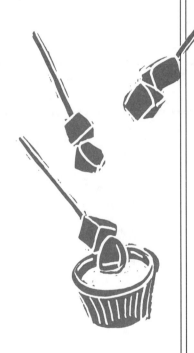

NUTRITIONAL ANALYSIS

Per 2 teaspoons sauce
17 calories
less than 1 g fat
0 cholesterol
100 mg sodium

Softening tortillas in a microwave makes them easy to cut and pliable enough to fit into miniature muffin cups. Once baked, they can be filled with your favorite combination; I am especially partial to this cornmeal one of sausage, black beans, and corn.

PREP TIME: 30 minutes

BAKE TIME: 5 minutes

ADVANCE PREP: May be refrigerated overnight or frozen up to 2 weeks.

TOSTADA CUPS WITH SAUSAGE AND BLACK BEANS

8 flour tortillas, 10 inches in diameter

Filling
½ pound low-fat spicy bulk sausage
¾ teaspoon salt
1 teaspoon ground cumin
⅓ cup yellow cornmeal
1 medium tomato, seeded and chopped (about ¾ cup) (see page 12)
½ cup frozen corn, thawed
½ cup canned black beans, drained

1 tablespoon minced pickled or fresh seeded jalapeños (see page 10)
1 can (4 ounces) chopped green chiles, drained
1 cup finely shredded regular or low-fat cheddar cheese

Garnish (optional)
Whole raw dried black beans, rinsed and dried
Small red and green chile peppers
Parsley or other greens

To Make Tostada Cups: Preheat oven to 300°F.

Fold 4 tortillas in half, place on a plate, cover, and microwave on high (100%) for 40 to 90 seconds, or until soft and pliable. Using a 2½-inch round cookie or biscuit cutter, cut rounds from each tortilla. Separate and press into 1½- to 1¾-inch muffin cups that are 1 inch deep. Repeat with remaining tortillas, making 48 cups. Bake for 20 minutes, or until very crisp and pale golden. (Cups may be stored, covered, overnight or frozen up to 1 month.)

To Make Filling: In a medium skillet, cook sausage, breaking it up with a fork until browned. Drain off fat. Pour 1 cup water into same skillet. Stir in salt and cumin. Place over medium heat until bubbles form around the edges but the water is not boiling. Slowly pour in cornmeal, whisking briskly until all is added. Stir for 1 minute. Remove from heat and stir in tomato, corn, beans, jalapeño, and green chiles. Spoon filling into cups, mounding the tops. Sprinkle with cheese. (Tostadas may be refrigerated overnight or frozen up to 2 weeks. Bring to room temperature on baking sheets in a single layer lightly covered with foil.)

To Bake: Preheat oven to 350°F.

Bake tostadas, uncovered, for 5 minutes, or until heated through and cheese melts. Serve warm or at room temperature. If desired, line a platter with a bed of black beans, arrange cups on top, and garnish with chiles and parsley.

MAKES: 48 tostadas.

ESPRESSO FUDGE CUPS

¼ pound (1 stick) unsalted
    butter or margarine
½ cup semisweet chocolate
    chips
2 large eggs
½ cup all-purpose flour
1 teaspoon instant espresso or
    coffee granules
¾ cup sugar
½ cup chopped pecans
24 pecan halves, for garnish, or
    Chocolate-Espresso Glaze

Chocolate-Espresso Glaze
    (optional)
2 ounces (scant ½ cup)
    semisweet chocolate chips
1 tablespoon unsalted butter or
    margarine
1 teaspoon light corn syrup
¼ teaspoon instant espresso or
    coffee granules
1 to 2 teaspoons Kahlúa
Small decorations either piped
    from colored frosting or
    purchased at a cake-
    decorating shop

Preheat oven to 350°F. Line twenty-four 1½-inch miniature muffin cups with paper liners.

To Make Batter: Place butter and chocolate in a medium microwavesafe bowl and microwave at 60% power for 1 to 2 minutes, or until smooth. Or melt butter and chocolate in heavy small saucepan over low heat. Remove from heat and whisk in eggs. Stir in flour, coffee powder, and sugar and mix well. Stir in chopped pecans. Spoon into muffin papers and if you don't wish to glaze the completed cups, top each with a pecan half.

To Bake: Bake for 17 to 20 minutes, or until the tops are set. Do not overbake or they will be dry instead of fudgy. Cool 2 to 3 minutes and remove to racks to cool completely.

To Make Chocolate Glaze: In a 4-cup microwavesafe bowl, melt chocolate, butter, corn syrup, coffee, and 1 teaspoon Kahlúa on high (100%), uncovered, for 1 to 3 minutes, stirring every minute, until smooth. Or melt in heavy saucepan over low heat, stirring until smooth. If too thick, thin with additional Kahlúa. Dip tops of cups into warm glaze. Garnish with frosting decorations. (Cups may be stored airtight at room temperature up to 2 days or frozen up to 1 month. Defrost, covered, in one layer at room temperature.)

MAKES: 24 cups.

F udgy brownies masquerade as petit pastries when baked in miniature muffin cups. I offer two garnishing alternatives: Before baking, top each with a pecan half or after baking, swirl with chocolate frosting and garnish with dainty frosting flowers or holiday motifs, either piped by hand or purchased at a cake decorating store.

PREP TIME: 15 minutes

BAKE TIME: 17 to 20 minutes

ADVANCE PREP: May be stored at room temperature up to 2 days or frozen.

NUTRITIONAL ANALYSIS

Per fudge cup (not including glaze)
114 calories
8 g fat
28 mg cholesterol
47 mg sodium

Per fudge cup (with glaze)
131 calories
9 g fat
29 mg cholesterol
49 mg sodium

Call these the great deceivers. They may look like ordinary cheesecake, but it's a cheesecake filled with white chocolate, lots of it. I haven't even attempted to reduce the calories or fat—some things are simply worth every bite.

PREP TIME: 30 minutes

BAKE TIME: 30 minutes to bake and 30 minutes with oven turned off

FREEZE TIME: 6 hours

ADVANCE PREP: May be frozen up to 1 month.

NUTRITIONAL ANALYSIS

Per square
146 calories
10 g fat
39 mg cholesterol
95 mg sodium

ALABASTER CHEESECAKE BITES

Chocolate Wafer Crust
1 box (8½ ounces) chocolate wafer cookies
6 tablespoons (⅔ stick) unsalted butter or margarine, melted
1 tablespoon sugar

Cheesecake Filling
10 ounces white chocolate, finely chopped, preferably Tobler Narcisse or Lindt Blancor
½ cup heavy cream
1 pound cream cheese, at room temperature

4 large eggs, separated
4 teaspoons vanilla extract

White Chocolate Topping
6 ounces white chocolate, finely chopped
¼ cup heavy cream
2 tablespoons white crème de cacao

Marbled Chocolate Shavings, for garnish (see page 101) (optional)
Fresh flowers, for garnish (see page 10)

To Make Crust: Preheat oven to 300°F. Line the bottom and sides of a 9 × 13-inch baking pan with heavy-duty aluminum foil, letting it extend 2 inches over short ends for handles. Grease or spray the foil. In a food processor with the metal blade, process cookies into crumbs. Add melted butter and sugar and pulse until combined. Reserve ⅓ cup for garnishing if not using shavings and press the remainder evenly into the bottom of the pan.

To Make Filling: Place chocolate in a medium bowl. Place cream in a 2-cup microwavesafe measure, cover with wax paper, and microwave on high (100%) for 1 to 2 minutes until it comes to a boil. Or heat cream on top of stove. Pour over chocolate, let stand 2 minutes, and stir smooth.

In large mixing bowl with electric mixer, beat cream cheese until smooth. Add egg yolks, one at a time, scraping sides of bowl frequently. Add chocolate mixture, and vanilla. Beat for 2 minutes. In small mixing bowl with clean beaters, beat egg whites to firm peaks and fold them into chocolate mixture. Pour filling evenly over the crust.

To Bake: Bake for 30 minutes, or until top has risen and is almost set. Turn off heat and leave in oven for 30 minutes. Transfer to a rack and cool to room temperature.

To Make Topping: Place chocolate in medium bowl. Microwave cream in 1-cup microwavesafe measure, covered with wax paper, on high (100%) for 30 to 90 seconds, or until it comes to a boil. Or heat on top of stove. Pour over chocolate and let stand 2 minutes. Stir in crème de cacao until smooth. Pour over the cool cheesecake. Sprinkle the top with reserved crumbs or chocolate shavings. When cool, cover and freeze at least 6 hours, or until firm. (Cheesecake may be frozen, covered, up to 1 month.)

To Cut: While frozen, using the foil as handles, lift the cheesecake from the pan and set on a work surface. With a chef's knife dipped in very hot water, cut frozen cake into 1½-inch squares. Return to freezer or refrigerate until ready to serve. Serve chilled. Garnish with Marbled Chocolate Shavings or fresh flowers, if desired.

MAKES: about 48 squares.

My German grandmother, Oma, was renowned for her butter cookies, which provided the master recipe for every pastry she ever made. In my adaptation, the lemon-nut pastry plays a dual role: It is both the base and the streusel-like topping that envelop a tangy lemon custard.

PREP TIME: 20 minutes

BAKE TIME: About 40 minutes

ADVANCE PREP: May be refrigerated for several days or frozen.

LEMON STREUSEL SQUARES

Lemon-Nut Pastry
2 medium lemons
⅓ cup sugar
1 cup shelled hazelnuts (filberts) (4 ounces)
¼ pound (1 stick) unsalted butter or margarine, cold and cut into 8 pieces
¾ cup all-purpose flour

Lemon Filling
2 large eggs

2 egg whites
¾ cup sugar
2 tablespoons unsalted butter or margarine, melted
⅓ cup fresh lemon juice (see page 11)
2 teaspoons all-purpose flour
¼ cup regular or light sour cream

Preheat oven to 350°F. Line an 8- or 9-inch square baking pan with heavy-duty foil, letting it extend an inch over the sides.

To Make Pastry: Using a sharp vegetable peeler, peel lemons, taking care to remove as little of the bitter white pith as possible. Place the peel in a food processor with the metal blade and process until finely chopped. Add sugar and process until peel is minced, about 1 minute. Add nuts and pulse to a medium chop. Remove ½ cup for the topping and set aside. Add butter and flour to processor and pulse until the mixture begins to hold together. Turn pastry into the prepared pan and press evenly into the bottom. Bake for 20 to 24 minutes, or until edges are golden and the top is set and very lightly colored.

To Make Filling: In same food processor bowl (no need to wash it), process eggs, egg whites, sugar, butter, lemon juice, and flour until blended. Pour filling over baked crust. Return to oven and bake 10 to 12 minutes, or until filling is barely set.

Crumble reserved lemon-nut mixture evenly over the filling. Return to oven and bake for 8 to 10 minutes more, or until filling is set. Remove from oven and cool to room temperature.

Remove from pan by lifting out foil. Place on cutting board, trim edges, and cut into 1½-inch squares. (Squares may be refrigerated for several days or frozen up to 1 month.) Serve chilled or at room temperature.

MAKES: 25 to 36 squares.

Change of Pace: Substitute walnuts, pecans, or pistachios for the hazelnuts.

RITA CALVERT'S SHORTBREAD ALMOND FLORENTINES

Pastry
½ pound plus 4 tablespoons
(2½ sticks) unsalted butter or
half butter and half margarine
1½ cups sugar
3 cups all-purpose flour
¾ cup cornstarch
¼ teaspoon salt

Topping
1 jar (12 ounces) apricot or
seedless raspberry preserves
or jam, melted (about 1 cup)
1⅓ cups sliced almonds (about
5 ounces)

To Make Pastry: Preheat oven to 325°F. Line a 15½ × 10½ × 1-inch jelly-roll pan with heavy-duty foil, leaving 2 inches overhanging on each short end. Grease the foil.

Place butter in a 4-cup microwavesafe measuring cup, cover with a paper towel, and microwave on high (100%) for 1 to 3 minutes, or until melted. Meanwhile in a food processor with the metal blade, pulse sugar, flour, cornstarch, and salt until mixed. With motor running, pour melted butter through feed tube and process until combined. Pat dough evenly into pan. Cover with a sheet of foil or wax paper and roll with a rolling pin to form an even layer.

To Bake and Top: Bake for 25 to 30 minutes, or until pale golden. Remove from oven and spread with melted preserves. Sprinkle evenly with almonds, pressing them gently into the preserves. Bake for 20 to 30 minutes more, or until jam is bubbling and edges are golden.

Remove from oven and cool 20 minutes. Using foil as handles, lift out and place on work surface. While still warm, cut into five 3-inch strips, then cut each lengthwise into ½- to ¾-inch bars. Cool on foil until firm. (Cookies may be stored in an airtight container for several days or frozen.)

MAKES: about 70 bars.

My assistant, Rita Calvert, is a woman of many talents. She is a food writer, stylist, and founder/president of Calvert Cedar Street Food Products. Her prized Florentine pastry recipe is one I make often. It's easy to prepare and feeds a crowd. A buttery rich crust is baked in a slow oven until crunchy, and then topped with preserves and sliced almonds.

PREP TIME: 20 minutes plus 30 minutes cooling and cutting

BAKE TIME: 45 to 60 minutes

ADVANCE PREP: May be stored airtight for several days or frozen.

NUTRITIONAL ANALYSIS

Per bar (with all butter)
95 calories
4 g fat
9 mg cholesterol
9 mg sodium

Free-form meringues are usually ultra-crisp, sugary shells that shatter when you bite into them. Not these. By beating a little vinegar into the egg whites, you get cups that bake dry on the outside but remain soft and tender within. You can even bake them on a humid day. Topped with swirls of bittersweet chocolate cream, they are celestial.

PREP TIME: Meringues, 35 minutes; truffle filling, 10 minutes plus chilling

BAKE TIME: 30 to 40 minutes

FREEZE TIME: At least 1 hour

ADVANCE PREP: May be frozen up to 2 weeks; do not refrigerate.

NUTRITIONAL ANALYSIS

Per meringue
82 calories
6 g fat
13 mg cholesterol
7 mg sodium

MINI MERINGUES WITH CHOCOLATE TRUFFLES

Meringue Shells
3 large egg whites, at room temperature
1 cup sugar
½ teaspoon white vinegar
½ teaspoon vanilla extract

Chocolate Truffle Filling
12 ounces semisweet chocolate, coarsely chopped (do not use chocolate chips)
2 cups heavy cream
2 teaspoons vanilla extract
¼ cup mini chocolate chips, for garnish (optional)

To Make Meringue: Line 2 large baking sheets with parchment paper or grease or spray them. Preheat the oven to 275°F. In a large mixing bowl with electric mixer on high speed, beat egg whites to firm peaks, about 3 minutes. Add 1 tablespoon sugar and beat 3 more minutes. Add 1 more tablespoon sugar and beat 3 minutes more, scraping sides once or twice. Very gradually mix in the remaining sugar, beating until the mixture is stiff and shiny like marshmallow creme. The total mixing time will be 15 to 20 minutes. Turn mixer to low speed and mix in vinegar and vanilla. Scrape sides, increase speed to high and beat for 1 minute.

To Form Shells: Fit a pastry bag with a ¼-inch star tip and fill with meringue. Pipe pinwheels about 1½ inches in diameter onto baking sheets. Pipe a border around the outer edge to form small cups. Or drop 1½-inch mounds of meringue at 2-inch intervals and use the back of a spoon to hollow out a shell.

To Bake: Bake for 30 to 40 minutes or until shells are very lightly colored and feel firm to the touch. If baking 2 sheets in 1 oven, rotate their positions after 15 minutes. Carefully loosen meringues with a spatula and cool completely. (Baked meringues may be stored, covered, at room temperature up to 2 days or frozen.)

To Make Filling: In a food processor with the metal blade, pulse chocolate until finely chopped. Bring cream to a boil. With the motor running, pour cream and vanilla through feed tube, processing until smooth. Remove to a medium bowl. Place in a bowl of ice water and stir constantly until thick enough to hold its shape and pipe. Or leave at room temperature, stirring occasionally, until thickened. If the chocolate gets too firm, it may be remelted.

To Assemble: Using a teaspoon, or a pastry bag fitted with a ½-inch star tip, pipe or spoon some chocolate into each meringue shell. Sprinkle with chocolate chips, if desired. Freeze until serving. (Filled shells may be frozen up to 2 weeks. Remove from freezer 10 minutes before serving. Do not refrigerate.) They may sit at room temperature for up to 4 hours.

MAKES: about 50 meringues.

INDEX